The Founding Texts of Economics

Smith's *Wealth of Nations*, Marx's *Capital*, and Keynes's *General Theory* are three paradigmatic texts which are foundational to any study of economics or political economy. Although they have long been abundantly quoted and commented on, these "Great Books" paradoxically are being read less and less, as the price of their success. The aim of this book is to encourage the reader to re-read these Texts, by providing "theoretical and conceptual entries" in the spirit of a reasoned dictionary. Hence the return to these works in the text, in statu nascendi, to shed light on their complexities, to loosen the imperialism of received ideas, and to underline their topicality from a theoretical point of view and to understand contemporary economic issues. For example, Adam Smith's view of the need to add a liberal state to the "system of natural liberty," Marx's view of the ability of the capitalist system to overcome temporarily but periodically its contradictions, or Keynes' view of the essential role of psychology in the decisions and behaviour of men in society.

This book is vital reading for anyone interested in the history of economic thought, the founding theories of political economy and the history of ideas more broadly.

Philippe Gilles is currently Professor of Economics and Dean of the Faculty of Economics, University of Toulon, France.

The Founding Texts of Economics

Reading Smith's *Wealth of Nations*, Marx's *Capital*, and Keynes's *General Theory*

Philippe Gilles

Authorised translation from the French language edition published by Classiques Garnier

Routledge
Taylor & Francis Group
LONDON AND NEW YORK

First published 2024
by Routledge
4 Park Square, Milton Park, Abingdon, Oxon OX14 4RN

and by Routledge
605 Third Avenue, New York, NY 10158

Routledge is an imprint of the Taylor & Francis Group, an informa business

British Library Cataloguing-in-Publication Data
A catalogue record for this book is available from the British Library

ISBN: 978-1-032-64897-2 (hbk)
ISBN: 978-1-032-64900-9 (pbk)
ISBN: 978-1-032-64905-4 (ebk)

DOI: 10.4324/9781032649054

Typeset in Times New Roman
by MPS Limited, Dehradun

**To Apolline, Camille, Cécile,
Marie-Christine, Thérèse,
and Simone Gilles**

Contents

General introduction

In a letter dated 5 July 1764, addressed to David Hume, Adam Smith (1987, p. 53), who resides in Toulouse, mentions for the first time the writing of the *Wealth of Nations* by specifying: "The Life which I led at Glasgow was a pleasurable, dissipated life in comparison of that which I lead here at Present. I have begun to write a book in order to pass away the time. You may believe I have very little to do." This apparent "casualness" contrasts, however, with the many letters Smith sent, before and at the time of the book's publication, to his publishers and translators (Abbé Blavet and Abbé Morellet, in particular), thanking the former, in a letter of 23 July 1782, for making it known "to the nation of Europe whose taste and judgement I most consider" (*ibid.*, p. 345).[1] As soon as it was available in French, P.-S. Dupont de Nemours, in a letter dated 19 June 1788, described the *Wealth of Nations* as "Livre excellent dont vous avez enrichi le monde" (Excellent book that you have enriched the world with, *ibid.*, p. 413), indicating that "les *Economistes* français [*i.e.* the Physiocrats] garderont pour vous autant de respect que vous daignez leur témoigner d'estime" (the French *Economists* will keep for you as much respect as you deign to show them esteem, *ibid.*, p. 413), and, as soon as it was published (9 March 1776), Hume, in a letter dated 1 April 1776 to Smith, expressed his enthusiasm:

> "Euge! Belle! Dear Mr Smith: I am much pleas'd with your Performance, and the Perusal of it has taken me from a State of great Anxiety. It was a Work of so much Expectation, by yourself, by your Friends, and by the Public, that I trembled for its Appearance; but am now much relieved. Not but that the Reading of it necessarily requires so much Attention, and the Public is disposed to give so little, that I shall still doubt for some time of its being very popular: But it has Depth and Solidity and Acuteness, and is so much illustrated by curious Facts, that it must at last take the public Attention. It is probably much improved by your last Abode in London. If you were here at my Fireside, I should dispute some of your Principles"(*ibid.*, p. 255)

Karl Marx, in a letter dated 17 April 1867, addressed to his friend Johann Philipp Becker, a militant of the First International, asks him to announce in

DOI: 10.4324/9781032649054-1

the press the upcoming publication of Book I of *Capital*: "It is without question the most terrible *missile* that has yet been hurled at the heads of the bourgeoisie (landowners included)" (Marxists Internet Archive, Marx emphasises) and, on April 30, replies to Sigfrid Meyer, a German socialist emigrated to New York:

> "Why then did I not answer you? Because I was the whole time at death's door. I thus had to make use of *every* moment when I was capable of work to complete my book [Capital] to which I have sacrificed my health, happiness, and family. I hope this explanation suffices. I laugh at the so-called 'practical' men and their wisdom. If one wanted to be an ox, one could, of course, turn one's back on the sufferings of humanity and look after one's own hide. But I should really have thought myself unpractical if I had pegged out without finally completing my book, at least in manuscript." (*ibid.*, Marx emphasises)

And, regarding the French translation edited by Maurice Lachâtre, Marx addressed him this letter, written in French, dated 18 March 1872:

> "J'applaudis à votre idée de publier la traduction de *Das Kapital* en livraisons périodiques. Sous cette forme, l'ouvrage sera plus accessible à la classe ouvrière et, pour moi, cette considération l'emporte sur toute autre. Voilà le beau côté de la médaille, mais en voici le revers: la méthode d'analyse que j'ai employée [...] rend assez ardue la lecture des premiers chapitres, et il est à craindre que le public français, toujours impatient de conclure, avide de connaître le rapport des principes généraux avec les questions immédiates qui le passionnent, ne se rebute parce qu'il n'aura pu tout d'abord passer outre. C'est là un désavantage contre lequel je ne puis rien si ce n'est toutefois prévenir et prémunir les lecteurs soucieux de vérité." (Marx, 1965, p. 543)[2]
>
> before concluding:
>
> "Il n'y a pas de route royale pour la science, et ceux-là seulement ont chance d'arriver à ses sommets lumineux qui ne craignent pas de se fatiguer à gravir ses sentiers escarpés." ("There is no royal road for science, and only those are lucky enough to reach its luminous peaks who are not afraid to tire themselves to climb its steep paths", *ibidem*)

From the beginning of 1935, John Maynard Keynes sensed that the content of his next book, the *General Theory of Employment, Interest and Money*, which had not yet been published, was likely to "revolutionise the economy", a "gigantic boast" as Virginia Woolf did not hesitate to affirm ("true I daresay"), on Sunday 6 January, in her Diary[3], but which he confirmed in a letter addressed on January 1 to his friend George Bernard Shaw:

> "To understand *my* state of mind, however, you have to know that I believe myself to be writing a book on economic theory which will largely revolutionise –not, I suppose, at once but in the course of the next ten years- the way the world thinks about economic problems. When my new theory has been duly assimilated and mixed with politics and feelings and passions, I can't predict what the final upshot will be in its effect on action and affairs. But there will be a great change, and, in particular, the Ricardian foundations of Marxism will be knocked away. I can't expect you, or anyone else, to believe this at the present stage. But for myself I don't merely hope what I say, in my own mind I'm quite sure." (Keynes, 2013, pp. 492–3, Keynes emphasises; see also Harrod, 1951, p. 462)

These different epistolary excerpts have one thing in common, showing the importance of the social, intellectual, and even scientific influence that Smith, Marx, and Keynes sensed from the content of their respective works, historical hindsight has not invalidated, but rather validated, these feelings and even these certainties.

This is because these three works are "paradigmatic books," Blaug's "great books" (1985, p. vii), those which, having provided theoretical answers to the great questions of Politics, have wisely focused on "the role of ideas and the role of action" to the point of "shap[ing] the course of events" (Galbraith, 1952, p. 71)[4]; works that have allowed the systematization of economic reasoning and analysis and, consequently, its autonomy in relation to other scientific disciplines, thus constituting the founding texts of Schools of thought. Thus, the contents of the *Wealth of Nations*, *Capital*, and the *General Theory* have in common that they conceive of a systematic representation of the economic laws of the dynamics of capitalism, both at the macro and micro levels. From this point of view, Smith, Marx, and Keynes are still alive and relevant today, and cannot be confined to intellectual history. Their ideas are still, in part, the basis for thinking about our future today, individually and collectively.

In other words, the content of these great books initiated the definition of "legitimate problems and methods of a research field," in this case, economics, "for succeeding generations [and still present] of practitioners" (Kuhn, 1970, p. 10). For that, they have in common two essential characteristics that constitute a *paradigm*: i) "Their achievement was sufficiently unprecedented to attract an enduring group of adherents away from competing modes of scientific activity"; ii) "it was sufficiently open-ended to leave all sorts of problems for the redefined group of practitioners to resolve" (*ibidem*). It is easy to understand why these works are abundantly quoted, commented and interpreted, but, at the same time, as a price of their success, less and less read directly and more and more through an intermediary, commentaries and secondary literature being logical and orderly, which is not the case with the great texts, characterized by a certain tediousness in reading. As Galbraith (1952, p. 72) notes for the *General Theory*:

> "Keynes' General Theory could not normally be read, even by the intelligent layman, unless he was schooled in the language and, even more, in the abstractions of economics. As a result its influence on practical affairs was almost entirely by proxy. It was not from Keynes but from his interpreters at first, second or third remove that most men learned of his ideas. Millions came to accept Keynes' conclusions who had never read a word he had written. More interesting, thousands came to be advocates of his proposals who, if asked, would have indignantly denied they were Keynesians. While everyone knows that Keynes was important and influential there is still a remarkable uncertainty as to just how or why."

By extrapolation, it follows that the analyses of Smith, Marx, and Keynes, contained in the *Wealth of Nations*, *Capital*, and the *General Theory*, have, at best, only a resemblance with what secondary literature reports from the study of these works. Where, precisely, the works of the inspirers are generally simplified or, conversely, unnecessarily complexified, vulgarized, and dogmatized, taking the form of intellectual legacies that carry controversies between epigones and then within new generations of interpreters, so many variants of the original thought, which distance us from it. Hence, the need to return to the source of the great books, keeping in mind the historical and ideological context of their conceptions,[5] in order to avoid two pitfalls: on the one hand, that of seeing, in the light of modern economic theory, only the errors and analytical limits that they contain, whereas they are often the heirs, "prisoners" of their historicities, and on the other hand, that of seeking at all costs the original avant-garde idea by over-interpreting some of their developments. As Blaug (1985, p. 1) sums it up, with efficiency, "The danger of arrogance toward the writers of the past is certainly a real one – but so is ancestor worship."

Ultimately, the return to the original texts, *in statu nascendi*, should make it possible to highlight the complexity of these works, to loosen the constraints of the vulgate and the imperialism of the "idées reçues" according to which: In the *Wealth of Nations*, liberalism, "laissez-faire" "laissez-passer" driven by an "invisible hand" express the *exclusive* forces of the "obvious and simple system of natural liberty"; in *Capital*, the decline of the capitalist mode of production becomes *inevitable* under the effect of its contradictions and antagonisms; the *General Theory* embodies the "triumphant" Macroeconomics, which admits only the State as a strategic agent, with the extension of its "traditional functions" summed up in a plea for public investment.

Confronted with these simplifications, these "ideological mutilations," the reinvestment in these great books, by the reappropriation of their contents while insisting on their unknown faces and the proposal, not so much of "readers' guides," as of "theoretical and conceptual entries" in the spirit of a reasoned dictionary, objects of the present book,[6] brings to light the detailed demonstrations made by Smith concerning the necessity of the State as "superintendent of the industry of private people" in order to direct it towards "the employments most suitable to the interest of society"; by Marx, on the capacity of the capitalist system, via the mobilization of the "credit system," of the technological dimension, or of "counteracting factors" for example, to overcome temporarily, but periodically, its contradictions; by Keynes, on the essential role played by psychology in the behaviour of men in society, who not only can but must foresee, with the possibility of being wrong. So many developments of a troubling topicality, so many incitements to re-read these great books, carrying rich teachings in times of questioning of the State and interrogations on the future of the "mixed economy" and public goods, of questioning on the "financial capitalism," of its autonomization with respect to the real economy up to the generalization of the speculative nature of behaviours, of the rise of individualism and the search for new forms of social cohesion.

Notes

1 "I am delighted with this translation and you have done me the greatest service that can be rendered to an author, by making my book known to the nation of Europe whose taste and judgment I most consider." Adam Smith to Abbé Blavet, Edinburgh, July 23, 1782.
2 "I applaud your idea of publishing the translation of *Das Kapital* in periodic issues. In this form, the work will be more accessible to the working class, and for me, this consideration outweighs all others. This is the beautiful side of the coin, but here is the other side: the method of analysis that I have used [...] makes the reading of the first chapters rather arduous, and it is to be feared that the French public, always impatient to conclude, eager to know the relation of the general principles to the immediate questions which impassion it, will not be put off because it will not have been able to get past it at first. It is there a disadvantage against which I cannot do anything if it is not however to warn and protect the readers anxious of truth"
3 "Then he [Maynard] read us a long magnificently spry and juicy letter from Shaw, on a sickbed, aged 77. The whole of economics twiddled round on his finger, with the usual dives and gives and colloquialities [...] M. [aynard]'s own letter said that he thinks he has revolutionised economics; in the new book he is writing [...] This he wrote in so many words; a gigantic boast; true I daresay. That was why we were asked to lunch not tea -that he may write his book in the soft exciting hours." (Woolf, 1935 in 1982, p. 272.)
4 It is interesting for our purposes to quote Galbraith's quote in full: "Certainly his final book, The General Theory of Employment Interest and Money shaped the course of events as only the books of three earlier economists - Smith's Wealth of Nations, Ricardo's Principles of Political Economy and Marx's Capital – have done."
5 At the limits of analogy, this return to the founding texts, of "fidelity to the work" (*Werktreue*), can be brought closer in spirit to the Historical Interpretation of Early Music Movement, which John Eliot Gardiner (2014, chap. 1, p. 7, 10) personifies and makes explicit with conviction: "To unlock the codes in the musical language of these Baroque masters, to close the gap between their world and ours, and to release the wellspring of their creative fantasy meant cultivating a radically different sonority. There was only one thing for it: to re-group using original (or replica) Baroque instruments. It was like learning a totally new language or taking up a new

instrument but with practically no one to teach you how to play it [...] Suddenly you could hear the music leap from the confines of its encasement. The moment these old instruments were let loose on music that had once been the exclusive preserve of the scaled-down modern symphony orchestra, what for years has seemed 'ye olde' and remote now sounded new-minted."

6 The first version of this work, written in French, was published in 2018 by Editions Classiques Garnier (Paris), then reissued in "pocket" format ("Classiques Jaunes") in 2020, under the title: "L'Actualité des Textes fondateurs: Adam Smith, Karl Marx et John Maynard Keynes". I would like to thank Editions "Classiques Garnier" for permission to use this first text. I would also like to thank Cécile Bastidon-Gilles (University of Toulon), Andy Humphries (Routledge Editions) and two anonymous reviewers for their comments and suggestions on the first versions of this text which, associated with their encouragement, have largely contributed to the realization of this work, for the content of which I remain, obviously, only responsible.

Part I

Adam Smith (Kirkcaldy 1723, Edinburgh, 1790) and "An Inquiry into the Nature and Causes of the Wealth of Nations" (1776)

Introduction

"An Inquiry into the Nature and Causes of the Wealth of Nations" (henceforth WON[1]) represents, for Schumpeter (1966, p. 181), "the most successful not only of all books on economics but, with the possible exception of Darwin's *Origin of Species*, of all scientific books that have appeared to this day," written by "the most famous of all economists." For Schumpeter, this success is deserved although WON does not contain "a single analytic idea, principle, or method that was entirely new in 1776 [...] and thought it cannot rank with Newton's *Principia* or Darwin's *Origin* as an intellectual achievement" (*ibid.*, pp. 184–185). So where does the importance come from and how is the posterity of WON explained?

The first element of response comes from the fact that WON plays the role of a paradigm (Kuhn, 1970) in Economics because it contains "accepted examples of actual scientific practice—examples which include law, theory, application, and instrumentation together—[which] provide models from which spring particular coherent traditions of scientific research" (*ibid.*, p. 10). Therefore, this "concrete scientific achievement" as "locus of professional commitment" (*ibid.*) founds WON as a "paradigm," *i.e.* the grouping of "universally recognized scientific achievements that for a time provide models, problems and solutions to a community of practitioners" (*ibid.*, p. viii).

Another explanation, in this line, is that WON embodies, in a striking way, what Schumpeter (1966, pp. 51–52, 143) calls a "Classical Situation," *i.e.* the epistemological autonomy of Economics coupled with an agreement on a field of knowledge that has brought to light specialized techniques of research and treatment of facts and of analytical interpretation: "Such a classical situation emerged in the second half of the eighteenth century and no such classical situation has ever emerged before [...] perhaps, with the peak success of that epoch, A. Smith's Wealth of Nations (1776) [...] [It] was the result of a merger of two types of work that are sufficiently distinct to justify separate considerations. There was the stock of factual knowledge and the conceptual apparatus that had slowly grown, during the centuries, in the studies of philosophers. And, semi-independent of this, there was a stock of facts and

DOI: 10.4324/9781032649054-3

concepts that had been accumulated by men of practical affairs in the course of their discussions of current political issues."

In this sense, in this Schumpeterian perspective, the content of WON illustrates this merger between Economic Thought, *i.e.* opinions on economic matters that dominate at a given moment in a given society (economic history), and Economic Analysis as the result of scientific work, a testimony to the specifically autonomous nature of Economics as a science, centred on the conditions that govern the wealth, and therefore the "material welfare" of Nations.[2] Another, more concise, expression of this fusional encounter is provided by K. Polanyi:

> "Adam Smith, it was true, treated material wealth as a separate field of study; to have done so with a great sense of realism made him the founder of a new science, economics." (Polanyi, 2001, p. 116)

But, in order to achieve this fusion, *i.e.* to make his purpose universal, Smith excludes from the search for this wealth, Nature in the physical sense (*Physis*), which is likely to differentiate territories and communities, and therefore countries, in favour of a common denominator, "labour," as he indicates on the first page of the Introduction to WON:

> "Whatever be the soil, climate, or extent of territory of any particular nation, the abundance or scantiness of its annual supply must, in that particular situation, depend upon those two circumstances [...] first, by the skill, dexterity, and judgement with which its labour is generally applied; and, secondly, by the proportion between the number of those who are not so employed." (WON, 1913, Introduction and Plan of the Work, p. 1)

This separation between physical and human nature is characteristic, for Polanyi (*ibid.*, p. 117), of Smith's thinking: "Political economy should be a human science; it should deal with that which was natural to man, not to Nature." This is another way, through the anthropology of economic value, of clarifying the "Classical situation," by showing that, starting with Smith and WON, it is not so much an assumed desire for independence between economic analysis and philosophy, but rather that "philosophical beliefs of economists are not relevant to the *validity* of the economic hypotheses they advance." (Blaug, 1985, p. 5; Blaug emphasises).

This fusion between economic analysis and thought takes the form, in WON, of imbrication of long detailed narratives of historical facts and periods ("the historical and descriptive methods of Adam Smiths" noted by Marx),[3] or even of voluminous digressions,[4] with short analytical paragraphs exposing real theorems, which, beyond the importance of the text,[5] makes particularly tedious reading,[6] even if the arguments are presented in a lively manner, in the form of pleadings or indictments depending on the case.[7] This tediousness is also noted with humour by Mark Blaug (1985, p. 35): "The practice of reading the expensive tomes of the eighteenth century from cover to cover seems to have almost wholly died out. Nowadays we read selections of Gibbon, Johnson, and Hume and confine ourselves to the first ten chapters of the *Wealth of Nations* [...] Let us assume, in a triumph of hope over experience, that people who read Smith's entire volume are not as rare as is sometimes believed."

Notes

1 Bibliographical references to WON will be linked, thereafter, as follows: (WON, I, IV, p. 17) for example will mean in The Wealth of Nations, Book I, Chap. IV, page 17.

2 This correlation between conceptual abstraction and empirical validity is also emphasized by Mathiot (1990, p. 94), for whom "This solidarity between the emergence of economic discourse as a new scientific discipline and the opening up of a new practical domain for agents is Smith's stroke of genius", or again, further on (*ibid.*, p. 104): "This analysis would remain a hollow formula if there were not a way of appearing and verifying its reality in practice. Here again, the originality and fruitfulness of the Smithian method shines through."

3 K. Marx, "The Poverty of Philosophy. Answer to the "Philosophy of Poverty" by M. Proudhon" (1847 in 1892, p. 33).

4 These digressions take the form, in Smith, of a series of examples ("sort"). Thus, following Chapter XI of Book I of WON, "Of the Rent of Land", there are no less than six digressions "concerning the Variations in the Value of Silver during the Course of the Four last Centuries", to the "Variations in the Proportion between the respective values of Gold and Silver", to the "Grounds of the Suspicion that the Value of Silver still continues to decrease", to the "Different Effects of the Progress of Improvement upon three different Sorts of Rude Produce", in order to reach the "Conclusion of the Digression concerning the Variations in the Value of Silver", then to the "Effects of the progress of Improvement upon the real price of Manufactures", for a total of 59 pages! It is the same in the middle of Chapter III of Book IV with a "Digression concerning Banks of Deposit, particularly concerning that of Amsterdam", or at the end of Chapter V of the same Book "Of Bounties", with a "Digression concerning the Corn Trade and Corn Laws".

5 WON consists of 5 Books: Book I "Of the Causes of Improvement in the Production Powers of Labour, and of the order according to which its produce is naturally distributed among the different ranks of the people", Book II "The Nature, Accumulation, and Employment of Stock", Book III "The Different Progress of Opulence in Different Nations", Book IV "Systems of Political Economy", Book V "The Revenue of the Sovereign or Commonwealth", for a total of about 1000 pages (depending on the edition). From this point of view, to quote Schumpeter (1966, p. 180), "Wealth of Nations was the mature result of a life's work"; "the first full-scale treatise on economics, containing as it does a solid core of production and distribution theory, followed by a review of the past in the light of these abstract principles, and concluding with a battery of policy applications" for Blaug (1985, p. 60).

6 Of which Smith is, at times, aware, challenging his reader: "I shall endeavour to explain, as fully and distinctly as I can, those three subjects in the three following chapters, for which I must very earnestly entreat both the patience and attention of the reader; his patience in order to examine a detail which may perhaps in some places appear unnecessarily tedious; and his attention in order to understand what may, perhaps, after the fullest explication which I am capable of giving it, appear

still in, some degree obscure. I am always willing to run some hazard of being tedious in order to be sure that I am perspicuous; and after taking the utmost pains that I can to be perspicuous, some obscurity may still appear to remain upon a subject in its own nature extremely astracted." (WON, I, IV, p. 22), or further on (WON, IV, p. 341): "I thought it necessary, though at the hazard of being tedious, to examine at full length this popular notion ...", or even: "Some of the foregoing reasonings and observations might perhaps have been more properly placed in those chapters of the first book [...] but I judged it more proper to reserve them for this chapter." (WON, IV, VI, p. 428).

7 "everywhere, the professor [A. Smith] turned his chair into a seat of judgement and bestowed praise and blame. And it was Adam Smith's good fortune that he was thoroughly in sympathy with the humors of his time. He advocated the things that were in the offing, and he made his analysis serve them." (Schumpeter, 1966, pp. 185–186).

1 From the pin manufacture to the division of labor as the birth of the economic subject, a condition for the opulence of nations

Let us take an example of this complexity of presentation, that of the beginning (Book I, chapter 1, pp. 3–10) of WON, relating to "the division of labour", discovered by Smith according to Marx (1892, p. 43), and within which is the famous passage about the "pin-maker" that Smith borrows, in part, from the article "Pin" in the Encyclopedia.[1] This short chapter is punctuated by digressions on the comparative price/quality ratios of Polish, French and English corn (WON, I, I, pp. 5–6), a description of the trades of a weaver, carpenter, smith or spinner (*ibid.*, p. 5) and an enumeration of all the trades and activities involved in the manufacture of a "woollen coat" (*ibid*, p. 9), in order to *implicitly illustrate* the superiority of exchange value over use value for the products of divided labor, to which is added the meticulous description of the division of labor at work in the pin manufacture, with mobilization of different trades and distinct operations:

> "One man draws out the wire, another straightens it, a third cuts it, a fourth points it, a fifth grinds it at the top for receiving the head: to make the head requires two or three distinct operations; to put it on, is a peculiar business; to whiten the pins is another; it is even a trade by itself to put them into the paper; and the important business of making a pin is, in this manner, divided into about eighteen distinct operations, which, in some manufactories, are all performed by distinct hands, though in others the same man will sometimes perform two or three of them. I have seen a small manufactory of this kind where ten men only were employed, and where some of them consequently performed two or three distinct operations." (WON, I, I, p. 4)

The division of labor as the historical embodiment of "labor value"

In addition to these numerous digressions, often illustrative after the fact, the content of this chapter 1 also exposes, in order to show the generality of the reasoning concerning the division of labor that can be applied indifferently on the macroeconomic (*i.e.* the social division) and microeconomic (*i.e.* the manufacturing division) levels,[2] the principles of an economic analysis with a

DOI: 10.4324/9781032649054-4

universal vocation: "labor" as the exclusive foundation of his theory of value where, consequently, the division of labor allows to specify the levels of development of societies, between "savage nations" (WON, I, Intro, p. 1), an "early and rude state of society" (WON, I, IV, pp. 17–18; V, p. 36) (without division of labor) and "civilized and thriving countries" (with division of labor, WON, I, I, p. 9; IV, p. 21). In other words, it invests labor with the unique capacity to constitute value, "the humanization of economic value" to use Polanyi's formula (2001, p. 132), where the division of labor is inscribed as a product of history.

If we understand the theory of value to mean the identification of the factors that explain why a good or service has an exchange value, then it is possible, in opposition to Blaug (1985, p. 39), to attribute to the content of Book I of WON, a Smithian theory of "labor value":

> "The value of any commodity to the person who possesses it, and who means not to use or consume it himself, but to exchange it for other commodities, is equal to the quantity of labour which it enables him to purchase or command. Labour is the real measure of the exchangeable value of all commodities" (WON, I, V, p. 22)

Referring to Hobbes, for whom, according to Smith, wealth is power (WON, I, V, p. 23), Smith enriches his theory of "labor value," which now has two dimensions: i) the theory of the quantity of labor in the sense of the quantity of labor that a commodity "incorporates"; ii) the theory of the disutility of labor in the sense of the quantity of labor that a commodity "makes it possible to obtain" ("can enable to purchase") on the market, by "delegating to another", willingly or unwillingly, through exchange, its production.

The first dimension, that of the quantity of work, is inscribed from the " early and rude state of society which precedes both the accumulation of stock and the appropriation of land" (WON, I, VI, p. 36). Originally, it refers to the quantity that a commodity costs to produce, which Smith illustrates with the famous example of the beaver.[3] In this primitive form, it is the quantity of non-divisible labor, and not its quality (*i.e.* the skills required ["ingenuity exercised"] and/or its "degrees of hardship", etc., WON, I, V, p. 23) that specifies value, the premise of Ricardian and Marxian theories of the value-quantity of labor. The second dimension, that of the disutility of labor, concerns the context of a "commercial society"[4] where the advantage of exchange prevails. It refers, precisely, to a qualitative dimension of work, by means of the doctrine of "toil and trouble", which allows for the division of labor, and which is the real price of everything:

> "The real price of everything, what everything really costs to the man who wants to acquire it, is the toil and trouble of acquiring it. What everything is really worth to the man who has acquired it, and who wants to dispose

of it or exchange it for something else, is the toil and trouble which it can save to himself, and which it can impose upon other people. What is bought with money or with goods is purchased by labour, as much as what we require by the toil of our own body. That money or those goods indeed save us this toil. They contain the value of a certain quantity of labour, which we exchange for what is supposed at the time to contain the value of an equal quantity." (WON, I, V, p. 22)

Within the framework of this "commercial society", on the basis of an innate and now legitimized propensity to exchange (*i.e.* "a certain propensity in human nature" and "the general disposition to exchange", WON, I, II, p. 10, 13), the division of labor grows with the expansion of the markets according to a cumulative dynamic,[5] to become an "impersonal form"[6] at the origin of all economic progress, allowing each individual to find his place in society:

> "As it is the power of exchanging that gives occasion to the division of labour, so the extent of this division must always be limited by the extent of that power, or, in other words, by the extent of the market. When the market is very small, no person can have any encouragement to dedicate himself entirely to one employment, for want of the power to exchange all that surplus part of the produce of his own labour, which is over and above his own occupation, for such parts of the produce of other men's labour as he has occasion for." (WON, I, III, p. 22)

Smith shows, here, that the division of labor impacts labor beyond the product's finality, *i.e.* responding to a need, in a context of the search for abundance of the social product, characteristic of an "advanced state of society" (WON, I, VI, p. 36). This dynamic requires a philosophical pre-requisite, that of emancipating divided labor from an "anthropology of needs" (Mathiot, 1990, p. 68), that we find in Hutcheson, Hume or Quesnay, for example, where Man, as a "being of need", is at the center of a Doctrine where the concepts of wealth, value, labor, etc. are, precisely, derived from this role of need, to replace it with a "moral anthropology of economic man" (*ibid.*, p. 69) in which the subject who profits from the exchange of his surplus replaces the subject who satisfies his needs, illustrating a cooperative game of exchange summarized by the formula "give me what I want, and you will get what you want", WON, I, II, p. 11). Thus:

> "It is not from the benevolence of the butcher, the brewer, or the baker, that we expect our dinner, but from their regard to their own interest. We address ourselves, not to their humanity but to their self-love; and never talk to them of our own necessities but of their advantages." (WON, I, II, p. 11)

To do this, the economic subject must have an "advantage" in exchanging the surplus, the fruit of divided labor, and he must be in a framework of division of labor that allows him to maximize it.

Let us take up these two points.

The framework of the (technical) division of labor allowing to increase productivity, and thus to maximize this surplus, is precisely described by Smith in terms of parcellisation and specialization of tasks in connection with the nascent machinery, on the basis of which F.W. Taylor, at the time of the second industrial revolution at the end of the nineteenth century, will build Scientific Management, *i.e.* Taylorism:

> "This great increase of the quantity of work, which, in consequence of the division of labour, the same number of people are capable of performing, is owing to three different circumstances: I. To the increase of dexterity in every particular workman; II. To the saving of the time which is commonly lost in passing from one species of work to another; III. To the invention of a great number of machines which facilitate and abridge labour, and enable one man to do the work of many." (WON, I, I, p. 6).

In detail, the first condition, "the improvement of the dexterity of the workman" is to reduce "every man's business to someone simple operation, and by making this operation the sole employment of his life" (*ibid.*, p. 6); the second, "saving the time", "commonly lost in passing from one sort of work to another", needs to allow the different trades "to be carried out in the same workhouse" (*ibid.*, p. 7) in order to remotivate the worker and to fight against "the habit of sauntering and of indolent careless application which is naturally, or rather necessarily, acquired by every country workman who is obliged to change his work and his tools [which] renders him almost always slothful and lazy, and incapable of any vigorous application" (*ibidem*). Finally, the machinery, result of this technical division of labor,[7] allows to "facilitated and abridged" the labour (*ibidem*). In this technical framework of the division of labor, a factor of well-being for a man (as a socio-technical condition for the maximization of an exchangeable surplus) in Book I, and not of enslavement of its "intellectual, social and martial virtues"[8] as developed in Book V (WON, V, I, p. 613), the economic subject appropriates the fruit of his divided labor and maximizes his personal interest as soon as, beyond the satisfaction of his primary needs, he takes "advantage" of exchanging his surplus. As a result, exchange becomes mutually advantageous since it allows the personal enrichment, and therefore the abundance, of all its actors and thus naturally leads to its generalization (to its universalism) within the market society, the guarantee of social prosperity. Thus, at the aggregate level, *i.e.* in the context of generalized exchange (or generalized division of labor), needs are satisfied by the exchange of surpluses, guaranteeing "general plenty or opulence", the economic subject, undifferentiated as to his legitimate interest in producing surplus, becoming a market subject:

"Every workman has a great quantity of his own work to dispose of beyond what he himself has occasion for; and every other workman being exactly in the same situation, he is enabled to exchange a great quantity of his own goods for a great quantity, or, what comes to the same thing, for the price of a great quantity of theirs. He supplies them abundantly with what they have occasion for, and they accommodate him as amply with what he has occasion for, and a general plenty diffuses itself through all the different ranks of the society." (WON, I, I, pp. 8–9).

This mutually advantageous interest, linked to exchange in a context of division of labor, functions as a (self-serving) benevolence towards others; benevolence, a natural feeling in which each individual shares the same moral purpose and which has the indirect but decisive consequence of making individuality the paradoxical foundation of the social relationship. This thesis of the existence of a natural and universal sense, oriented towards the feeling of benevolence, capable of grasping moral properties independently of any convention and therefore of any rationalism is the basis of Adam Smith's moral philosophy, inherited from his Master, Francis Hutcheson,[9] holder of the Chair of Moral Philosophy and Professor at the University of Glasgow. In the tradition of the scholastics and the philosophers of natural law, Smith's moral philosophy is based on the hypothesis of altruism, or, more precisely, of the coexistence *of man in a situation of abundance* of self-interest with (self-interested) benevolence towards others, which can also be compared to the " cordial affection" contained in Book III of David Hume's Treatise on Human Nature (1739). This apparent contradiction is resolved by the " sympathy" that drives individuals, enabling them to put themselves in another's role and imagine how we would feel if we were in her or his situation. In other words, sympathy enables us to project ourselves into the situation occupied by another, in order to imagine what our affects might then be, *i.e.* what the feelings and sufferings of another might be. But Smith, faced with this level of abstraction, and compared to his glorious predecessors, "comes back to earth", seeks to found a practical and operational philosophy, a "palatable and persuasive" meaning of Moral according to Hirschman (2013, pp. 18–19), a junction between moral and social theory allowing man to fulfill his overriding motivation: to improve his condition and, consequently, to better our condition. Therefore, knowing that, for man, the good, unlike the true, cannot be learned, the question is how can the good (or virtues) of the "general system" prevail over the evil (or vices) of the particular? In order to propose a moral philosophy likely to bring together the moral sense of practice, on the one hand, and the individual moral sense of the common interest, on the other, Smith operates, in the first place, an ideological "sleight of hand" by replacing the mandevillian terms (contained in The Fable of the Bees: or, Private Vices, Publick Benefits, 1714) that are too connoted with "passion" and "vice" by neutral terms such as " advantage" or "interest". Then, in a second step, he shows that it is the fulfillment of the conditions of increased general welfare, that is, the realization of a "civilized and thriving nation" where "the produce of the whole labour of the society is so great, that all are often abundantly supplied, and a workman, even of the lowest and poorest order, if he is frugal and industrious, may enjoy a greater share of the necessaries and conveniences of life than it is possible for any savage to acquire" (WON, Introduction, pp. 1–2), which allows the main springs of human action to converge:

> "By holding that ambition, the lust for power, and the desire for respect can all be satisfied by economic improvement, Smith undercut the idea that passion can be pitted against passion, or the interests against the passions. This whole train of thought becomes suddenly incomprehensible, if not nonsensical, and there is a return to the stage [...] when the major passions were considered to be a solid bloc and to feed on each other." (Hirschman, 2013, p. 110).

The advantage to the exchange and the desire for unlimited enrichment as conditions to the opulence of nations

It is in the supreme stage of realization of the advantage, for each, of exchanging his surplus within the abundance, for all, permitted by the division of labor, making the exchange mutually advantageous, that Smith allows the identification of passions with interests within the market economy, a guarantor of prosperity through the fulfillment of personal interests:

> "It is thus the private interests and passions of individuals naturally dispose them to turn their stock towards the employments which in ordinary cases are most advantageous to the society. But, if from this natural preference, they should turn too much of it towards those employments, the fall of profit in them and the rise of it in all others, immediately dispose them to alter this faulty distribution. Without any intervention of law, the private interests and passions of men naturally lead them to divide and distribute the stock of every society, among all the different employments carried on in it, as nearly as possible in the proportion which is most agreeable to the interest of the whole society." (WON, IV, VII, p. 492).

In fact, the Smithian economic subject, producer of surplus, by obeying his own interests, in a context of abundance, contributes to the public interest as an echangist, illustration of the natural harmonization of interests. Let us emphasize, here, the increasingly close connection between the two terms "public interest" and "abundance". Now, in a context of abundance, characterized by a high degree of predictability and constancy of motives and behaviors dictated by interest alone, this reasoning can easily be extended to society as a whole, since free competition on the factor market tends to equalize the "net advantages" of factors in all activities, and consequently allows for an optimal allocation of resources between activities:

> "in a society where things were left to follow their natural course, where there was perfect liberty, and where every man was perfectly free both to choose what occupation he thought proper, and to change it as often as he though proper. Every man's interest would prompt him to seek the advantageous, and to shun the disadvantageous employment." (WON, I, X, p. 76)

As we can see, for this mutually advantageous interest to operate, a society of opulence (or in the process of being so, WON, I, VII, p. 42) is required, necessary but not sufficient condition, because it is necessary, also, that this opulence is shared (condition of second rank), even in an unequal way when:

i the inequality of wealth and land, inherited or produced, results in a desire for unlimited enrichment,[10] and accumulation of capital which will increase the capacity of the society to wage,[11] and therefore to prosper:

> "The proportion between capital and labour [...] seems everywhere to regulate the proportion between industry and idleness. Wherever capital predominates, industry prevails: wherever revenue, idleness. Every increase or diminution of capital, therefore, naturally tends to increase or diminish the real quantity of industry, the number of productive hands, and, consequently, the exchange value of the annual produce of the land and labour of the country, the real wealth and revenue of all its inhabitants. Capitals are increased by parsimony, and diminished by prodigality and misconduct. Whatever a person saves from his revenue he adds to his capital, and either employs it himself in maintaining an additional number of productive hands, or enables some other person to do so by lending it to him for an interest, that is, for a share of the profits." (WON, II, III, p. 259)

ii the inequality of "wages and pecuniary wages and profit" (WON, I, X, p. 77) is justified by "the different employments of labour and stock", that is "certain circumstances in the employments themselves, which, either really or at least in the imaginations of men, make up for a small pecuniary gain in some, and counter-balance a great one in others." (*Ibidem*).

Let's take up these two points, whose common denominator is that, for Smith, inequality between men is merely the product of social structures and the socialization of individuals; Smithian anthropology therefore postulates the natural equality of men.

i The first shows that the accumulation of capital comes, from the first period of the advanced state of society, from labor itself,[12] workers who, thanks to "an uncommon degree of dexterity and ingenuity and superior resistance to hardship" (WON, I, VI, p. 36), have made it possible to generate a surplus well above their immediate needs[13]:

> "As soon as stock has accumulated in the hands of particular persons, some of them will naturally employ it in setting to work industrious people, whom they will supply with materials and subsistence, in order to make a profit by the sale of their work, or by what their labour adds to the value of the materials. In exchanging the complete manufacture either money, for labour, or for other goods, over and above what may be sufficient to pay the price of the materials, and the wages of the workmen, something must be given for the profits of the undertaker of the work who hazards his stock in this adventure." (WON, I, VI, p. 37).[14]

It is, therefore, the accumulation of capital, as "the whole stock of materials and wages which he advanced" (*ibidem*), which makes it possible to generate profits, "a different name for the wages of a particular sort of labour, the labour of inspection and direction"[15] (*ibid.*), even though they are not fixed by the quantity and nature of this "labour of inspection and direction" but result from "the value of the stock employed [...] in proportion to the extent of this stock" (*ibid.*) to which is added the employer's ability to extract an "additional quantity" of profit compared to the advance of wages and the furnishing of materials (WON, I, VI, p. 38), suggesting, here, the future theories of profit based on "exploitation" (Sismondi) and "surplus labor" (Marx).[16] Moreover, the rate of profit "varies more or less with the certainty or uncertainty of the returns [...] The ordinary rate of profit always rises more or less with the risk" even if this dynamic is not rigorously proportional "or so as to compensate it completely" since the "Bankruptcies are most frequent in the most hazardous trades" (WON, I, X, p. 86). Finally, the rate of profit varies according to "the extent of the market" (*ibid.*, p. 88). It is, therefore, this conception of capital accumulation, and its allocation, which conditions future opulence, made possible by the surplus of previous labor, which makes the logic of unlimited enrichment, and thus the inequality of possessions, compatible with the interest of all. The latter can then be understood as the realization of the "full employment" of the factors of production; "productive labour"[17] being what produces wealth, the enrichment of all remaining subordinate to the wealth of a few as long as the latter are satisfied with "hospitality without luxury and liberality without ostentation" (WON, V, III, p. 724), therefore that this wealth is, mainly, mobilized to the accumulation, to the employment of this " productive labor", and not to prodigality (or "misconduct") that tend "to diminish the funds destined for the maintenance of productive labour" although the "Great nations are never impoverished by private, though they sometimes are by public prodigality and misconduct" (WON, II, III, pp. 262–263), misconducts involving luxurious spending and the use of " unproductive labor".[18] In this sense, Smith's satisfaction with the general interest has more to do with the growth of the nation's wealth than with the way it is shared:

> "The real recompense of labour, the real quantity of the necessaries and conveniences of life which it can procure to the labourer, has during the course of the present century, increased perhaps in a still greater proportion than its money price [...] it is not the money price of labour only, but its real recompense, which has augmented. Is this improvement in the circumstances of the lower ranks of the people to be regarded as an advantage or as an inconveniency to the society? [...] what improves the circumstances of the greater part can never be regarded as an inconveniency to the whole. No society can surely be flourishing and happy of which the far greater part of the members are poor and miserable. It is but equity, besides, that they who feed, clothe, and lodge the whole body of the people, should have such a share of the produce of their own labour as to be themselves tolerably well fed, clothed, and lodged." (WON, I, VIII, pp. 60–61)

ii Wage inequalities (WON, I, X, "Inequalities arising from the Nature of the Employments themselves", p. 77 and ff) are explained and justified by *a*) the relative attractiveness of jobs (*i.e.* "the agreeableness or disagreeableness of the employments", *Ibid.*, p. 77), with wages varying positively with the disutility of work,[19] the same reasoning applies to profits[20]; *b*) the cost (human and financial) of acquiring the necessary qualification for each of them, introducing the modern concept of "human capital"[21]. Smith shows, here, that the cost of a man's education and training can be considered as an investment in the expectation, with a reasonable time horizon "regard being had to the very uncertain duration of human life" (*ibid.*, p. 78), of future gains (analogous to an investment in physical capital), economically justified when it is more than amortized, within "a reasonable time" by the related wage differentials[22]; *c*) the regularity of employment induced, in particular, by the seasonality of certain activities, and/or the precariousness of manufacturing employment mainly made up of "journeyman"[23]; *d*) the trust and responsibility demanded of the " liberal professions", such as physicians and lawyers, to whom we entrust, respectively, "our life and reputation" (*ibid.*, p. 81), and certain employees, such as executives and managers, to pay for insurance against theft and disclosure of secrets (*e.g.* trade secrets, *ibid.*, p. 131)[24]; *e*) the probability of achieving anticipated earnings given the uncertainty of outcomes for certain types of jobs (*i.e.* "the probability or improbability of success in them" (*ibid.*, p. 81). Smith is, here, at the foundation of modern economic analysis of choices in an uncertain future. Using the references of lotteries and insurance (*ibid.*, pp. 83–84), Smith shows that men tend to overvalue the chances of uncertain gains compared to losses, so they are weakly "risk averse" or "risk lovers", due to "the natural confidence which every man has more or less, not only in his own abilities, but in his own good fortune [...] The contempt of risk and the presumptuous hope of success." (*ibid.*, p. 82, 84)[25]:

"The over-weening conceit which the greater part of men have of their own abilities, is an ancient evil remarked by the philosophers and moralists of all ages. Their absurd presumption in their own good fortune has been less taken notice of. It is, however, if possible still more universal. There is no man living who when in tolerable health and spirits, has not some share of it. The chance of gain is by every man more or less over-valued, and the chance of loss is by most men undervalued, and by scarce any man, who is in tolerable health and spirits, valued more than it is worth." (WON, I, X, p. 83)

As a result, occupations that can be estimated to have relatively high but uncertain earnings have lower average wage rates than occupations whose earnings can be predicted with certainty. Indeed, men always overestimate their chances of success in these risky professions (the "liberal professions" of law, for example, *ibid.*, p. 82), where "all the most generous and liberal spirits are eager to crowd into them" (*Ibidem*), although they are, in the end, "very poorly rewarded, in terms of monetary gain" (*Ibidem*); the same reasoning can be applied to the differential rates of profit between different branches of industry (*ibid.*, p. 86 ff): "In all the different employments of stock, the ordinary rate of profit varies more or less with the certainty or uncertainty of the returns [...] The ordinary rate of profit always rises more or less with the risk. It does not, however, seem to rise in proportion to it, or so as to compensate it completely." (*ibid.*, p. 86).

Here, as often in WON (*cf. supra*), general reasoning takes precedence over detailed developments, and from the point of view of readability "the devil is in the details": if competition does not equalize the pecuniary returns of the different occupations and the different "uses of capital", it ultimately equalizes the "net benefits" of the different occupations and branches of industry, *i.e.* the sum of the pecuniary and non-pecuniary benefits, the differences in earnings being compensated by one or more of the five factors (*a, b, c, d, e*) detailed earlier:

"The five circumstances above mentioned, though they occasion considerable inequalities in the wages of labour and profits of stock, occasion none in the whole of the advantages and disadvantages, real or imaginery, of the different employments of either. The nature of those circumstances is such, that they make up for a small pecuniary gain in some, and counterbalance a great one in others." (WON, I, X, p. 89)

It is market mechanisms, within a framework of perfect competition, and thus within "the obvious and simple system of natural liberty" (WON, IV, IX, p. 540), that will harmoniously reconcile private interests and economic efficiency; in other words, competition, by equalizing rates of return and limiting excessive gains, and thus by ensuring the equivalence of exchanges (no one loses out on the market), leads to an optimal allocation of labor and capital between activities, thus maximizing well-being. The "invisible hand" is held out to us.

Notes

1 Written by Alexandre Deleyre for the 1st edition of the Encyclopedia (" Encyclopédie, ou Dictionnaire raisonné des Sciences, des Arts et des Métiers, par une Société de Gens de Lettres, mis en ordre et publié par M. Diderot, et quant à la Partie Mathématique, par M. d'Alembert", Tome 5, 1755, p. 804–8), this article begins as follows: "The pin is of all the mechanical works the thinnest, the most common, the least precious, and yet one of those which require perhaps the most combinations: from which it follows that art, as well as nature, displays its prodigies in small objects, and that industry is as limited in its views, as it is admirable in its resources; for a pin undergoes eighteen operations before entering the trade", eighteen operations that are described by Smith in WON (I, p. 4). Marx, from the very first pages of "A Contribution to the Critique of Political Economy" (1859), in his "Historical Notes on the Analysis of Commodities", refers to this manufacture of pins by A. Smith, as an illustration of the advantage of the Division of Labor as a productive force, specifying, in a footnote, that W. Petty had done it before him using the manufacture of a watch. (Marx, 1965, p. 305)

2 "The effects of the division of labour, in the general business of society, will be more easily understood, by considering in what manner it operates in some particular manufactures." (WON, I, I, p. 3).

3 "If among a nation of hunters, for example, it usually costs twice the labour to kill a beaver which it does to kill a deer, one beaver should naturally exchange for, or be worth two deer. It is natural that what is usually the produce of two days' or two hours' labour, should be worth double of what is usually the produce of one day's or one hour's labour." (WON, I, VI, p. 36). In this simple model of a society of hunters, with two goods (deer and beaver) and only one "mode of production" (hunting), relative prices are governed by relative labor costs: a beaver will be exchanged for two deers if it takes twice as long to kill it. In this case, the price is determined by supply alone, which considerably limits the theoretical insights of this model. But suppose that the exchange value becomes one fallow deer for one beaver (for reasons of demand, *i.e.* undifferentiated preferences (tastes) and consumption patterns for both; and/or reasons of supply, *i.e.* it still takes one hour (versus two) to kill a deer, but deers are farther from the initial hunting point than beavers), then the beaver "producer" will relatively abandon his activity (which costs him two hours) in favor of that of two deers, with which he could now buy two beavers. It follows that deer hunting will increase and beaver hunting will decrease until the exchange value is effectively equalized (for an explanation, see Blaug, 1985, pp. 41–42).

4 "When the division of labour has been once thoroughly established, it is but a very small part of a man's wants which the produce of his own labour can supply. He supplies the far greater part of them by exchanging that surplus part of the produce of his on labour, which is over and above his own consumption, for such parts of the produce of other men's labour as he has occasion for. Every man thus lives by exchanging, or becomes in some measure a merchant, and the society itself grows to be what is properly a commercial society." (WON, I, IV, p. 17).

5 "the division of labour [...] so far as it can be introduced, occasions, in every art, a proportionable increase of the productive powers of labour. The separation of different trades and employments from one another, seems to have taken place, in consequence of this advantage [...] Every workman has a great quantity of his own work to dispose of beyond what he himself has occasion for; and every other workman being exactly in the same situation, he is enabled to exchange a great quantity of his own goods for a great quantity, or, what comes to the same thing, for the price of a great quantity of theirs. He supplies the abundantly with what they have occasion for, and they accommodate him as amply with what he has occasion for, and a general plenty diffuses itself through all the different ranks of the society." (WON, I, I, p. 5, 8–9).

6 "Among men [...], the most dissimilar geniuses are of use to one another; the different produces of their respective talents, by the general disposition to truck, barter, and exchange, being brought, as it were, into a common stock, where every man may purchase whatever part of the produce of other men's talents he has occasion for." (WON, I, II, p. 13).

7 "the invention of all those machines by which labour is so much facilitated and abridged, seems to have been originally owing to the division of labour. Men are much more likely to discover easier and readier methods of attaining any object, when the whole attention of their minds is directed towards that single object, than when it is dissipated among a great variety of things. But in consequence of the division of labour, the whole of every man's attention comes naturally to be directed towards some one very simple object [...] Whoever has been much accustomed to visit such manufactures, must frequently have been shown very pretty machines, which were the inventions of such workmen, in order to facilitate and quicken their own particular part of the work." (WON, I, I, pp. 7–8).

8 "In the progress of the division of labour, the employment of the far greater part of those who live by labour, that is, of the great body of the people, comes to be confined to a few very simple operations; frequently to one or two. But the understandings of the greater part of men are necessarily formed by their ordinary employments. The man whose life is spent in performing a few simple operations, of which the effects, too, are, perhaps, always the same, or very nearly the same, has no occasion to exert his understanding, or to exercise his invention in finding out expedients for removing difficulties which never occur. He naturally loses, therefore, the habit of such exertion, and generally becomes as stupid and ignorant as it is possible for a human creature to become. The torpor of his mind renders him, not only incapable of relishing or bearing a part in any rational conversation, but of conceiving any generous noble, or tender sentiment, and, consequently, of forming any just judgement concerning may, even, of the ordinary duties of private life. Of the great and extensive interests of his country, he is altogether incapable of judging" (WON, V, I, p. 613).

9 Francis Hutcheson (1694–1746), Professor of Moral Philosophy at Glasgow University, was Smith's teacher (he was one of his students from 1737 to 1740) and one of his predecessors in this Chair.

10 This desire for unlimited enrichment is associated, for Marx, to greed: "The only wheels which political economy sets in motion are greed and the war amongst the greedy" while: "The worker may only have enough for him to want to live, and may only want to live in order to have that." (Marx, 1977, p. 67, 112).

11 It is indeed a question of capital accumulation, therefore of productive investment, Smith warning against the dangers of prodigality and speculation (WON, IV, I, p. 330): "No complaint [...] is more common than that of a scarcity of money. This complaint [...] is not always confined to improvident spendthrifts. It is sometimes general [...] Over-trading is the common cause of it. Sober men, whose projects

have been disproportioned to their capitals, are as likely to have neither wherewithal to buy money, nor credit to borrow it, as prodigals whose expense has been dispropotioned to their revenue. Before their projects can be brought to bear, their stock is gone, and their credit with it." Smith draws some lessons from this as to the reasons for holding money, to be compared with those contained in Say's law (*ibid.*, p. 331–2): "Goods do not always draw money so readily as money draws goods, in the long run, they draw it more necessarily than even it draws them. Goods can serve many other purposes besides purchasing money, but money can serve no other purpose besides purchasing goods. Money necessarily runs after goods, but goods do not always or necessarily run after money. The man who buys, does not always mean to sell again, but frequently to use or to consume; whereas he who sells, always means to buy again. [...] It is not for its own sake that men desire money, but for the sake of what they can purchase with it." We find, here, the "general formula of the commodity", exposed by Marx at the beginning of Book I of Capital (1990, p. 200 and ff), within which money (M) (and not capital) spent (and not advanced) serves as a neutral intermediary in the process of exchange of commodities (C), a simple correspondence of use values: "The direct form of the circulation of commodities is C-M-C, the transformation of commodities into money and the re-conversion of money into commodities: selling in order to buy [...] The path C-M-C proceeds from the extreme constituted by one commodity, and ends with the extreme constituted by another, which falls out of circulation and into consumption. Consumption, the satisfaction of needs, in short use-value, is therefore its final goal." (*ibid.*, p. 247, 250). For a development, see below Chap. 4.

12 "Labour was the first price, the original purchase money that was paid for all things. It was not by gold or by silver, but by labour, that all the wealth of the world was originally purchased; and its value, to those who possess it, and who want to exchange it for new productions, is precisely equal to the quantity of labour which it can enable them to purchase [...] But though labour be the real measure of the exchangeable value of all commodities, it is not that by which their value is commonly estimated. It is often difficult to ascertain the proportion between two different quantities of labour. The time spent in two different sorts of work will not always alone determine this proportion. The different degrees of hardship endured, and of ingenuity exercised, must likewise be taken into account." (WON, I, V, p. 23).

13 Which raises the problem of the allocation of savings. For Smith, money fulfils the three traditional functions of i) a unit of account ("In consequence of its being the measure of value, we estimate that of all other commodities by the quantity of money which they will exchange for.", WON, IV, I, p. 323), ii) as an intermediary for exchanges ("In consequence of its being the instrument of commerce, when we have money we can more readily obtain whatever else we have occasion for than by means of any other commodity", *ibid.*), and iii) as a reserve of value, but only for a short time because "It is not for its own sake that men desire money, but for the sake of what they can purchase with it" (*Ibid.*, p. 332). Therefore, if we exclude the *prolonged* hoarding of income, as Say will repeat in his law, money is reduced to serving as a means of exchange, and saving (or non-consumption) is necessarily identical to investment (or accumulation): "Every man of common understanding will endeavour to employ whatever stock he can command in procuring present enjoyment or future profit. If it is employed in procuring present enjoyment, it is a stock reserved for immediate consumption. If it is employed in procuring future profit, it must procure this profit either by staying with him, or by going from him. In the one case it is afixed, in the other,it is circulating capital. A man must be perfectly crazy who, where there is tolerable security, does not employ all the stock

he commands, whether his own or borrowed of other people, in some one or other of those three ways." (WON, II, I, p. 214).

14 Or even: "The industry of the society can augment only in proportion as its capital augments, and its capital only in proportion to what can be gradually saved out of its revenue." (WON, IV, II, p. 347).

15 It is understandable, therefore, that Smith often uses the expression "the wages of labour" on purpose, which, outside this context, would be a tautology.

16 "the whole produce of labour does not always belong to the labourer. He must in most cases share it with the owner of the stock which employs him. Neither is the quantity of labour commonly employed in acquiring or producing any commodity, the only circumstance which can regulate the quantity which it ought commonly to purchase, command, or exchange for. An additional quantity, it is evident, must be due for the profits of the stock which advanced the wages and finished the materials of that labour." (WON, I, VI, p. 38). For a comment on Marx (1977, p. 26).

17 "There is one sort of labour which adds to the value of the subject upon which it is bestowed: there is another which has no such effect. The former, as it produces a value, may be called productive; the latter, unproductive. Thus the labour of a manufacturer adds, generally, to the value of the materials which he works upon, that of his own maintenance and of his master's profit. The labour of a menial servant, on the contrary, adds to the value of nothing." (WON, II, III, p. 253). Therefore, "A man grows rich by employing a multitude of manufacturers: he grows poor by maintaining a multitude of menial servants." (*ibid.*, p. 254). It should be noted that this unproductive labour extends, in Smith's case, to all trades and all functions, particularly service functions, especially services that do not directly serve industry. Here, Smith's central idea is that productive labor is incorporated into the production of objects and that this added value endures through the object sold beyond the labor performed: "The sovereign, for example, with all the officers both of justice and war serve under him, the whole army and navy, are unproductive labourers. They are the servants of the public, and are maintained by a part of the annual produce of the industry of other people. Their service, how honourable, how useful, or how necessary soever, produces nothing for which an equal quantity of service can afterwards be procured. The protection, security, and defence of the commonwealth, the effect of their labour this year, will no purchase its protection, security, and defence for the year to come" (*ibid.*, p. 254). The same applies to churchmen, lawyers, physicians, "men of letters of all kinds", but also to players, buffoons, musicians, etc. (*Ibidem*) We shall see, later, that Smith will (in Books IV and V) substantially modify this assessment, by showing the usefulness, indeed the necessity, of many of his occupations and functions for the accomplishment of the "system of natural liberty".

18 "every prodigal appears to be a public enemy, and every frugal man [holder of savings that can be accumulated, Ph.G.] a public benefactor." (WON, II, III, p. 262), and further (WON, IV, I, pp. 323–324): "A frugal man, or a man eager to be rich, is said to love money; and a careless, generous, or a profuse man, is said to be indifferent about it. To grow rich is to get money [...] A rich country, in the same manner as a rich man, is supposed to be abounding in money.".

19 "The wages of labour vary with the ease or hardship, the cleanliness or dirtiness, the honourableness or dishonourableness of the employment." (*ibid.*, p. 77).

20 "Disagreeableness and disgrace affect the profits of stock in the same manner as the wages of labour." (*ibid.*, p. 78).

21 "The wages of labour vary with the easiness and cheapness, or the difficulty and expense of learning the business." (*ibid.*, p. 78).

22 "The work which he [a man educated] learns to perform, it must be expected, over and above the usual wages of common labour, will replace to him the whole expense of his education, with at least the ordinary profits of an equally valuable capital. It must do this too in a reasonable time, regard being had to the very uncertain duration of human life, in the same manner as to the more certain duration of the machine." (*ibid.*, p. 78).

23 "The wages of labour in different occupations vary with the constancy or inconstancy of employment [...] The high wages of those workmen are not so much the recompense of their skill, as the compensation for the inconstancy of their employment." (*ibid.*, pp. 79–80).

24 "Such confidence could not safely be reposed in people of a very mean or low condition. Their reward must be such, therefore, as may give them that rank in the society which so important a trust requires", especially since, in conjunction with the previous accumulation of human capital (*see above, b*) "The long time and the great expense which must be laid out in their education, when combined with this circumstance, will necessarily enhance still further the price of their labour." (*ibid.*, p. 81).

25 This important work by Smith on lotteries makes it possible to show that agents do not behave in the same way with respect to gains and losses, an issue central to the contemporary "prospect theory" developed by Kahneman & Tversky from 1979 onwards, and which earned the former the Nobel Prize in Economics in 2002 (Tversky died in 1996). Thus, contrary to Smith's theory, in which the agent favors risky gain, in Kahneman & Tversky's model (1979), which was constructed from experimental work, agents suffer more from a loss than they enjoy an equivalent gain, *i.e.* "loss aversion". Second, agents prefer certainty to randomness in situations of gain and randomness to certainty in situations of loss, with an aversion to risk for gain and an affection for risk for loss. Thus, when we are sure of winning a certain amount, we prefer not to take the risk of winning less. Conversely, when one is sure of losing, the desire to avoid this loss may lead one to accept taking a risk.

Bibliography

Blaug, Mark (1985). *Economic Theory in Retrospect* (1962). Cambridge: Cambridge University Press, fourth edition.

Hirschman, Albert Otto (2013). *The Passions and the Interests. Political Arguments for Capitalism before its Triumph* (1977). Princeton and Oxford: Princeton University Press, "Princeton Classics".

Hume, David (1739). *A Treatise on Human Nature: being An Attempt to introduce the experimental Method of Reasoning into Moral Subjects*, London, Printed for John Noon, at the White-Hart, near Mercer's-Chapel in Cheapside.

Kahneman, Daniel & Tversky, Amos (1979). Prospect Theory: An Analysis of Decisions under Risk. *Econometrica*, *47*(2), march, 263–291.

Kuhn, Thomas Samuel (1970). *The Structure of Scientific Revolutions* (1962), Second Edition, Enlarged, Chicago: The University of Chicago Press, International Encyclopedia of Unified Science.

Marx, Karl (1892). *The Poverty of Philosophy. Answer to the "Philosophy of Poverty" by M. Proudhon* (1874). Moscow: Foreign Languages Publishing House.

Marx, Karl (1965). *Œuvres Economie*, Tome I, Paris, Edition établie et annotée par Maximilien Rubel, Editions Gallimard, NRF, coll. "Bibliothèque de la Pléiade".

Marx, Karl (1977). *Economic and Philosophic Manuscripts of 1844*. Moscow: Progress Publishers, fifth revised edition.

Marx, Karl (1990). *Capital. A Critique of Political Economy*, Volume I (1867), Translated by Ben Fowkes. London: Penguin Books in association with New Left Review, Penguin Classics.

Mathiot, Jean (1990). *Adam Smith. Philosophie et Economie. De la sympathie à l'échange*. Paris: PUF, coll. "Philosophies" n° 24.

Polanyi, Karl (2001). *The Great Transformation. The Political and Economic Origins of Our Time* (1944). Boston (Mass.): Beacon Press.

Schumpeter, Joseph Alois (1966). *History of Economic Analysis* (1954), New York: Oxford Universty Press, sixth printing.

Smith, Adam (1913). *An Inquiry Into the Nature and Causes of the Wealth of Nations* (1776). London: George Routledge & Sons, Limited; New York, E.P. Dutton and Co.

2 From the conditions of the opulence of individuals to that of nations

The market and the "invisible hand"

The universal character of this equivalence of exchanges, which can be brought closer to the third Newtonian law of equality of action and reaction[1] applied to all elementary exchanges, *i.e.* the equality of supply and demand actions, allows Smith to construct, from it, the economic and social order, marked by the interdependence of all prices and incomes, and regulated by the Market, the embodiment of the compatibility of agents' revenues with the prices of goods.

The market: from the practice of exchange to the providential manifestation of the "invisible hand"

Although Smith is very wary of demonstrations based on analogy,[2] there are in WON implicit links between the laws that govern the functioning of markets and the three Newtonian laws constitutive of classical Mechanics, (*i.e.* Dynamics or Newton's laws of motion) contained in *Philosophiae Naturalis Principia Mathematica* (1687; Mathematical Principles of Natural Philosophy), successively the "Law of Inertia" (WON, I, V), the "law of forces" (WON, I, VI), the "law of Action and Reaction" (WON, I, VII). Thus, the Market is at the same time, the place where any action is opposed to an equal reaction, where the actions of the two forces are reciprocal, and the order within which, in the absence of external forces, the quantity of motion of this system remains constant:

> "The quantity of every commodity brought to market naturally suits itself to the effectual demand. It is the interest of all those who employ their land, labour, or stock, in bringing any commodity to the market, but the quantity should never exceed the effectual demand; and it is the interest of all other people that it should never fall short of that demand. If at any time it exceeds the effectual demand, some of the component parts of its price must be paid below their natural rate. If it is rent, the interest of the landlords will immediately prompt them to withdraw a part of their land; and if it is wages or profit, the interest of the labourers in the one case, and of their employers in the other, will prompt them to withdraw a part of

DOI: 10.4324/9781032649054-5

their labour or stock from this employment. The quantity brought to market will soon be no more than sufficient to supply the effectual demand. The parts of its price will rise to their natural rate, and the whole to its natural price." (WON, I, VII, p. 44).

A symmetrical reasoning of convergence towards the natural price is brought when, on the contrary, "the quantity brought to market is fall[ing] short of the effectual demand" (*Ibidem*). The reference to Newton is even more explicit when Smith states that "the natural price is the central price, to which the price of all commodities are continually gravitating." (*Ibidem*).

Here we find Smith's desire to scientifically found a practical moral philosophy anchored in the economist's own "reality", since he favours reasoning in terms of prices and market quantities, to the detriment of an "abstract face to face" between supply and demand, showing that the Market embodies the actual practice of exchange. In this framework, imperfection (or disequilibrium), here "when the quantity of any commodity exceeds the effectual demand" or "If, on the contrary, the quantity brought to market should at any time fall short of the effectual demand" (WON, I, VII, p. 44) on the contrary, when "the quantity brought to the market remains for some time below effective demand", is not synonymous with failure or impotence of the system, which would then be caught in default, but refers to an acceptable result in the best of all possible worlds (we will come back to this below), much preferable to the idealized result of an abstract system. Smith reverses, here, the traditional forms of economic normativity, in favor of a norm rooted in the experience or actual practice of the rule, taking the form of a plurality of interrelated relations or situations, as illustrated by the gravitation of "market prices" around the "natural price":

"The actual price at which any commodity is commonly sold is called its market price. It may either be above, or below, or exactly the same with its natural price [...] The natural price is the central price, to which the price of all commodities are continually gravitating. Different accidents may sometimes keep them suspended a good deal above it, and sometimes force them down even somewhat below it. But whatever may be the obstacles which hinder them from settling in this centre of repose and its continuance, they are constantly tending towards it." (WON, I, VII, p. 43, 44).

There is thus a space of real variations in connection with the "effectual demand", the well-named one,[3] which functions less as a norm than as a delimitation of a space of possible exchanges, the one that is sufficient "to effectuate the bringing of the commodity to market" (*ibid.*, p. 43), and it is in this space that the Market operates, the realized exchange fixing the quantities and the related unique price. In this framework, "equilibrium is not a matter of calculation, but of practice", to use Mathiot's formula (1980, p. 111) where "it is from the interplay of differences, effectively observed in the exchanges carried out, that the fixing of the natural price as a center of gravitation for these differences is established" (*ibidem*). And the regulation of the market, *i.e.* the compensation of these differences, the result of behaviour in terms of individual interests adopted by the agents in this space, is in no way idealized, but participates in an empirical process in terms of prices and quantities that is temporally *asymmetrical*, with compensation (by trial and error) by prices when there is excess demand, and compensation (quasi-instantaneous) by quantities in the case of a shortfall of demand (or of relative overproduction):

> "The market price of any particular commodity, though it may continue long above, can seldom continue long below, its natural price. Whatever part of it was paid below the natural rate, the persons whose interest it affected would immediately feel the loss, and would immediately withdraw either so much land, or so much labour, or so much stock, from being employed about it, that the quantity brought to market would soon be no more than sufficient to supply the effectual demand. Its market price would soon rise to the natural price. This at least would be the case where there was perfect liberty." (WON, I, VII, p. 48).

As we can see, by accepting the reality of deviations as the origin and finality (as far as their correction is concerned) of the Market, and thus by rejecting the identity between natural price and market price, Smith allows the moral agent, animated by feelings and passion, to become, in this necessarily socialized space that is the Market, an economic agent. He becomes at once the actor of prices and the subject of income, the exchanger and the producer of commodities, demonstrating that Smithian individualism cannot be interpreted in an analytical grid that would oppose the individual to the social, the Smithian subject going far beyond the "simple calculating man", the *homo oeconomicus* retained by Political Economy. At the same time, each individual agent can only exert a negligible influence on the total market situation, while the result of all these individual actions determines the price. But if the Market appears, with evidence, as the "manager" of the gaps between the natural price and the market prices, by mobilizing, through perfect competition and its dynamic effects of individual incentive, the personal interests endowed with this function of correction of the gaps (*i.e.* the gravitation towards the natural price), nothing shows that this management is also optimal (in conformity with the general interest). This optimality would require that these interests be subject to a norm decreed by the Market and converge towards it, the Market functioning, then, as a superior Order, imposing itself on individuals. It is here that Smith mobilizes the metaphor of the "invisible hand" (see box), according to which each agent, by seeking only his private interest, contributes to wealth and the common welfare, thus guaranteeing a socially optimal result independent of individual conscious wills:

"the annual revenue of every society is always precisely equal to the exchangeable value of the whole annual produce of its industry, or rather is precisely the same thing with that exchangeable value. As every individual, therefore, endeavours as much as he can both to employ his capital in the support of domestic industry, and so to direct that industry that its produce may be of the greatest value, every individual necessarily labours to render the annual revenue of the society as great he can. He generally, indeed, neither intends to promote the public interest, nor knows how much he is promoting it. By preferring the support of domestic to that of foreign industry, he intends only his own security; and by directing that industry in such a manner as its produce may be of the greatest value, he intends only his own gain, and he is in this, as in many other cases, led by an invisible hand to promote an end which was no part of his intention. Nor is it always the worse for the society that it was no part of it. By pursuing his own interest he frequently promotes that of the society more effectually than when he really intends to promote it." (WON, IV, II, p. 345).

Adam Smith's "invisible hands"

Smith used this notion of "invisible hand" in two other of his works. In his "History of Astronomy" contained in "his" *Essays on Philosophical Subjects* (1795, p. 25), "the invisible hand of Jupiter", mobilized by Smith, is inscribed "in the first ages of the world, [where] the lowest and most pusillanimous superstition supplied the place of philosophy", among savages for whom "notions are guided altogether by wild nature and passion [where] every object of nature, by its beauty or greatness, its utility or hurtfulness, is considerable enough to attract his attention, and whose operations are not perfectly regular, is supposed to act by the direction of some invisible and designing power" (*Ibidem*). Here we are, therefore, at the opposite end of the spectrum from the "invisible hand principle", which, in order for the natural convergence of individual behaviors towards the satisfaction of the general interest to operate, requires that individuals be endowed with "Sympathy", *i.e.* a natural disposition to share the passions of others. However, in savage societies (*cf. supra*), behaviour is entirely guided by wild nature and passion, where scientific reasoning and explanation are absent, hence the recourse to the "invisible hand" as a providential explanation. We can, here, note Smith's fascination with Newton's Natural Philosophy and his desire to use it to scientifically establish his representation of social life (*cf. supra*). In this line, we can follow Diemer & Guillemin (2012, p. 338) when they argue that "The invisible hand, which is the mechanism that ensures the articulation between individual inclinations and social life, is reminiscent of the harmony of celestial bodies. It brings to mind a higher presence that watches over the world." The other reference, contained in the *Theory of moral sentiments* (1759 in 1761, IV, I, pp. 273–274) refers to the question, already addressed by Mandeville, of the relationship between the desire for unlimited enrichment, represented by the consumption of luxuries, in this case, the lavish spending of landowners, and the satisfaction of the needs of the population, thus the improvement of the condition of all, represented by the consumption of basic necessities (for survival and social reproduction), in this case wheat: "The produce of the soil maintains at all times nearly that number of inhabitants which it is capable of maintaining. The rich only select from the heap what is most precious and agreeable. They consume little more than the poor, and in spite of their natural selfishness and rapacity, though they mean only their own conveniency, though the sole end which they propose from the labours of all the thousands whom they employ, be the gratification of their own vain and insatiable desires, they divide with the poor the produce of all their improvements. They are led by an invisible hand to make nearly the same distribution of the necessaries of life, which would have been made, had the earth been divided into equal portions among all its habitants, and thus without knowing it, advance the interest of the society, and afford means to the multiplication of the species [...] In ease of body and peace of mind, all the different ranks of life are nearly upon a level, and the beggar, who suns himself by the side of the highway, possesses that security which kings are fighting for." *The Theory of Moral Sentiments* seems, here, to be the philosophical precondition or justification for WON: Smith, by means of the study of the various feelings and passions proper to man, comes to the conclusion that the principal motives of human action, of the "great mob of mankind", lie in the need for increased material well-being, and that, precisely, the improvement of material conditions makes it possible to satisfy, in the better-off, the needs for consideration, power and ambition. From then on, WON is seen as the search for conditions to satisfy this generalized economic promotion.

It is advisable to specify, here, the raison d'être of this "invisible hand", in other words, to identify the immediate causes, which make it possible, and the deep causes, which make it necessary, this force which makes men, by spontaneously indulging their particular passions, contribute "unconsciously" to the collective good and the general interest, by the objectification of their unintentional actions within a framework of natural harmonization of interests.

The immediate causes refer to the context of abundance described above, a condition for the accomplishment of the "system of natural liberty" which, through the mutual advantage of exchange associated with a desire for unlimited enrichment, thus through the system of "optimism" (in the proper sense of this term, from "optimum", the best, or "the best of all possible worlds"[4]), allows, on the one hand, a confusion between interest and sentiment, and thus to channel or contain passions; on the other hand, to give rise to the feeling of "compensatory social interest". Thus, for example, the love of glory, the thirst for honour, dignity, consideration and recognition can be opposed to the strict pursuit of wealth for purely private ends and lead to unintended and socially beneficial consequences of certain behaviours.

The root cause of the "invisible hand" refers to the "guiding providence" described by J. Viner (1927, p. 202) in the context of a "harmonious order in nature manifesting itself through the instincts of the individual man" (*ibid.*, p. 199), *i.e.* this "beneficent Nature" variously named by Smith ("the great Director of Nature", "the final cause", "the Author of Nature", "the great judge of hearts", "an invisible hand", "Providence", "the divine Being" and, in rare circumstances, "God", *ibid.*, p. 202). And in order to preserve this natural order, "designed and guided by a benevolent God", *ibid.*, p. 208), Providence has "fashioned the constitution of external nature as to make its processes favorable to man", in other words, has "implanted *ab initio* in human nature such sentiments as would bring about, through their ordinary working, the happiness and welfare of mankind" (*ibid.*, p. 202). Thus, Providence addresses the unconscious of men in order to show them that certain actions, of which they could doubt the interest, have positive aspects to be taken into account, giving rational intelligibility to these spontaneous actions which, a priori, seem to be devoid of it, and ensuring a "complete harmony between the general interests of society and the particular interests of individuals" (*ibid.*, p. 209). In this framework, "coercion", the fear of the "divine menace", as a transcendence calling upon the faculty of judging men, can constitute a "recall the order". Here, the "invisible hand", as a manifestation of Providence, is the regulator of the human order constituted by private self-interested actions. The invisible hand in question refers, in this case, both to this Providence, but also to the non-intentionality of the consequences of actions motivated by inclinations inscribed in human nature (*i.e.* a "wonderful spontaneity" of Leibniz[5]). In other words, it is without knowing it that men do good, according to a logic of action invisible to their conscience:

> "Every individual is continually exerting himself to find out the most advantageous employment for whatever capital he can command. It is his own advantage, indeed, and not that of the society, which he has in view. But the study of his own advantage, naturally, or rather necessarily leads him to prefer that employment which is most advantageous to the society." (WON, IV, II, p. 343)

"Free trade": from principle to reality

In this "obvious and simple system of natural liberty" (WON, IV, IX, p. 540), in which each person maximizes his or her own satisfaction, the "laissez-faire", "laissez passer", "laisser faire les hommes et laisser passer les marchandises", a maxim "popularized" by Vincent de Gournay (1712–1759), is the vehicle (as "continuous sources of actions") for maximizing the satisfaction of the entire community (as "continuous sources of wealth"):

> "The principle of laissez-faire had arrived to harmonise Individualism and Socialism, and to make at one Hume's Egoism with the greatest Good of the Greatest Number [...] The Individualism of the political philosophers pointed to laissez-faire. The divine or scientific harmony (as the case might be) between private interest and public advantage pointed to laissez-faire. But above all, the ineptitude of public administration strongly prejudiced the practical man in favour of laissez-faire - a sentiment which has by no means disappeared" (Keynes, "The End of Laissez-faire", 1926, pp. 11–12)

The "laissez-faire" approach was already present in Smith's earlier demonstrations of free concurrence (or perfect concurrence) as a condition for the optimal allocation of resources, and of a decentralized pricing system as a condition for capital accumulation and income growth through the extension of the market and the division of labor. These virtues of optimization of the general welfare linked to "laissez-faire" are manifested on the "domestic market" but also operate, according to a similar logic, for "foreign trade" thanks to the freedom of trade ("laissez-passer"), justified by a common sense argument: the advantage to trade between individuals (*cf. supra*) can be transposed to that of nations, which is the foundation of the theory of the absolute advantages of international trade:

> "What is prudence in the conduct of every private family, can scarce be folly in that of great kingdom. If a foreign country can supply us with a commodity cheaper than we ourselves can make it, better buy it of them with some part of the produce of our own industry, employed in a way in which we have some advantage [...] The general industry of the country is not employed with the greatest advantage when it is thus directed towards an object which it can buy cheaper than it can make. [it] is thus turned away from a more, to a less advantageous employment, and the exchangeable value of its annual produce, instead of being increased, according to the intention of the lawgiver, must necessarily be diminished by every such regulation [...] As long as the one country has those advantages, and the other wants them, it will always be more advantageous for the latter rather to buy of the former than to make." (WON, IV, II, p. 346, 347)

According to this theory of absolute advantages, not to be confused with Ricardo's theory of relative (or comparative) advantages[6] (*cf.* box), the international specialization of countries (*i.e.* the international division of labor) allows for an efficient allocation of factors of production for each country, and increases global wealth and collective welfare. International trade thus becomes a positive-sum game (win/win) subject to absolute advantages, *i.e.* when the production costs of country A are lower for a product than those of another country B.

Absolute advantages (Smith), Relative advantages (Ricardo)

For Smith, it is in a country's interest to specialize in those productions that it can obtain at the lowest cost compared to competing countries. This absolute advantage can result from favorable natural conditions (agriculture and mining activities with easy operating conditions), low production costs (real wages, price of productive consumption), and high productivity of the factors of production (qualification of the labor force, incorporated technologies). In this context, let us assume two countries (A, B), with two factors of production (labor and nature) and two goods (x, y), to which correspond, in autarky, the quantities of labor necessary (expressed in hours) to produce, respectively, these two goods:

	Country A	*Country B*
Good x	100 h.	300 h.
Good y	300 h.	100 h.

Here, Country A (which spends 100 hours producing x and 300 hours producing y) has an absolute advantage in x, while Country B (which spends 300 and 100 hours respectively on x and y) has an absolute advantage in y. Under the assumptions of constant returns, international factor immobility and perfect inter-sectoral mobility, each of the two countries has an interest in specializing in the product for which it has an absolute advantage. Total production thus increases from 4 or ($2x + 2y$) in a situation of autarky, to 8 or ($4x + 4y$) in a situation of international division of labor, as long as Country A employs the 300 hours needed by y to produce x, and symmetrically for Country B. Or, for an unchanged total production (4), the number of hours needed decreases from 800 to 400. But what if one country (A or B) can produce at a lower cost and without volume limitation (absence of supply constraints) the two products x and y that both countries need? In this case, it would be in the interest of one country to buy the other's products without being able to sell anything in return, according to the theory of absolute advantages, which then reaches a dead end. Ricardo, in chapter VI of *On the Principles of Political Economy, and Taxation* (*op. cit.*), will resolve this dilemma according to which openness to exchange leads, in this case, to the impossibility of exchange (*ibid.*, p. 160 and ff.), by showing that even with an absolute advantage/disadvantage, the internal ratio of costs implies specialization in production in which the disadvantage (advantage) is the lesser (greater), with relative or comparative costs (or advantages) taking precedence. With the same assumptions as before, Ricardo constructs a "two-country, two-goods" model (*ibid.*, p. 170), presenting the amount of labor hours needed in autarky to produce cloth and wine in England and Portugal (*ibid.*, pp. 160–170):

	England	*Portugal*
Cloth	100 h.	90 h.
Wine	120 h.	80 h.

Here, Portugal has absolute advantages in both goods, but it has an interest in specializing in the production where its relative cost is lowest (where its relative advantage is highest). Similarly, England has an interest in specializing in the production where its relative cost is lowest (where its relative disadvantage is lowest). Thus, England will use the 120h. freed by the abandonment of the production of wine for the production of cloth, having, henceforth, for this one of 220h., that is to say, a production of 2,2 units of cloth. Portugal will use the 90h. freed by the abandonment of the production of cloth to the production of wine, that is 170h. and a production of 2,125 units of wine. World production will be 4,325 units (instead of 4 in autarky) or, for a constant total production (4 units), the use of about 360h. of work instead of 390h., "free trade" being, in any case, preferable to autarky: "It is quite as important to the happiness of mankind, that our enjoyments should be increased by the better distribution of labour, by each country producing those commodities for which by its situation, its climate, and its other natural or artificial advantages it is adapted, and by their exchanging them for commodities of other countries." (Ricardo, *op. cit.*, p. 153).

But as soon as this plea for "free trade" was asserted, Smith was quick to admit numerous departures from this principle, "restraints on the freedom of trade" (*Restraints upon the importation from foreign countries of such goods as can be produced at home* [WON, IV, II, pp. 342–359], *Restraints upon the importation of goods of almost all kinds, from those countries with which the balance is supposed to be disadvantageous* [WON, IV, III, pp. 359–364]) required by situations in which "it may be advantageous to lay some burden upon foreign, for the encouragement of domestic industry" (WON, IV, II, p. 351 and ff.). These protectionist measures are legitimized in order to i) defend industries "necessary for the defence of the country" (*ibid.*, p. 351), hence, for example, the justification of "The act of navigation"[7]; ii) when "some tax is imposed at home upon the produce of the latter" (*ibid.*, p. 352) and that the national productions are, thus, unfairly competed by foreign productions less (or not) imposed[8]; iii) to gradually restore the competitive functioning of the internal market when it has been disrupted or even deteriorated by "the insolent outrage of furious and disappointed monopolists" (*ibid.*, p. 358) and/or by the "exclusive privileges of corporations" which destroy "the natural liberty of exercising the kind of industry that pleases his Majesty's subjects" pp. 357–358)[9]; iv) to preserve infant industries[10] (*ibid.*, pp. 358–359); and finally v) as "revenge" against foreign customs barriers, "when some foreign nation restrains by high duties or prohibitions the importation of some of our manufactures into their country" (*ibid.*, p. 354). This series of reasons for deviating from, or even invalidating, the principle of "free trade", whose accumulation of situations justifying protectionism approximates the totality of possible economic configurations, naturally leads Smith to agree that "free trade" between nations often leads (*i.e.* apart from the "ideal" situation of absolute advantage) to socially undesirable results, rendering utopian the very principle of total freedom of trade, and making its practice impractical in the light of industrial interests:

> "To expect, indeed, that the freedom of trade should ever be entirely restored in Great Britain, is as absurd as to expect that an Oceania or Utopia should ever be established in it. Not only the prejudices of the public, but what is much more unconquerable, the private interests of many individuals, irresistibly oppose it." (WON, IV, II, p. 358)

However, if these situations that are harmful to "free trade" (notably situations of imperfect competition, especially monopolies) are not, for Smith, the result of a dysfunction of the "obvious and simple system of natural liberty" but rather of "the skill of that insidious and crafty animal, vulgarly called a statesman or politician, whose councils are directed by the momentary fluctuations of affairs" (*ibid.*, p. 355), whose "short-term" vision is poorly matched to the "general interest of society":

> "The legislature, were it possible that its deliberations could be always directed, not by the clamorous importunity of partial interests, but by an extensive view of the general good, ought upon this very account, perhaps, to be particularly careful neither to establish any new monopolies of this kind, nor to extend further those which are already established. Every such regulation introduces some degree of real disorder into the constitution of the state, which it will be difficult afterwards to cure without occasioning another disorder." (WON, IV, II, p. 359)

As we can see, these "clamorous importunity of partial interests" that Smith deplores show his lucidity with respect to the naive and simplistic doctrine of the spontaneous harmony of interests, that of the strictly individualistic conception of the general interest. Smith is not content to assert that a free-market economy guarantees, through the powerful motive of self-interest, the general welfare, the "best of all worlds". He is concerned with the institutional conditions (or structures) that can guide, canalize and secure the pecuniary motives and beneficial play of market forces; in other words, Smith is aware that "i) self-interest is just as likely to thwart as to promote the public welfare; ii) the market mechanism fosters harmony but not unless it was surrounded by an appropriate legal and institutional framework." (Blaug, 1985, p. 63).

In fact, the benefits of competition require more than "laisser faire, laisser passer", in the infinitive as in V. de Gournay's maxim (see above), or, in the imperative, "laissez faire, laissez passer"[11], as a doctrinaire principle defended by the Physiocrats, hence Smith's analytical reorientation[12] at the beginning of Book IV, towards *Political Economy*:

> "Political economy, considered as a branch of the science of a statesman or legislator, proposes two distinct objects: first, to supply a plentiful revenue or subsistence for the people, or, more properly, to enable them to provide such a revenue or subsistence for themselves; and secondly, to supply the state or commonwealth with a revenue sufficient for the public services. It proposes to enrich both the people and the sovereign [...] I shall endeavour to explain both as fully and distinctly as I can." (WON, IV, Introduction, p. 323).

It is the study of Books IV and V of WON, entitled respectively "Of Systems of Political Economy" (devoted to a critical analysis of the "system of commerce" and the "system of agriculture", *i.e.* the Mercantilists and the Physiocrats) and "Revenue of the Sovereign or Commonwealth" (a veritable Treatise on Public Finances), that constitutes the subject of the following developments.

Notes

1 Let us recall that Smith was fascinated by Physics, in particular Newtonian, and that he wrote "The Principles which lead and direct Philosophical Enquiries; illustrated by the History of Astronomy" and "illustrated by the History of Ancient Physics" published posthumously in 1795 in his "Essays on Philosophical Subjects" (respectively, Smith, 1795, pp. 1–93 and 95–111). His first words in the Preface are as follows: "Wonder, Surprise, and Admiration, are words which, though often confounded, denote, in our language, sentiments that are indeed allied, but that are in some respects different also, and distinct from one another. What is new and singular, excites that sentiment which, in strict propriety, is called Wonder; what is unexpected, Surprise; and what is great or beautiful, Admiration." (*ibid.*, p. 3).

2 "Yet an analogy of this kind, it would seem, far from a demonstration, could afford, at most, but the shadow of probability.", "History of Astronomy" in *Essays on Philosophical Subjects*, *op. cit.*, p. 75.

3 in reference to the problematic translation of "effective demand" in the General Theory. Cf. infra, chap. 7.

4 "*Die beste aller möglichen Welten*", "the best (optimum) among all possible worlds" from *Théodicée* de G.W. Leibniz (*Theodicity: Essays on the Goodness of God, the Freedom of Man, and the Origin of Evil*, 1710, "Essays on the justice of God and the freedom of man in the origin of evil", 1951, I, § 8), optimal combination between God's goodness, man's freedom and his courage in the face of evil adversity. This divine optimization of the world supported by Leibniz will be criticized and even mocked by Candide (Voltaire) in the face of Pangloss (Leibniz), denouncing this naive conception of the world consisting in a blindness in the face of "evil", in favor of a rationalization of human processes in order to make superstition and irrationality recede. For Marx's "best of all possible worlds", see below chap. 4, and Keynes', Part 3, Introduction.

5 "It is well to show, notwithstanding, how this dependence of voluntary actions does not fundamentally preclude the existence within us of a wonderful spontaneity, which in a certain sense makes the soul in its resolves independent of the physical influence of all other creatures. This spontaneity, hitherto little recognized, which exalts our command over our actions to the highest pitch, is a consequence of the System of Pre-established Harmony" (G.W. Leibniz, Theodicity: Essays on the Goodness of God, the Freedom of Man, and the Origin of Evil, 1710, "Essays on the justice of God and the freedom of man in the origin of evil", 1951, I, § 59).

6 contained in Chapter VI "On Foreign Trade" of the first edition of *On the Principles of Political Economy, and Taxation* (1817, pp. 146–185). It is interesting to note that the Ricardian conception of the "invisible hand" at the international level is contained precisely in this Chapter VI (*ibid.*, pp. 156–7): "Under a system of perfectly free commerce, each country naturally devotes its capital and labour to such employments as are most beneficial to each. This pursuit of individual advantage is admirably connected with the universal good of the whole. By stimulating industry, by rewarding ingenuity, and by using most efficaciously the peculiar powers bestowed by nature, it distributes labour most effectively and most economically: while, by increasing the general mass of production, it diffuses general benefit, and binds together by one common tie of interest and intercourse, the universal society of nations throughout the civilized world."

7 "The defence of Great Britain depends very much upon the number of its sailors and shipping. The act of navigation, therefore, very properly endeavours to give the sailors and shipping of Great Britain the monopoly of the trade of their own country, in some cases, by absolute prohibitions, and in others by heavy burdens upon the shipping of foreign countries. [So] all ships, of which the owners, masters, and three-fourths of the mariners are not British subjects, are prohibited, upon pain of forfeiting ship and cargo, from trading to the British settlements and plantations, or from being employed in the coasting trade of Great Britain." (*ibid.*, p. 351). The "Act of Navigation", in question here, is a series of protectionist laws passed from 1651 onwards (abolished in 1849) by the English Parliament, during the term of office of the Lord Protector, Oliver Cromwell. Their original purpose (*i.e.* in the context of the civil wars of 1642 to 1651) was to finance the construction of a navy, and to weaken the colonies controlled by the Royalist opposition following the emigration of the Cavaliers (*i.e.* the cavalry of the "Royalists" at war with the "Parliamentarians"), by preventing them from trading with other countries. It is therefore singular, in 1776, to continue to invoke the security of the country: "As defence [...] is of much more importance than opulence, the act of navigation is, perhaps, the wisest of all the commercial regulations of England." (*ibid.*, p. 352).

8 "Subsistence becomes necessarily dearer in consequence of such taxes; and the price of labour must always rise with the price of labourer's subsistence. Every commodity, therefore, which is the produce of domestic industry, though not immediately taxed itself, becomes dearer in consequence of such taxes, because the labour which produces it become so. Such taxes, therefore, are really equivalent [...] to a tax upon every particular commodity produced at home. In order to put domestic upon the same footing with foreign industry, therefore, it becomes necessary, they think, to lay some duty upon every foreign commodity, equal to this enhancement of the price of the home commodities with which it can come into competition." (*ibid.*, p. 353).

9 These situations of imperfect competition (monopoly and/or corporations), perceived as "real encroachments upon natural liberty" (*ibid.*, p. 358) can themselves be the result of protectionist measures when the domestic manufactures concerned "by means of high duties or prohibitions upon all foreign goods which can come into competition with them, have been so far extended as to employ a great multitude of hands." (*ibid.*, p. 356). In this case, trade liberalization must be progressive ("by slow gradations and with a good deal of reserve ad circumspection", *ibid.*) in order to avoid the collapse of the domestic market: "Were those high duties and prohibitions taken away all at once, cheaper foreign goods at the same kind might be poured so fast into the home market, as to deprive all at once many thousands of our people of their ordinary employment and means of subsistence. The disorder which this would occasion might, no doubt, be very considerable." (*ibid.*). This reflection by Smith is not unrelated to the contemporary problem of "too big to fail", *i.e.* the need to support (here by the gradual or even partial dismantling of tariff and non-tariff protection) an economic actor (here the monopolist) when its only defect (here its bankruptcy) directly threatens the overall stability of the system (here the domestic market), or even triggers a systemic risk (in this case, the entire economy through contagion), even if the low substitutability of domestic products compared to imported goods (through non-price or comparative qualitative competitiveness) and the intersectoral mobility of the labor factor (*ibid.*, pp. 356–357) would mitigate these effects.

10 "The undertaker of a great manufacture, who, by the home markets being suddenly laid open to the competition of foreigners, should be obliged to abandon his trade, would no doubt suffer very considerably. That part of his capital which had usually been employed in purchasing materials and in paying his workmen might, without much difficulty, find another employment. But part of it which was fixed in workhouses, and in the instruments of trade, could scarce be disposed of without considerable loss. The equitable regard, therefore, to his interest requires that changes of this kind should never be introduced suddenly, but slowly, gradually, and after a very long warning." (*ibid.*, pp. 358–359).

11 It's worth noting that Keynes's "The end of laissez-faire" (1926) has been translated into French as "La fin du laisser-faire".

12 M. Blaug (1985, p. 57) is more definite: "The introduction to Book IV defines political economy as a branch of statecraft, a definition in violent opposition to the whole tenor of the *Wealth of Nations*."

Bibliography

Blaug, Mark (1985). *Economic Theory in Retrospect* (1962). Cambridge: Cambridge University Press, fourth edition.

Diemer, Arnaud & Guillemin, Hervé (2012). "Adam Smith et la physique de Newton". *Œconomia*, *2*(3), septembre, 327–363.

Keynes, John Maynard (1926). *The End of Laissez-Faire*, London, Published by Leonard & Virginia Woolf at the Hogarth Press, 52 Tavistock Square.

Leibniz, Gottfried Wilhelm (1951). *Essays on the Goodness of God, the Freedom of Man and the Origin of Evil* (1710). London: Routledge & Kegan Paul Ltd.

Mathiot Jean (1990). *Adam Smith. Philosophie et Economie. De la sympathie à l'échange*. Paris: PUF, coll. "Philosophies" n° 24.

Ricardo, David (1817). *On the Principles of Political Economy, and Taxation*. London: John Murray, Albemarle-Street.

Smith, Adam (1761). *The Theory of Moral Sentiments* (1759), London, Printed for A. Millar, in the Strand; and A. Kincaid and J. Bell, in Edinburgh, second edition.

Smith, Adam (1913). *An Inquiry Into the Nature and Causes of the Wealth of Nations* (1776), London: George Routledge & Sons, Limited; New York, E.P. Dutton and Co.

Smith, Adam (1795). *Essays on Philosophical Subjects*, London, Printed for T. Cadell Jun. and W. Davies in the Strand; and W. Creech, Edinburg.

Viner, Jacob (1927). Adam Smith and Laissez Faire. *Journal of Political Economy*, *35*(2), april, 198–232.

3 From spontaneity to the "System of natural liberty"

The state as "superintendent of the industry of private people, charged with directing it towards the employments most suitable to the interest of society"

As Polanyi (2001, p. 35) argues, "Nowhere has liberal philosophy failed so conspicuously as in its understanding of the problem of change. Fired by an emotional faith in spontaneity, the common-sense attitude toward change was discarded in favor of a mystical readiness to accept the social consequences of economic improvement, whatever they might be.". In other words, opulence creates the conditions for blind confidence in the supposedly harmonious virtues of optimizing well-being—individual and therefore collective, since private interests are effectively harmonized with social interests—devolved to the free market system. In this case, the collective interest joins the arithmetic additivity of individual satisfactions, where the static efficiency conditions of the general equilibrium are met, with competition providing the stimulus for dynamic individual incentive effects (*cf. supra*) in a context of change oriented to "progress of the society towards real wealth and greatness" and increasing "the real value of the annual produce of its land and labour." (WON, IV, IX, p. 540). However, continues Polanyi (*ibid.*, p. 39), "A belief in spontaneous progress must make us blind to the role of government in economic life. This role consists often in altering the rate of change, speeding it up or slowing it down as the case may be; if we believe that rate to be unalterable—or even worse, if we deem it a sacrilege to interfere with it—then, of course, no room is left for intervention." It is from this "naïve" philosophy of the "spontaneous harmony of interests" (or Leibniz's System of Pre-established Harmony, *cf. supra*), where confidence in the automaticity of equilibrium in a market of perfect competition is absolute (*i.e.* an omniscient and omnipotent "invisible hand", a rampart against any organized collective action, *a fortiori* the State), that Smith stands out, as he had begun to do with his many concessions to "free trade". He recognizes the complexities and shortcomings of the "obvious and simple system of natural liberty", cases of conflicts of interest where the spontaneity of self-interest leads to socially undesirable or, minima, sub-optimal results, where without collective regulation and planning, a "pure" market economy remains subject only to the rules of individual behavior; in other words, situations that reveal the presumption of maximum social well-being and raise the problem of the conditions required to achieve it:

DOI: 10.4324/9781032649054-6

> "All systems [*i.e.* the Commercial or Mercantile System and the Agricultural Systems] either of preference or of restraint, being thus completely taken away, the obvious and simple system of natural liberty establishes itself of its own accord. Every man, as long as he does not violate the laws of justice, is left perfectly free to pursue his own interest his own way, and to bring both his industry and capital into competition with those of any other man, or order of men. The sovereign is completely discharged from a duty, in the attempting to perform which, he must always be exposed to innumerable delusions, and for the proper performance of which no human wisdom or knowledge could ever be sufficient: the duty of superintending the industry of private people, and of directing it towards the employments most suitable to the interest of the society." (WON, IV, IX, p. 540)

Henceforth, the "obvious and simple system of natural liberty" becomes, for Smith, the "system of natural liberty" (WON, pp. 540–541), *i.e.* the move away from a system governed exclusively by natural laws,[1] which, powerless against the manifestation of biased interests, calls for the gradual and natural institutionalization of the state, conceived essentially as an institution of justice, liberty and security, to protect the natural and acquired rights of the individual.

The liberal conception of the State: regalian functions and education as responses to the failings of private interest and civic virtues

This liberal conception of the State means, first and foremost, that natural processes must not be hindered, in other words, public interventionism is subordinate to the free exercise of natural liberty, on pain of becoming a system subversive of the very object it sets out to achieve, namely the maximization of the collective interest, *i.e.* society's progress towards opulence:

> "What is the species of domestic industry which his capital can employ, and of which the produce is likely to be of the greatest value, every individual, it is evident, can, in this local situation, judge much better than any statesman or lawgiver can do for him. The statesman, who should attempt to direct private people in what manner they ought to employ their capitals, would not only load himself with a most unnecessary attention, but assume an authority which could safely be trusted to no single person, to no council or senate whatever, and would nowhere be so dangerous as in the hands of a man who had folly and presumption enough to fancy himself fit to exercise it." (WON, IV, II, p. 345)

All the more so since, beyond the effectiveness of "natural liberty", the State is liable to mismanage its own funds by using them for unproductive expenditure, in contrast to private individuals who, driven by their own interests, for the vast majority of them steer clear of "misconduct" such as prodigality (*cf. supra*):

> "Great nations are never impoverished by private, though they sometimes are by public prodigality and misconduct [while] it can seldom happen, indeed, that the circumstances of a great nation can be much affected either by the prodigality or misconduct of individuals; the profusion or imprudence of some, being always more than compensated by the frugality and good conduct of others." (WON, II, III, p. 263 [and] 262)[2]

Faithful to his method of reconciling conceptual abstraction and empirical validation, this liberal conception of Government, beyond affirming the principle of the secondarity of Politics to the "system of natural liberty", is also justified, according to Smith, by experience, since the general opulence resulting from "frugality and good private conduct" persists despite the errors committed by the State:

> "This frugality and good conduct, however, is upon most occasions, it appears from experience, sufficient to compensate, not only the private prodigality and misconduct of individuals, but the public extravagance of government. The uniform, constant, and uninterrupted effort of every man to better his condition, the principle from which public and national, as well as private opulence is originally derived, is frequently powerful enough to maintain the natural progress of things toward improvement, in spite both of the extravagance of government, and of the greatest errors of administration." (WON, II, III, p. 264)

This subjugation of the political finds some of its origins in Thomas Aquinas' conception of the State or political authority, or of the "political community [*communitas*]" in his *Summa Theologiae, Prima pars*. In terms of its origins and purpose, the State is conceived solely in terms of the utilitarian goals that individuals could not achieve without its help,[3] with the aim of tending towards a "perfect community", one that serves the higher goods that "family communities" cannot provide; a *regimen unius* capable of directing, above all, subjects towards unity, *i.e.* towards the good that is the final cause of government. The raison d'être of the State is thus the Common Good (*multitudo socialis*), the interest of the community, rationally perceived, *i.e.* conceived in terms of the interest of others, within a framework that defends individual liberties, which cannot be reduced to membership of the "political community". For example, for Thomas Aquinas, property is not contrary to the natural law, but results from human reason, since men attach greater importance to what they own than to what belongs to many, *a fortiori* to all. Consequently, social order can become harmonious if individual possessions are guaranteed and if, at the same time, there is no reason to quarrel over the collective use of public goods; the creation and maintenance of unity and peace among subjects being the prerequisites of social life (*pax* or *tranquillitas regni/civitatis*). So, "private property owes its origin, in part, to the necessity of avoiding a chaotic struggle for goods, and government its origin to the necessity of enforcing peace and order." (Schumpeter, 1966, p. 119).

In other words, it is on the basis of indefectible respect for this individual free exercise, which enables private interests to be reconciled with economic efficiency, that the role of the State, as guarantor of the unhindered development of this free exercise, must be situated. In the "system of natural liberty", the State must enable the optimality of the competitive economy to be achieved, *i.e.*:

i guarantee a secure institutional framework for the optimal allocation of resources required for the production and distribution of exchangeable goods. Here, the State mobilizes its regalian functions of Defense and Justice,[4] respectively "the duty of protecting the society from the violence and invasion of other independent societies" (*ibid.*, p. 540), and "the duty of protecting, as far as possible, every member of the society from the injustice or oppression of every other member of it, or the duty of establishing an exact administration of justice" (*ibidem*);

ii overcome market failures by producing public goods for which the private costs of production exceed the social costs, guaranteeing their availability without exclusivity and universal consumption without rivalry[5]:

> "the duty of erecting and maintaining certain public works and certain public institutions, which it can never be for the interest of any individual, or small number of individuals, to erect and maintain, because the profit could never repay the expense to any individual or small number of individuals, though it may frequently do much more than repay it to a great society." (WON, IV, IX, p. 540)

Let's take a closer look at these functions of government (see also Viner, 1927, p. 217 and ff).

For Smith, justice and defense require, first and foremost, specific administrations staffed by civil servants who must be protected, by their status and remuneration, from the ordinary pressures of the market or other powers. The public service, thus defined, is driven by a general principle: "Public services are never better performed than when their reward comes only in consequence of their being performed, and is proportioned to the diligence employed in performing them." (WON, V, I, p. 563), and this "rewarding" of public servants, *i.e.* the techniques and levels of their remuneration, must: i) make the pursuit of their own interests compatible with the advancement, through their contribution, of the general interest; ii) guarantee the impartiality of their actions and decisions and avoid corruption:

"Fixed salaries were appointed to the judges, which were supposed to compensate to them the loss of whatever might have been their share of the ancient emoluments of justice [...] The circumstances of those salaries being paid by the crown can nowhere much diminish the necessary expense of a law suit. But it was not so much to diminish the expense as to prevent the corruption of justice that the judges were prohibited from receiving any present or fee from the parties." (WON, V, I, pp. 562–563)

By evoking the obligation to devote oneself entirely to one's duties,[6] and the duties of obedience,[7] probity and neutrality,[8] Smith outlines the modern principles governing public service and the rule of law.

As far as Defense is concerned, Smith (*ibid.*, pp. 541–555) shows that with "the progress of manufactures and the improvement in the art of war", in other words "when the art of war [...] has gradually grown to be a very intricate and complicated science" (*ibid.*, p. 544), it has become necessary to design and establish a "standing army" (*ibid.*, p. 547) (*i.e.* a professional army):

"The art of war [...] as it is certainly the noblest of all arts, so in the progress of improvements it necessarily becomes one of the most complicated among them. The state of the mechanical, as well as of some other arts, with which it is necessarily connected, determines the degree of perfection to which it is capable of being carried at any particular time. But in order to carry it to this degree of perfection, it is necessary that it should become the sole or principal occupation of a particular class of citizens, and the division of labour is as necessary for the improvement of this as of every other art [...] The practice of military exercises is the sole or principal occupation of the soldiers of a standing army, and the maintenance or pay which the state affords the mis the principal and ordinary fund of their subsistence." (WON, V, I, pp. 546–547)

And it's the "wisdom of the state", especially in "industrious and wealthy nations",[9] combined with the prudence of the State[10] who are behind these measures in favor of "a standing army", the only means by which "the civilization of any country can be perpetuated, or even preserved for any considerable time." (*ibid.*, p. 553), and can be established "a regular government through the remotest provinces of the empire [or] in countries which could not otherwise admit of any" (*ibid.*, p. 554). Smith concludes by responding to the concerns of "Men of republican principles" that a "standing army" may be "dangerous to liberty", by setting out the conditions for subordinating the army to civil power, making the existence of a "standing army" compatible with respect for "republican principles":

"where the military force is placed under the command of those who have the greatest interest in the support of the civil authority, because they have

> themselves the greatest share of that authority, a standing army can never be dangerous to liberty." (WON, V, I, p. 554)

On the contrary, because of the climate of security it provides, the "standing army" can even be "favourable to liberty" (*ibid.*, p. 554), enabling the whole authority of government thanks to the "security which it gives to the sovereign", enabling him to make decisions with peace of mind and serenity,[11] guaranteeing the "peace of every citizen" and "the security of magistrate endangered by every popular discontent" and, finally, ensuring political and institutional stability, which, without the "standing army", could be threatened "where a small tumult is capable of bringing about in a few hours a great revolution." (*ibid.*, p. 554).

The administration of justice is also a condition for the proper functioning of the "system of natural liberty", insofar as it enables the protection of persons, property and possession,[12] and the guarantee of personal rights and obligations contracted between citizens[13]:

> "If a nation could not prosper without the enjoyment of perfect liberty and perfect justice, there is not in the world a nation which could ever have prospered." (WON, IV, IX, p. 529)

And in a context of opulence, where wealth accumulates and inequalities increase, the defense of property becomes one of the central elements in the preservation of prosperity, and therefore of national cohesion: i) because the fate of the nation depends on the protection of the conditions for the exercise of personal freedom (love of country being a sentiment derived from a love of self) and the regulation of "passions which prompt to invade property" (WON, V, I, p. 556) and thus threaten society,[14] the "civil government [becoming] indispensably necessary for its own preservation." (*ibid.*, p. 559); ii) because it generates a wealth of nation, guaranteeing the fulfillment of the virtuous dynamic of unlimited enrichment, exchange advantage, and capital accumulation (*cf. above*):

> "In all countries where there is tolerable security, every man of common understanding will endeavour to employ whatever stock he can command in procuring present enjoyment or future profit. If it is employed in procuring present enjoyment, it is a stock reserved for immediate consumption. If it is employed in procuring future profit, it must procure this profit either by staying with him, or by going from him. In the one case it is fixed, in the other it is circulating capital. A man must be perfectly crazy who, where there is tolerable security, does not employ all the stock he commands, whether his own or borrowed of other people, in some one or other of those three ways." (WON, II, I, p. 214)

If this Justice is to be rendered impartially and fairly, and therefore effectively from the point of view of the "system of natural liberty", it is necessary, in order to limit arbitrariness and prevent abuse and corruption, in the tradition of Locke and Montesquieu, for there to be a separation of powers:

> "The separation of the judicial from the executive power seems originally to have arisen from the increasing business of the society, in consequence of its increasing improvement [...] upon the impartial administration of justice depends the liberty of every individual - the sense which he has own security. In order to make every individual feel himself perfectly secure in the possession of every right which belongs to him, it is not only necessary that the judicial should be separated from the executive power, but that it should be rendered as much as possible independent of that power. The judge should not be liable to be removed from his office according to the caprice of that power. The regular payment of his salary should not depend upon the good will or even upon the good economy of that power." (WON, V, I, pp. 565–566)

Like Defense and Justice, Education, both "the education of youth" (WON, V, I, pp. 596–618) and "the instruction of people of all ages" (*ibid.*, pp. 618–642), contributes to the maintenance and fortitude of the rule of law by enabling the stability of power, which in turn contributes to "the general benefit of the whole society" (*ibid.*, p. 643):

> "Though the state was to derive no advantage from the instruction of the inferior ranks of people, it would still deserve its attention that they should not be altogether uninstructed. The state, however, derives an inconsiderable advantage from their instruction. The more they are instructed, the less liable they are to the delusions of enthusiasm and superstition, which, among ignorant nations, frequently occasions the most dreadful disorders. An instructed and intelligent people, besides, are always more decent and orderly than an ignorant and stupid one [...] In free countries, where the safety of government depends very much upon the favourable judgment which the people may form of its conduct, it must surely be of the highest importance that they should not be disposed to judge rashly or capriciously concerning it." (WON, V, I, p. 618)

This function of preserving and even restoring order is particularly important in the context of division of labor, a source of intellectual and cultural impoverishment for "the great body of the people", and especially for the parcel worker, whose "dexterity at his own particular trade seems, in this manner, to be acquired at the expense of his intellectual, social, and martial virtues." (*ibid.*, p. 613), all of which contribute to political instability and the degeneration of society:

> "In some cases, the state of the society necessarily places the greater part of individuals in such situations as naturally form in them, without any

> attention of government, almost all the abilities and virtues which that state requires, or, perhaps, can admit of. In other cases [*i.e.* "in the progress of the division of labour"], the state of the society does not place the greater part of individuals in such situations, and some attention of government is necessary, in order to prevent the almost entire corruption and degeneracy of the great body of the people [...] But in every improved and civilized society, this is the state into which the labouring poor, that is, the great body of the people, must necessarily fall, unless government takes some pains to prevent it." (WON, V, I, p. 613)

Here, Smith is confronted with a problem new to him, an internal contradiction in his reasoning. Until now, the State, through its regalian functions (Defense, Justice), only operated in response to the failings of private interest, acting where individual initiative could not, in the "system of natural liberty" where the economic function of the division of labor (as contained in Book I, *cf. supra*) was central to the improvement of well-being (*i.e.* opulence). With his reasoning on Education, in Book V, he highlights the dehumanizing character of this "same" division of labor, in other words, its (in) human consequences, with the economic virtues of the division of labor "suddenly" coming into conflict with the loss of civic virtues it provokes in individuals. Thus, Smith's proposals in terms of education are primarily ethical and moral, not economic (the accumulation of human capital, for example), in line with civic humanism, where man's freedom and fullness lie in his participation in civic life, which requires intellectual and moral capacities, in terms of autonomy and humanity, to do so. Yet these capacities cannot be exclusively motivated by utility and regulated by the law, and are at odds with the "torpor of his mind" (*ibid.*, p. 613) resulting from the division of labor. In this context, courage and the will to serve the general interest collide with the spontaneity of personal interests, and "the great body of the people" sees the noblest characteristics of the human character fade away:

> "In the progress of the division of labour, the employment of the far greater part of those who live by labour, that is, of the great body of the people, comes to be confined to a few very simple operations; frequently to one or two. But the understandings of the greater part of men are necessarily formed by their ordinary employments. The man whose whole life is spent in performing a few simple operations [...] has no occasion to exert his understanding, or to exercise his invention in finding out expedients for removing difficulties which never occur. He naturally loses, therefore, the habit of such exertion, and generally becomes as stupid and ignorant as it is possible for a human creature to become. The torpor of his mind renders him, not only incapable of relishing or bearing a part in any rational conversation, but of conceiving any generous, noble, or tender sentiment, and, consequently, of forming any just judgement concerning many, even, of the ordinary duties of private life. Of the great and

extensive interest of his country, he is altogether incapable of judging." (WON, V, I, p. 613)

Consequently, "in a civilized and commercial society", this situation, where "all the nobler parts of the human character may be, in a great measure, obliterated and extinguished in the great body of the people" (*ibid.*, p. 614), can arise "unless government takes some pains to prevent it" (*ibid.*, p. 613). It is through public education, which fosters the practice of fundamental civic virtues, that the state must operate, first and foremost for the common people[15] who "have little time to spare for education" and who "as soon as they are able to work, must apply to some trade by which they can earn their subsistence," the trade "generally so simple and uniform as to give little exercise to the understanding; while, at the same time, their labour is both so constant and so severe, that it leaves them little leisure and less inclination to apply to, or even to think of, anything else" (*ibid.*, p. 615), an observation to be compared with Marx's alienation.[16] On the contrary, "The employments in which people of some rank or fortune spend the greater part of their lives, are not, like of the common people, simple and uniform. They are, almost all of them, extremely complicated, and such as exercise the head more than the hands. The understandings of those who are engaged in such employments can seldom grow torpid for want of exercise [and they] are seldom such as harass them from morning to night", leaving to "well-born people" "a good deal of leisure, during which they may perfect themselves in every branch either of useful or ornamental knowledge" (*ibid.*, p. 615). But even if, adds Smith, "the common people cannot, in any civilized society, be so well instructed as people of some rank and fortune", "the most essential parts of education, however, to read, write, and account, can be acquired at so early a period of life, that the greater part even of those who are to be bred to the lowest occupations, have time to acquire them before they can be employed in those occupations" (*ibid.*, p. 615). This is the minimum common educational good that the State can and must facilitate, encourage and even impose, inspired by the Scottish "parish schools", which were virtually free of charge,[17] in which "the master being partly, but not wholly, paid by the public; because, if he was wholly, or even principally, paid by it, he would soon learn to neglect his business"[18] (*ibid.*, p. 616). In addition, the government must be vigilant about the content of teaching, so that "instead of a little smattering of Latin, which the children of the common people are sometimes taught, and which can scarce ever be of any use to them", they are instructed in "the elementary parts of geometry and mechanics", likely to be applied in the exercise of their future trades, and thanks to which they could "improve in those principles, necessary introduction to the most sublime, as well as to the most useful, sciences." (*ibid.*, p. 616).[19] The State can also encourage the best children by awarding merit-based scholarships,[20] and, by awarding national diplomas, the whole mass of the people in a context of compulsory schooling.[21] In the final analysis, this is a genuine plea by Smith for public education, with State aid for buildings, but with teachers' remuneration mainly dependent on tuition fees (in order to maintain an incentive for teachers to improve, *cf. supra*), awarding state diplomas (and not by the Church, often with strict limitations on the part of testators), with the primary aim of combating every kind of "mental mutilation" (*ibid.*, p. 618), in other words, to restore intellectual, social, civic and "martial" virtues (*ibidem*) in order to train free citizens, respectful of customs, laws and the government itself:

> "An instructed and intelligent people [...] are always more decent and orderly than an ignorant and stupid one. They feel themselves, each individually, more respectable, and more likely to obtain the respect of their lawful superiors, and they are therefore more disposed to respect their superiors." (WON, V, I, p. 618)

An educated people, therefore capable of making informed political choices, in full knowledge of the facts, a prerequisite for greater democratic representation of the people:

> "[An instructed and intelligent people] are more disposed to examine, and more capable of seeing through the interest complaints of faction and sedition, and they are, upon that account, less apt to be misled into any wanton or unnecessary opposition to the measures of government." (*ibidem*)

State economic action: from public works and services to taxation and banking regulation

At the same time as exercising its (regalian) functions of preserving and even restoring order through Defense, Justice, and Education, the State must carry out economic action, the other duty of the sovereign or republic, a duty that consists of "erecting and maintaining those public institutions and those public works which, though they may be in the highest degree advantageous to a great society, are, however, of such a nature that the profit could never repay the expense to any individual or small number of individuals, and which it therefore cannot be expected that any individual or small number of individuals should erect or maintain." (WON, V, I, p. 566). The purpose of these "expenses required of public Works and public Institutions" (*ibidem*) is different from the previous regalian functions, in that these investments and (collective) public services, intended to "facilitate the commerce of the society" (*ibidem*), have the function of compensating for the insufficiencies, or even failings, of individual initiative in stimulating the creation of certain wealth necessary to the general interest (*i.e.* opulence), a new manifestation of the limits of the effectiveness of individual spontaneity in making the "system of natural liberty" "obvious and simple".

Smith begins by listing those "public Works and Institutions for facilitating the commerce of the society designed to facilitate the company's trade" (*ibid.*, p. 567):

"the erection and maintenance of the public works which facilitate the commerce of any country, such as good roads, bridges, navigable canals, harbours, etc., must require very different degrees of expense in the different periods of society, is evident without any proof." (WON, V, I, p. 567)

But this evidence does not immediately (*i.e.* as early as the following paragraph) preclude the question of financing these investments and public works expenses, the answer to which will determine the nature of these goods:

"It does not seem necessary that the expense of those public works should be defrayed from that public revenue, as it is commonly called, of which the collection and application are in most countries assigned to the executive power. The greater part of such public works may easily be so managed, as to afford a particular revenue sufficient for defraying their own expense, without bringing any burden upon the general revenue of the society." (*ibidem*)

Smith's answer is that these infrastructures must be financed by appropriate tolls, paid mainly by users,[22] proportional to usage,[23] according to the "user pays" logic, premises of external cost internalization and marginal social cost pricing models,[24] any remaining share being financed by local resources, where their use is limited, with this decentralization helping to rationalize expenditure (*i.e.* avoid disproportionate projects, for example),[25] or financed by general tax revenues (in the case of "the post-office", for example, *ibid.*, p. 567).

These goods are, therefore, first and foremost collective goods, insofar as they are indivisible, their production costs cannot be imputed to a particular individual, and their consumption respects the property of non-rivalry, since they can be consumed simultaneously by several people without the quantity consumed by one diminishing the quantities available for the others (subject to saturation or congestion), so that the marginal cost of an additional use is zero. On the other hand, in Smith's mind, the consumption of these goods is made exclusive (*i.e.* the possibility of excluding a user from use), since only those who pay a "tax or toll" (*ibid.*, p. 567) can use them; in other words, the toll system is akin to an access control device that ensures the exclusivity of these goods, which become club goods, or toll goods.

These infrastructures, which facilitate the transport and trade of goods, extend the size of the market, intensify the division of labor and thus promote opulence, do not require the same levels of maintenance, which has an impact on the choice of operating systems:

"A high-road, though entirely neglected, does not become altogether impassable, though a canal does. The proprietors of the tolls upon a high-road, therefore, might neglect altogether the repair of the road, and yet continue to levy nearly the same tolls. It is proper, therefore, that the tolls for the maintenance of such a work should be put under the management of commissioners or trustees." (WON, V, I, p. 569)

In other words, public services are responsible for some of the operation and maintenance activities required for the proper use of these facilities, and here again, they make up for the shortcomings of private interest in fulfilling the general interest, even if "the abuses which the trustees have committed in the management of those tolls" (*ibid.*, p. 569) need to be corrected, by being vigilant about the recruitment and working conditions of staff dedicated exclusively to these missions[26] (*ibid.*, pp. 349–351), or "a special administration" (*ibid.*, p. 573), which must also control the allocation of toll revenues:

> "a tax upon carriages in proportion to their weight, though a very equal tax when applied to the sole purpose of repairing the roads, is a very unequal one when applied to any other purpose, or to supply the common exigencies of the state." (WON, V, I, p. 570)

While Smith had clearly stated, at the end of Book IV (*Ibid.*, pp. 540–541), that only "three duties of great importance, indeed, but plain and intelligible to common understandings" were to be fulfilled by the sovereign in "the system of natural liberty", his regalian functions of protection (*i.e.* duties of protection inside and outside the country) and his interventionism as a substitute for the failings of private interests (*i. e.* the duty of erecting and maintaining certain public works and public institutions) that we have just seen, there are, in fact, four, since Smith, in Book II of WON, forcefully demonstrates the need for state regulation in the banking field, by the introduction of "regulations" which, for him, are nothing less than "a manifest violation of that natural liberty which it is the proper business of law, not to infringe, but to support" (WON, II, II, p. 249).[27] What is this all about?

Witnessing the Scottish banking crisis of 1765 (*ibid.*, p. 250) and, above all, the bankruptcy of the Ayr Bank in 1772 (*ibid.*, p. 240),[28] and referring to one of the prohibitions, that of small-denomination notes ("ten and five shilling bank notes", *ibidem*), stemming from the Scottish Banking Act of 1765, designed to protect agents against the insolvency of banks, Smith wonders about the functioning (and drifts) of the banking system.[29] After emphasizing the role of banks in economic development, insofar as they enable the financing of the economy, *i.e.* "the maintenance of industry" (*ibid.*, p. 224),[30] he first points out the dangers of issuing and discounting securities (*i.e.* bills of exchange) and of excess liquidity when "the circulating money of any country" exceeds its absorption capacity, *i.e.* "the whole value of the annual produce" (*ibid.*, p. 224), knowing furthermore that "the whole paper money of every kind which can easily circulate in any country never can exceed the value of the gold and silver of which it supplies the place, or which (the commerce being supposed the same) would circulate there, if there was no paper money." (*ibid.*, p. 227).

The first problem is therefore the overabundance of paper, when there is "more of this paper than was necessary for transacting the business" (*ibid.*, p. 228), or when "the circulation has been overstocked with paper money" (*ibid.*, p. 229), thus provoking contagious defiance (*i.e.* a "run") among private individuals:

> "Many people would immediately perceive that they had more of this paper than was necessary for transacting their business at home, and as they could not send it abroad, they would immediately demand payment of it from the banks [...] There would be a run upon the banks to the whole extent of this superfluous paper, and, if they showed any difficulty or backwardness in payment, to a much greater extent; the alarm, which this would occasion, necessarily increasing the run upon the banks." (WON, II, II, p. 228)

Hence the need for banks to comply with debt and liquidity ratios.[31]

A second problem arises from the assessment of the reputation and credibility of borrowers (*i.e.* counterparty risk) and the projects to be financed, which is not unrelated to the previous point:

> "The over-trading of bold projectors in the United Kingdom has been the original cause of this excessive circulation of paper money. What a bank can with propriety advance to a merchant or undertaker of any kind, is not either the whole capital with which he trades, or even any considerable part of that capital: but that part of it only which he would otherwise be obliged to keep by him unemployed, and in ready money, for answering occasional demands. If the paper money which the bank advances never exceeds this value, it can never exceed the value of the gold and silver which would necessarily circulate in the country if there was no paper money; it can never exceed the quantity which the circulation of the country can absorb and employ." (WON, II, II, p. 231)

Indeed, while "banking companies of Scotland were for a long time very careful to require frequent and regular repayments from all their customers, and did not care to deal with any person [and to assess] his fortune or credit", enabling the bank "to make some tolerable judgement concerning the thriving or declining circumstances of their debtors, without being obliged to look out for any other evidence besides what their own books afforded them" (*ibid.*, p. 232), wider access to credit has led to an increase in information asymmetry between lenders and borrowers (*i.e.* when business is no longer confined within more reasonable bounds, to use Smith's terminology, *ibid.*, p. 228), a factor in adverse selection[32] and the misjudgment of risks and their traceability:

> "a bank which lends money, perhaps to five hundred different people, the greater part of whom its directors can know very little about, is not likely to be more judicious in the choice of its debtors than a private person who lends out his money among a few people whom he knows, and in whose sober and frugal conduct he thinks he has good reason to confide. The debtors of such a bank as that whose conduct I have been giving some account of, were likely, the greater part of them, to be chimerical projectors, the drawers and redrawers of circulating bills of exchange, who would employ the money in extravagant undertakings, which, with all the assistance that could be given them, they would probably never be able to complete, and which, if they should be completed, would never repay the expense which they had really cost." (*ibid.*, pp. 242–243)

This has led to an increase in speculative behaviour, through cavalier or pyramid effects (*i.e.* the Ponzi scheme), where artificial transactions in securities, *i.e.* the continuous exchange of drafts between operators ("This practice was called raising money by circulation", *ibid.*, p. 237), artificially increases returns and their values, thus feeding a fraudulent financial scheme that consists of remunerating customer investments essentially with funds provided by new entrants:

> "some of those traders had recourse to an expedient which, for a time, served their purpose, though at a much greater expense, yet as effectually as the utmost extension of bank credits could have done. This expedient was no other than the well-known shift of drawing and re-drawing; the shift to which unfortunate traders have sometimes recourse when they are upon the brink of bankruptcy [...] Though the drawer, acceptor, and endorsers of the bill should, all of them, be persons of doubtful credit, yet still the shortness of the date gives some security to the owner of the bill. Though all of them may be very likely to become bankrupts, it is a chance if all become so in so short a time. "The house is crazy, says a weary traveller to himself, and will not stand very long; but it is a chance if it falls to-night, and I will venture, therefore, to sleep in it to-night"." (*ibid.*, pp. 235–236)

This technique of manipulating financial information, aimed at creating false appearances about the evolution of returns and asset prices, undermines the mechanisms of trust and transparency, making informational asymmetry almost irreducible, particularly in the context of a financial market made up of several banks:

> "When two people, who are continually drawing and re-drawing upon one another, discount their bills always with the same banker, he must immediately discover what they are about, and see clearly that they are trading, not with any capital of their own, but with the capital which he

advances to them. But this discovery is not altogether so easy when they discount their bills sometimes with one banker, and sometimes with another, and when the same two persons do not constantly draw and re-draw upon one another, but occasionally run the round of a great circle of projectors, who find it for their interest to assist one another in this method of raising money, and to render it, upon that account, as difficult as possible to distinguish between a real and a fictitious bill of exchanges; between a bill drawn by a real creditor upon a real debtor, and a bill for which there was properly no real creditor but the bank which discounted it; nor any real debtor but the projector who made use of the money." (*ibid.*, pp. 238–239)

Moreover, this technique amplifies the interconnection of bank balance sheets ("such payments only put into one coffer what had the moment before been taken out of another", *ibid.*, p. 240), thus increasing contagion phenomena and systemic risk, a "fatal circle" from which banks cannot escape without "incurring a considerable loss, and perhaps, too, even some degree of discredit [and increasing], in the long-run, the real distress of the country" (*ibid.*, p. 241).

We are, once again, far from the "obvious and simple system of natural liberty" and, faced with this endangerment of collective well-being, Smith, in keeping with two of his principles, banks are i) at the service of production which is ii) the true wealth of nations,[33] sets out some prudential measures:

"To restrain private people [...] from receiving in payment the promissory notes of a banker, for any sum whether great or small, when they themselves are willing to receive them; or, to restrain a banker from issuing such notes, when all his neighbours are willing to accept of them, is a manifest violation of that natural liberty which it is the proper business of law, not to infringe, but to support [...] The obligation of building party walls, in order to prevent the communication of fire, is a violation of natural liberty, exactly of the same kind with the regulations of the banking trade which are here proposed." (WON, II, II, p. 249)

This prudential regulation is designed to force banks to be "more circumspect in their conduct", to return to behaviors that are more "advantageous to the public" (*ibid.*, p. 253), those that, in a context of increased competition, enable the fulfillment of the general interest.

The first recommendation is to restrict access to financial securities to professional bankers, major industrialists and traders, who alone are in a position to assess the risks involved, and to raise the minimum amounts in order to exclude the poorly-informed public, who are therefore vulnerable to these same risks:

"If bankers are restrained from issuing any circulating bank notes, or notes payable to the bearer, for less than a certain sum; and if they are subjected to the obligation of an immediate and unconditional payment of such bank notes as soon as presented, their trade may, with safety to the public, be rendered in all other respects perfectly free." (WON, II, II, p. 253)

The second, like his criticism of the concentration of large companies and the growing separation between ownership and exploitation of invested capital, is to encourage interbank competition:

> "The late multiplication of banking companies in both parts of the United Kingdom, an event by which may people have been much alarmed, instead of diminishing, increases the security of the public. It obliges all of them to be more circumspect in their conduct, and, by not extending their currency beyond its due proportion to their cash, to guard themselves against those malicious runs, which the rivalship of so many competitors is always ready to bring upon them. It restrains the circulation of each particular company within a narrower circle, and reduces their circulating notes to a smaller number." (*ibid.*, p. 253)

Thirdly, to ensure the compartmentalization of the banking market in order to limit the risks of contagion:

> "By dividing the whole circulation into a greater number of parts, the failure of any one company, an accident which, in the course of things, must sometimes happen, becomes of less consequence to the public." (*ibid.*, p. 253)

In order to enable the fulfillment of these "several duties of the sovereign" which "necessarily supposes a certain expense" (WON, IV, IX, p. 540), the end of WON (V, II, "Sources of the General or Public Revenue of the Society"; V, III, "Of Public Debts") contains a veritable treatise on public finance charged with answering two main questions:

- "what are the different methods in which the whole society may be made to contribute towards defraying the expenses incumbent on the whole society, and what are the principal advantages and inconveniences of each of those methods?", in other words, the "sources of the general or public revenue of the society", *i.e.* taxes, the primary source of public financing (WON, V, II, pp. 644–723);

- "what are the reasons and causes which have induced almost all modern governments to mortgage some part of this revenue, or to contract debts, and what have been the effects of those debts upon the real wealth, the annual produce of the land and labour of the society?", *i.e.* public debt, the second source of public financing (WON, V, III, pp. 723–760).

The chapter on taxes begins with the "four maxims" that should govern all tax collection, guided by the principles of fairness and efficiency, which guarantee the ability, and therefore the willingness, to pay: i) "The subjects of every state ought to contribute towards the support of the government, as nearly as possible in proportion to their respective abilities; that is, in proportion to the revenue which they respectively enjoy under the protection of the state." (WON, V, II, p. 651); ii) "The tax which each individual is bound to pay, ought to be certain, and not arbitrary. The time of payment, the manner of payment, and the quantity to be paid, ought all to be clear and plain to the contributor, and to every other person." (*ibid.*, p. 652); iii) "Every tax ought to be levied at the time, or in the manner, in which it is most likely to be convenient for the contributor to pay it." (*ibidem*); iv) "Every tax ought to be so contrived as both to take out and to keep out of the pockets of the people as little as possible over and above what it brings into the public treasury of the state." (*ibidem*).

Considering these Principles, Smith is unfavorable to the taxation of profit, since profit "is the compensation, and in most cases it is no more than a very moderate compensation, for the risk and trouble of employing the stock" (*ibid.*, p. 671), and that it would be passed on *in fine* to the price of the goods, "in which case the final payment of the tax would fall altogether upon the consumers of those goods" (*ibid.*, p. 671). Smith was also very circumspect about the taxation of capital income, firstly because of the difficulties of valuing assets other than real estate (*ibid.*, pp. 672–673),[34] and secondly because of the international mobility of capital:

> "The proprietor of stock is properly a citizen of the world, and is not necessarily attached to any particular country. He would be apt to abandon the country in which he was exposed to a vexatious inquisition, in order to be assessed to a burdensome tax, and would remove his stock to some other country, where he would either carry on his business, or enjoy his fortune more at his case." (WON, V, II, p. 672)

Smith is also opposed to any "taxes upon the wages of labour", insofar as the direct tax upon the wages "can have no other effect than to raise the wages of labour somewhat higher than the tax" (*ibid.*, p. 686), directly if the demand for labour is perfectly inelastic ("full employment" regime), and indirectly when this wage inflation is reflected in the "ordinary or average price of provisions" (*ibidem*), which is the basis for wage setting (subsistence wage theory).

This analysis of the impact (or externalities) of these different taxes on economic activity leads Smith to favor the taxation of the landlord (*i.e.* "Taxes upon the rent of land; produce of land; rents of houses" (*ibid.*, p. 653 ff), as these assets are easily identifiable, which is useful for assessing "a land tax" (*ibid.*, p. 653) and for "the transference of property" (*ibid.*, p. 680), and reflect the inequality of individuals' wealth; with tax fairness consisting, in this case, in taking account of these "different degrees of wealth" and restraining prodigality:

> "The necessaries of life occasion the great expense of the poor. They find it difficult to get food, and the greater part of their little revenue is spent in getting it. The luxuries and vanities of life occasion the principal expense of the rich; and a magnificent house embellishes and sets off to the best advantage all the other luxuries and vanities which they possess. A tax upon house rents, therefore, would in general fall heaviest upon the rich; and in this sort of inequality there would not, perhaps, be anything very unreasonable. It is not very unreasonable that the rich should contribute to the public expense, not only in proportion to their revenue, but something more than in that proportion. The rent of houses, though it in some respects resembles the rent of land, is in one respect essentially different from it. The rent of land is paid for the use of a productive subject. The land which pays it produces it. The rent of house is paid for the use of an unproductive subject. Neither the house nor the ground which it stands upon produce anything." (WON, V, II, p. 666)

Finally, Smith supports the principle of indirect "taxes upon consumable commodities" (*ibid.*, p. 690 and ff): "The state not knowing how to tax directly and proportionably the revenue of its subjects, endeavours to tax it indirectly by taxing their expense which, it is supposed, will in most cases nearly in proportion to their revenue. Their expense is taxed by taxing the consumable commodities upon which it may be laid out." (*ibid.*, pp. 690–691). In order to guarantee the fairness and proportionality of these taxes in relation to people's incomes and lifestyles, the taxation of "necessaries goods" should be avoided as far as possible, in favor of the taxation of "luxuries goods," with the setting of these taxes depending, implicitly, on the elasticity of demand for these different goods.

In addition to taxes, the other public resource is debt. Smith, faithful to the classical prejudice against public spending (financed by taxation and/or the issue of state bonds), which necessarily diverts productive labor into unproductive jobs, criticizes, in particular in the context of a "commercial country abounding with every sort of expensive luxury", the allocation of this debt financing "all the costly trinkets which compose the splendid but insignificant pageantry of the court [and] the same frivolous passions [influencing] the sovereign" (WON, V, III, p. 725), and insists on this eviction effect, which is particularly damaging to the nation's opulence:

> "The public funds of the different indebted nations of Europe, particularly those of England, have [...] been represented as the accumulation of a great capital superadded to the other capital of the country, by means of which its trade is extended, its manufactures multiplied, and its lands cultivated and improved much beyond what they could have been by

means of that other capital only. [We didn't] consider that the capital which the first creditors of the public advanced to government, was, from the moment in which they advanced it, a certain portion of the annual produce turned away from serving in the function of a capital to serve in that of a revenue; from maintaining productive labourers to maintain unproductive ones, and to be spent and wasted, generally in the course of the year, without even the hope of any future reproduction." (WON, V, III, p. 739)

In this context, public debt is akin to a charge on the prosperity of future generations, a sort of capture of future opulence, since it is guaranteed by the ability of governments to collect taxes on future income; a charge that can be partially eliminated if the debt is used to finance public goods (see above). However, this crowding-out effect is all the more important as these investments in state notes are particularly attractive:

"The necessities of the state render government upon most occasions willing to borrow upon terms extremely advantageous to the lender. The security which it grants to the original creditor, is made transferable to any other creditor, and, from the universal confidence in the justice of the state, generally sells in the market for more than was originally paid for it. The merchant or moneyed man makes money by lending money to government, and instead of diminishing, increases his trading capital. He generally considers it as a favour, therefore when the administration admits him to a share in the first subscription for a new loan. Hence the inclination or willingness in the subjects of a commercial state to lend." (*ibid.*, p. 727)

Moreover, as the ease with which governments can raise funds does not encourage them to economize,[35] they may be faced with the risk of over-indebtedness[36] or even sovereign default or bankruptcy:

"The progress of the enormous debts which at present oppress, and will in the long-run probably ruin, all the great nations of Europe, has been pretty uniform. Nations, like private men, have generally begun to borrow upon what may be called personal credit, without assigning or mortgaging any particular fund for the payment of the debt; and when this resource has failed them, they have gone on to borrow upon assignments or mortgages of particular funds [...] When national debts have once been accumulated to a certain degree, there is scarce, I believe, a single instance of their having been fairly and completely paid. The liberation of the public revenue, if it has ever been brought about at all, has always been brought about by a bankruptcy; sometimes by an avoed one, but always by a real one, though frequently by a pretended payment." (WON, V, III, p. 727 and 744).

Notes

1 This is how Marx, in Book I of Capital (1990, I, chap. 6, p. 280), ironically describes this system of natural liberty: "This is in fact a very Eden of the innate rights of man. It is the exclusive realm of Freedom, Equality, Property and Bentham. Freedom, because both buyer and seller of a commodity [...] contract as free persons, who are equal before the law. Their contract is the final result in which their joint will finds a common legal expression. Equality, because each enters into relation with the other, as with a simple owner of commodities, and they exchange equivalent for equivalent. Property, because each disposes only of what is his own. And Bentham, because each looks only to his own advantage [...] And precisely for that reason, either in accordance with the pre-established harmony of things, or under the auspices of an omniscient providence, they all work together to their mutual advantage, for the common weal, and in the common interest."

2 or, about the Government of England: "The orderly, vigilant, and parsimonious administration of such aristocracies [...] is extremely proper [...] for the management of a mercantile project of this kind. But wheter such a government as that of England (which, whatever may be its virtues, has never been famous for good economy; which, in time of peace, has generally conducted itself with the slothful and negligent profusion that is, perhaps, natural to monarchies; and, in time of war, has constantly acted with all the thoughtless extravagance that democracies are apt to fall into) could be safely trusted with the management of such a project, must, at least, be a good deal more doubtful [...] No two characters seem more inconsistent than those of trader and sovereign." (WON, V, II, pp. 645–646).

3 conception not so far removed from Keynes's "The End of Laissez-Faire" (1926, pp. 46–47): "The most important *Agenda* of the State relate not to those activities which private individuals are already fulfilling, but to those functions which fall outside the sphere of the individual, to those decisions which are made by *no one* if the State does not make them. The important thing for Government is not to do things which individuals are doing already, and to do them a little better or a little worse; but to do those things which at present are not done at all." (Keynes emphasises).

4 The regalian function of monetary issuance was discussed earlier in WON (I, IV, p. 19): "To prevent such abuses [*i.e.* counterfeit money], to facilitate exchanges, and thereby to encourage all sorts of industry and commerce, it has been found necessary, in all countries that have made any considerable advances towards improvement, to affix a public stamp upon certain quantities of such particular metals as were in those countries commonly made use of to purchase goods. Hence the origin of coined money, and of those public offices called mints".

5 We will see later that Smith's system of tolls and the functioning of the education system (notably the private remuneration of teachers), by limiting access to these goods, which become non-rival goods (indivisibility of use) but excludable by price, bring them closer to being "club goods".

6 "In every profession, the exertion of the greater part of those who exercise it is always in proportion to the necessity they are under of making that exertion. This necessity is greatest with those to whom the emoluments of their profession are the only source from which they expect their fortune, or even their ordinary revenue and subsistence." (WON, V, I, p. 597). For example, "by maintening and employing a certain number of citizens in the constant practice of the military exercices, the state may render the trade of a soldier a particular trade, separate and distinct from all others." (*ibid.*, p. 547), as well as "The administration of justice became so laborious and so complicated a duty as to require the undivided attention of the persons to whom it was entrusted." (*ibid.*, p. 565).

7 "Regularity, order, and prompt obedience to command, are qualities which, in modern armies, are of more importance towards determining the fate of battles, than the dexterity and skill of the soldiers in the use of their arms." (*ibid.*, p. 548).

8 "When the judicial is united to the executive power, it is scarce possible that justice should not frequently be sacrificed to what is vulgarly called politics. The persons entrusted with the great interests of the state may, even without any corrupt views, sometimes imagine it necessary to sacrifice to those interests the rights of a private man." (*ibid.*, p. 566). The same applies to "the authority of fortune or the distinction of birth": "Birth and fortune are evidently the two circumstances which principally set one man above another. They are the two great causes which naturally establish authority and subordination among men" to prevent "his birth and fortune thus naturally procure him some sort of judicial authority" to establish "the impartial administration of justice [on which] depends the liberty of every individual – the sense which he has of his own security." (*ibid.*, p. 566, 559, 566); in other words, to prevent the subordination of the justice system to the private interests of the powerful and "politicians".

9 "That wealth [...] which always follows the improvements of agriculture and manufactures, and which in reality is no more than the accumulated produce of those improvements, provokes the invasion of all their neighbours. An industrious, and upon that account a wealthy nation, is of all nations the most likely to be attacked; and unless the state takes some new measures for the public defense, the natural habits of the people render them altogether incapable of defending themselves." (*ibid.*, p. 546).

10 "it is the wisdom of the state only which can render the trade of a soldier a particular trade, separate and distinct from all others." (*ibid.*, p. 546).

11 "The security which [the standing army] gives to the sovereign renders unnecessary that troublesome jealousy which, in some modern republics, seems to watch over the minutest actions, and to be at all times ready to disturb the peace of every citizen." (*ibid.*, p. 554).

12 "It is only under the shelter of the civil magistrate that the owner of that valuable property, which is acquired by the labour of many years, or perhaps of many successive generations, can sleep a single night in security" particularly as "He is at all times surrounded by unknown enemies, whom, though he never provoked, he can never appease, and from whose injustice he can be protected only by the powerful arm of the civil magistrate continually held to chastise it. The acquisition of valuable and extensive property, therefore, necessarily requires the establishment of civil government." (*ibid.*, p. 556).

13 This concerns all areas, for example, the financial sector: "When the law does not enforce the performance of contracts, it puts all borrowers nearly upon the same footing with bankrupts or people of doubtful credit in betterregulated countries." (WON, I, IX, p. 74; see also, WON, II, II, p. 236), commercial and private leases: "Originally the courts of law gave damages only for breach of contract. The court of Chancery, as a court of conscience, first took upon it to enforce the specific performance of agreements." (WON, V, I, p. 564) and employment: "What are the common wages of labour, depends everywhere upon the contract usually made between those two parties, whose interests are by no means the same. The workmen desire to get as much, the masters to give as little as possible." (WON, I, VIII, p. 51).

14 "Wherever there is great property, there is great inequality. For one very rich man, there must be at least five hundred poor, and the affluence of the rich excites the indignation of the poor, who are often both driven by want and prompted by envy to invade his possessions. It is only under the shelter of the civil magistrate that the owner of that valuable property [...] can sleep a single night in security [...] The

acquisition of valuable and extensive property, therefore, necessarily requires the establishment of civil government. Where there is no property, or at least, none that exceeds the value of two or three days' labour, civil government is not so necessary." (*ibid.*, p. 556).

15 "The education of the common people requires, perhaps, in a civilized and commercial society, the attention of the public more than that of people of some rank and fortune [who] are generally eighteen or nineteen years of age before they enter upon that particular business, profession, or trade, by which they propose to distinguish themselves in the world. They have before that full time to acquire, or, at least, to fit themselves for afterwards acquiring, every accomplishment which can recommend them to the public esteem, or render them worthy of it. Their parents or guardians are generally sufficiently anxious that they should be so accomplished, and are, in most cases, willing enough to lay out the expense which is necessary for that purpose." (*ibid.*, pp. 614–615).

16 With classical economists such as Smith, Mill or Say: "Division of labour is a convenient, useful means—a skilful deployment of human powers for social wealth; but it reduces the ability of each person taken individually" or for Mill: "human activity is reduced to mechanical motion. Division of labour and use of machinery promote wealth of production. Each person must be entrusted with as small a sphere of operations as possible" hence "the examination of division of labour and exchange is of extreme interest, because these are perceptibly alienated expressions of human activity and essential power as a species activity and species power" and the conclusion that: "Division of labour and exchange are the two phenomena which lead the political economist to boast of the social character of his science, while in the same breath he gives unconscious expression to the contradiction in his science—the motivation of society by unsocial, particular interests [...] Wealth—production—is explained by division of labour and exchange. The impoverishment of individual activity, and its loss of character as a result of the division of labour, are admitted." (Marx, 1844 in 1977, pp. 126–127).

17 "The public can facilitate this [*i.e.* most essential parts of education] acquisition, by establishing, in every parish or district, a little school, where children may be taught, for a reward so moderate, that even a common labourer may afford it" (*ibid.*, p. 616).

18 This logic of disincentive remuneration (*ibid.*, p. 597) also applies to universities, since wages are based on hours worked and not on the quality of teaching, or, more generally, the absence of remuneration based on results, which ultimately destroys the motivation to do any job well: "In other universities the teacher is prohibited from receiving any honorary or fee from the pupils, and his salary constitutes the whole of the revenue which he derives from his office. His interest is, in this case, set as directly in opposition to his duty as it is possible to set it. It is the interest of every man to live as much at his ease as he can; and if his emoluments are to be precisely the same whether he does or does not perform some very laborious duty, it is certainly his interest, at least as interest is vulgarly understood, either to neglect it altogether, or, if he is subject to some authority which will not suffer him to do this, to perform it in as careless ad slovenly a manner as that authority will permit." (*ibid.*, p. 598) particularly as "If the authority to which he is subject resides in the body corporate, the college or university, of which he himself is a member, and in which the greater part of the other members are, like himself, persons who either are or ought to be teachers, they are likely to make a common cause, to be all very indulgent to one another, and every man to consent that his neighbour may neglect his duty provided he himself is allowed to neglect his own. In the University of Oxford, the greater part of the public professors have for these

many years, given up even the pretence of teaching." (*ibidem*); Adam Smith was educated in Oxford.

19 In Smith's mind, the primary function of education is not to train individuals for the job market, or to be exclusively vocational, but to turn them into citizens. Consequently, the state must guarantee the scientific production and dissemination of knowledge, even if this knowledge is not directly relevant to the needs of the economy or the market: "Were there no public institutions for education, no system, no science, would be taught for which there was not some demand; or which the circumstances of the times did not render it either necessary, or convenient, or, at least, fashionable to learn." (*ibid.*, p. 612). This positioning is not unrelated to the debate on the Knowledge Economy, and the competitive knowledge economy as a factor in sustainable growth. On this subject, *cf.* B. Readings, *The University in ruins*, Cambridge (Mass.), London, Harvard University Press, 1996.

20 "The public can encourage the acquisition of those most essential parts of education by giving small premiums and badges of distinction to the children of the common people who excel in them." (*ibid.*, p. 616).

21 "The public can impose upon almost the whole body of the people the necessity of acquiring those most essential parts of education, by obliging every man to undergo an examination or probation in them before he can obtain the freedom in any corporation, or be allowed to set up any trade, either in a village or town corporate." (*ibid.*, p. 616).

22 "A highway, a bridge, a navigable canal, for example, may in most cases be both made and maintained by a small toll upon the carriages which make use of them: a harbour, by a moderate port duty upon the tonnage of the shipping which load or unload in it." (*ibid.*, p. 567).

23 "When the carriages which pass over a highway or a bridge, and the lighters which sail upon a navigable canal, pay toll in proportion to their weight or their tonnage, they pay for the maintenance of those public works exactly in proportion to the wear and tear which they occasion of them [...] When the toll upon carriages of luxury, upon coaches, post-chaises, etc., is made somewhat higher in proportion to their weight, than upon carriages of necessary use, such as carts, wagons, etc., the indolence and vanity of the rich is made to contribute in a very easy manner to the relief of the poor, by rendering cheaper the transportation of heavy goods to all the different parts of the country." (*ibid.*, p. 568).

24 According to this approach, prices (for transport, for example) must be equal to the additional short-term cost created by an additional infrastructure user, and pricing at marginal social cost (*i.e.* the private cost directly linked to infrastructure use + external costs, loss of time for other users, pollution, etc.) leads to a more efficient use of existing infrastructure. Moreover, since the user pays for the additional cost he imposes on society (*i.e.* "in proportion to the wear and tear which they occasion", "the wear and tear which that carriage occasions of the roads" for Smith, *ibid.*, p. 567, 570), such pricing contributes to equity between users and non-users and establishes a direct link between the use of common resources and payment according to the "polluter pays" or "user pays" principle.

25 "When high roads, bridges, canals etc., are in this manner made and supported by the commerce which is carried on by means of them, they can be made only where that commerce requires them, and consequently where it is proper to make them. Their expense, too, their grandeur and magnificence, must be suited to what that commerce can afford to pay. They must be made consequently as it is proper to make them. A magnificent high road cannot be made through a desert country where there is little or no commerce, or merely because it happens to lead to the

country villa of the intendant of the province, or to that of some great lord to whom the intendant finds it convenient to make his court." (*ibid.*, p. 568).

26 "If the meanness and poverty of the trustees of turnpike-roads render it sometimes difficult at present to oblige them to repair their wrong, their wealth and greatness would render it ten times more so in the case which is here supposed." (*ibid.*, p. 571).

27 "Such regulations may, no doubt, be considered as in some respects a violation of natural liberty. But those exertions of the natural liberty of a few individuals, which might endanger the security of the whole society, are, and ought to be, restrained by the laws of all governments; of the most free, as well as of the most despotical." (*ibid.*, p. 249).

28 See David Hume's letter to Adam Smith, dated 27 June 1772, concerning the bankruptcy of the Ayr bank (Smith, 1987, p. 228).

29 "The Scotch banks, no doubt, paid all of them very dearly for their own imprudence and inattention. But the Bank of England paid very dearly, not only for its own imprudence, but for the much greater imprudence of almost all the Scotch banks." (*ibid.*, p. 231). Finally, let's not forget that John Law ("the famous Mr. Law", *ibid.*, p. 243) was also Scottish.

30 "that the trade and industry of Scotland, however, have increased very considerably [...] and that the banks of issue have contributed a good deal to this increase, cannot be doubted." (*ibid.*, p. 225) and, further on: "It is not by augmenting the capital of the country, but by rendering a greater part of that capital active and productive than would otherwise be so, that the most judicious operations of banking can increase the industry of the country." (*ibid.*, p. 245).

31 "the expenses peculiar to a bank consist chiefly in two articles: first, in the expense of keeping at all times in its coffers for answering the occasional demands of the holders of its notes, a large sum of money, of which it loses the interest; and, secondly, in the expense of replenishing those coffers as fast as they are emptied by answering such occasional demands." (*ibid.*, p. 228).

32 "The debtors [are] chimerical projectors, the drawers and redrawers of circulating bills of exchange, who employ the money in extravagant undertakings [to the detriment of] the sober and frugal debtors of private persons [...] more likely to employ the money borrowed in sober undertakings which were proportioned to their capitals, and which, though they might have less of the grand and the marvellous, would have more of the solid and the profitable, which would repay with a large profit whatever had been laid out upon them [...] The success of this operation, therefore, without increasing in the smallest degree the capital of the country, would only have transferred a great part of it from prudent and profitable, to imprudent and unprofitable undertakings." (*ibid.*, pp. 242–243).

33 "It is not by augmenting the capital of the country, but by rendering a greater part of that capital active and productive than would otherwise be so, that the most judicious operations of banking can increase the industry of the country." (*ibid.*, p. 245).

34 "The nations accordingly, who have attempted to tax the revenue arising from stock, instead of any severe inquisition of this kind, have been obliged to content themselves with some very loose, and, therefore, more or less arbitrary estimation. The extreme inequality and uncertainty of a tax assessed in this manner can be compensated only by its extreme moderation, in consequence of which every man finds himself rated so very much below his real revenue, that he gives himself little disturbance though his neighbour should be rated somewhat lower." (*ibid.*, pp. 672–673).

35 "The government of such a state is very at to repose itself upon this ability and willingness of its subjects to lend it their money on extraordinary occasions. It

foresees the facility of borrowing, and therefore dispenses itself from the duty of saving." (*ibid.*, p. 727).

36 when, for example, "the new taxes were imposed for the sole purpose of paying the interest of the money borrowed upon them" (*ibid.*, p. 736).

Bibliography

Keynes, John Maynard (1926). *The End of Laissez-Faire*, London, Published by Leonard & Virginia Woolf at the Hogarth Press, 52 Tavistock Square.

Leibniz, Gottfried Wilhelm (1951). *Essays on the Goodness of God, the Freedom of Man and the Origin of Evil* (1710). London: Routledge & Kegan Paul Ltd.

Marx, Karl (1977). *Economic and Philosophic Manuscripts of 1844*. Moscow: Progress Publishers, fifth revised edition.

Marx, Karl (1990). *Capital. A Critique of Political Economy*, Volume I (1867), Translated by Ben Fowkes. London: Penguin Books in association with New Left Review, Penguin Classics.

Polanyi, Karl (2001). *The Great Transformation. The Political and Economic Origins of Our Time* (1944). Boston (Mass.): Beacon Press.

Schumpeter, Joseph Alois (1966). *History of Economic Analysis* (1954). New York: Oxford Universty Press, sixth printing.

Smith, Adam (1913). *An Inquiry into the Nature and Causes of the Wealth of Nations* (1776). London: George Routledge & Sons, Limited; New York, E.P. Dutton and Co.

Smith, Adam (1987). *The Correspondence of Adam Smith*. In E.C. Mossner & I.S. Ross eds., The Glasgow Edition of the Works of Adam Smith. Indianapolis: Liberty Fund, Inc.

Viner, Jacob (1927). Adam Smith and Laissez Faire. *Journal of Political Economy*, *35*(2), april, 198–232.

Part II

Karl Marx (Trier, 1818, London, 1883) and "Capital. A Critique of Political Economy" ("Das Kapital. Kritik der Politischen Oekonomie") (1867)

Introduction

April 1867: Marx has finished writing Book I of Capital and travels to Hamburg to take the manuscript to the publisher himself. In a letter dated the 17th to his friend Johann Philipp Becker, a militant of the I° Internationale, he informs him of the purpose of this trip and asks him to announce the forthcoming publication of his book in the press: "It is without question the most terrible missile that has yet been hurled at the heads of the bourgeoisie (landowners included)."

Capital. A Critique of Political Economy (henceforth Capital), from the original title *Das Kapital. Kritik der politischen Oekonomie* (Hamburg, Verlag von Otto Meisner, 1867), "Marx's major thought, his great obsession" for M. Rubel (in Marx, 1965, p. 537), a work sustained from 1844 to his death, *i.e.* almost forty years during which Marx wrote Capital, in its four books, but only giving its definitive form to Book I, with Books II, III and IV, which remained in draft form, being published after his death.

> "This work, whose first volume I now submit to the public, forms the continuation of my book Zur *Kritik der Politischen Ökonomie*, published in 1859 [...] What I have to examine in this work is the capitalist mode of production, and the relations of production and forms of inter-course [*Verkehrsverhältnisse*] that correspond to it [...] The second volume of this work will deal with the process of the circulation of capital (Book II) and the various forms of the process of capital in its totality (Book III), while the third and last volume (Book IV) will deal with the history of the theory. I welcome every opinion based on scientific criticism. As to the prejudices of so-called public opinion, to which I have never made concessions, now, as ever, my maxim is that of the great Florentine: "*Segui il tuo corso, e lascia dir le genti!*" [Follow your path and let people tell you!]" (Marx, 1990, Preface, I, p. 89, 90, 93)[1]

Like Smith's WON (*cf.* Part I), reading Capital is demanding, "a major undertaking" to quote Blaug (1985, p. 266), not only because of its length, repetitive and unfinished character, but also because of the complexity of a text filled with "analytical riddles and Hegelian 'contradictions'" (*ibidem*)

DOI: 10.4324/9781032649054-8

likely to make "quite arduous [its] reading [assez ardue [sa] lecture]" (Marx, Letter to Maurice Lachâtre, French editor of Capital, 18 March 1872, in Marx, 1965, p. 542). Alongside this prolixity and its repetitive, unfinished aspects, also noted by Schumpeter (1966, pp. 391–392), the tediousness of Capital can be explained by Marx's desire to write a scientific treatise, to conceive society scientifically by specifying the laws of operation of the "capitalist mode of production" (henceforth CMP) and to derive from them the true law of value that "the human mind", *a fortiori* political economy, has so far sought in vain. This recourse to the authority of science, in order to abstract oneself from "the most violent, sordid and malignant passions of the human breast, the Furies of private interest" (Marx, 1990, p. 92), is evident as early as the Preface to Book I: "Beginnings are always difficult in all sciences. The understanding of the first chapter, especially the section that contains the analysis of commodities, will therefore present the greatest difficulty." (*ibid.*, p. 89) and Marx continues:

> "the complete body is easier to study than its cells. Moreover, in the analysis of economic forms neither microscopes nor chemical reagents are of assistance. The power of abstraction must replace both. But for bourgeois society, the commodity-form of the product of labour, or the value-form of the commodity, is the economic cell-form. To the superficial observer, the analysis of these forms seems to turn upon minutiae. It does in fact deal with minutiae, but so similarly does microscopic anatomy [...] The physicist either observes natural processes where they occur in their most significant form, and are least affected by disturbing influences [or] makes experiments under conditions which ensure that the process will occur in its pure state. What I have to examine in this work is the capitalist mode of production, and the relations of production and forms of intercourse that correspond to it." (Preface, *ibid.*, p. 90)[2]

The abstraction required to specify the "natural laws of capitalist production" (*ibid.*, p. 91) and the "natural laws of its movement" (*ibid.*, p. 92) is coupled in Capital with the use of facts and historical examples, provided by "the social statistics", "used as the main illustration of the theoretical developments" (*ibid.*, pp. 90–91). Within this framework, "the development of the economic formation of society is viewed as a process of natural history", the study of which requires a "free scientific inquiry" where, for example, the capitalist and the landowner are studied as "personifications of economic categories", as "bearers of particular class-relations and interests" (*ibid.*, p. 92).

In Capital, Marx conceived an elaborate theory of capitalism as a "specific mode of production" (*ibid.*, I, pp. 1023–1025) *sui generis* (*ibid.*, p. 1035), *i.e.* the CMP, historically dated and therefore contingent, whose dynamics refer to the conditions and mechanisms of capital accumulation, both microeconomic (individual capital) and macroeconomic (social capital). At both levels, accumulation is confronted with the contradictions inherent in the capitalist system, synthesized in the contradiction between the *social* character of production and the *private* character of ownership of the means of production and economic decisions, within a framework that makes this accumulation possible, the use of money as capital. However, for Marx, in capitalism, "Widerspruch ist nicht Widersinn"—in other words, "contradiction is not impossibility"—the system's contradictions constitute endogenous dynamics, where crises (and their overcoming) illustrate the periods during which the system shows its capacity to overcome, temporarily, its contradictions, resembling real pulsations. "Crisis" then appears as a means (as a propitious moment) to overcome, temporarily and brutally, some of the contradictions generated by the CMP dynamic:

> "Crises are never more than momentary, violent solutions for the existing contradictions, violent eruptions that re-establish the disturbed balance for the time being." (Marx, 1991, III, p. 357)

The widespread occurrence of crises in space, and the repetition of this regulatory process throughout history, form the basis for the idea of periodicity, and hence the concept of "cycle", which henceforth grasps the "crisis" as a moment in the cycle (its turning point) and analyzes it in relation to its periodic return. Marx thus abandons a pathological conception of "crisis", with its extraordinary character, in favour of an analysis of economic physiology in which "crisis" loses its accidental character to become a necessary moment in the normal functioning of the capitalist system, thereby reviving the original scientific understanding of the concept of "crisis" contained in the Hippocratic corpus (see box).

"Crisis" in Hippocrates' corpus

In the great treatises of the School of Cos, *i.e.* the Hippocratic *corpus*, Hippocrates, in his treatise *The Nature of Man, De natura homini*, sets out his conception of the individual's body, which is composed, according to "the theory of four constituent humours", of four "primary elements or particular elements of the nature of man and of all the others": "The human body contains blood, phlegm [or pituitum], yellow bile and black bile. These are the things that make up its constitution and cause its pain and health. Health is primarily that state in which these constituent substances are in the correct proportion to each other, both in strength and quantity, and are well mixed. Pain occurs when one of the substances presents either a deficiency or an excess, or is separated in the body and not mixed with the others." (Hippocrates, 1983, §4, p. 5–6/25). The properties of each of these correspond to each of the four seasons, each humour predominating in the season which shares the same nature: blood, hot and wet, predominates in spring; yellow bile, hot and dry, in summer; black bile, cold and dry, in autumn; and phlegm, cold and wet, in winter. When these four humours are in the right mixing ratio (*i.e.* "eucrasia" or *Krasis*, *i.e.* balance), they enable the person to be healthy, but when they are in disharmony (*i.e.* "dyscrasia" or imbalance), they cause disease and, eventually, crisis. Indeed, the first, most acute phase of the disease is that of the alteration of the "raw humors", often produced by external causes (climates and seasons). For the disease to be cured, the raw humours must be cooked by organic heat: this is "coction" (*i.e.* fever), which consists in thickening them and attenuating their dominant quality: "in some cases, the fever resolved at a time different from those given above without reaching a crisis. In most of these, the fever returned after a short interval and the crisis was reached in one of the usual periods." (*Epidemics*, Book I, §3, *ibid.*, p. 6/54). Finally, the "cooked humours" are eliminated, the last period of the disease, that of resolution-healing, that of the "crisis": "Whenever there is danger, watch out for all ripe discharges that flow from every part of the body at their due times and for favourable and critical abscess formation. Ripeness shows that the crisis is at hand and that recovery is certain. On the other hand, what is raw and immature, as well as unfavourable abscess formation, denotes the failure to reach a crisis, pain, prolongation of the malady, death or relapse." (*ibid.*, §11, p. 15/54).

Crudity, coction, crisis—these are the three phases through which diseases pass, the three periods according to Hippocrates. Consequently, *an incurable disease is one that never reaches crisis.* In the first (pre) scientific field where "crisis" comes into play, it is therefore a necessary element in regulating the organism, a return to equilibrium.

In line with his "humoral theory", in which "crisis" is a natural phenomenon insofar as the living organism is endowed with a spontaneous medicinal force, Hippocrates laid the foundations of expectant medicine by recommending that we follow and listen to nature in order to promote the completeness of crises and not to thwart its useful instincts, as he describes in several of his *Aphorisms*, for example, §20 and §21: "When a disease has attained the crisis, or when a crisis has just passed, do not disturb the patient with innovation in treatment either by the administration of drugs or by giving stimulants. Let them be." and "The progress of a disease should be so guided, where guidance is needed, so that it develops in the most favourable manner according to its natural tendency." (*Aphorisms*, I, p. 6/67)

Marx, in Capital, is thus simultaneously led to criticize and reject the CMP because of the consequences of its antagonisms, and to recognize its formidable endogenous dynamic where contradictions not only do not rhyme with impossibility but become *stimuli* for development: "The mechanism of the capitalist production process removes the very obstacles it temporarily creates" (I, XXV, p. 770), or again:

> "The periodical devaluation of the existing capital, which is a means, immanent to the [CMP], for delaying the fall in the profit rate and accelerating the accumulation of capital value by the formation of new capital, disturbs the given conditions in which the circulation and reproduction process of capital takes place, and is therefore accompanied by sudden stoppages and crisis in the production process [...] Capitalist production constantly strives to overcome these immanent barriers, but it overcomes them only by means that set up the barriers afresh and on a more powerful scale." (III, XV, p. 358)

Schumpeter (1966, pp. 391–392) recommends "a reader's guide" to grasp the complexity of this Marxian model of the dynamics of capitalism, which is supposed to uncover its autogenous mechanism,[3] while warning that "there is no point whatever in tackling Marx without preparation". It is this preparation that motivates the content of the next chapter.

Notes

1 Bibliographical references to Capital refer to the relevant Book (I, II, III or IV) and the chapter from which the quotation is taken. Thus, for example, Marx (I, VII, p. 283) means in Capital, Book I, Chapter 7, page 283.

2 Later (I, I, p. 127), Marx again uses scientific analogies, such as "a simple geometrical example" to explain "exchange value". Similarly, he uses chemistry, in this case, the respective properties of butyric acid and propyl formate, to explain the relative form of the value of two goods (*ibid.*, p. 141), or "the scientific dissection of the air" for the value of the products of labour (*ibid.*, p. 167), or "the law of gravity" for the social labour time required as a law (*ibid.*, p. 168), *etc.*

3 *i.e.* the mechanism which, endowed with intrinsic rationality, makes it possible to find, in this dynamic, a constant defined by laws of change; in other words, the mechanism whose operation alone, without recourse to external factors, transforms a given state of society into another state.

4 From the theory of value to the transformation of "surplus value" into "profit" and "value" into "production price"

From the "Fetishim of the commodity and its secret" to the "General formula of capital"

Marx begins "classically" with Capital. Following in the footsteps of Smith (WON, I, IV, pp. 21–22) (see Part I) and Ricardo (1817, pp. 1–48), he reminds us, in his first chapter "The Commodity", that every commodity, which is "first of all, an external object, a thing which through its qualities satisfies human needs of whatever kind" (*ibid.*, I, I, p. 125), is embodied in a use-value ("The usefulness of a thing makes it a use-value", *ibid.*, p. 126), that is only realized by "use or consumption" and forms "the material content of wealth, whatever its social form may be." (*ibid.*, p. 126); and exchange-value that appears as "first of all as the quantitative relation, the proportion, in which use-values of one kind exchange for use-values of another kind. This relation changes constantly with time and place" (*ibidem*). Logically, a good produced only becomes a commodity if it is useful, *i.e.* if it meets a need, a condition of value, and on this basis, commodities are the object of an exchange that gives the private labor that created them a social character: "As use-values, commodities differ above all in quality, while as exchange-values they can only differ in quantity, and therefore do not contain an atom of use-value. If then we disregard the use-value of commodities, only one property remains, that of being products of labour." (*ibid.*, p. 128). But this exchanged labor then abandons its "concrete forms" (those of the turner, the mason or the spinner, for example), to metamorphose into a "congealed quantity of homogeneous human labor [representing] the same phantom-like objectivity" (*ibidem*), *i.e.* becomes equal and indistinct human labor:

> "If we make abstraction from its use-value, we abstract also from the material constituents and forms which make it a use-value. It is no longer a table, a house, a piece of yarn or any other useful thing. All its sensuous characteristics are extinguished. Nor is it any longer the product of the labour of the joiner, the mason or the spinner, or of any other particular kind of productive labour. With the disappearance of the useful character of the products of labour, the useful character of the kinds of labour

DOI: 10.4324/9781032649054-9

embodied in them also disappears; this in turn entails the disappearance of the different concrete forms of labour." (I, I, p. 128)

And this standardization, resulting from the dispossession of workers' know-how, makes it possible to calculate the quantum of labor, *i.e.* the "socially necessary labour-time" (*ibid.*, p. 129) to produce a good:

> "Socially necessary labour-time is the labour-time required to produce any use-value under the conditions of production normal for a given society and with the average degree of skill and intensity of labour prevalent in that society [...] What exclusively determines the magnitude of the value of any article is therefore the amount of labour socially necessary, or the labour-time socially necessary for its production." (*ibid.*, p. 129)

The result is that i) the substance of value lies in this socially undifferentiated labor, whose quantity is measured by the duration of work, ii) the values of all commodities are equal expressions of the same unit, human labor, and can be replaced by each other, iii) concrete labor, *i.e.* the "expenditure of human strength" destined for a specific form of productive activity (linen and coat, as Marx's example, *ibid.*, p. 139 ff), is metamorphosed into "abstract human labour", socially equalized and undifferentiated labor, in order to express the value of the commodity (*ibid.*, p. 150), iv) to understand the transformation of the product of labor into a commodity, it is necessary to correct those economists who "are misled by the fetishism attached to the world of commodities, or by the objective appearance of the social characteristics of labour" and to steer them away from their "dull and tedious dispute over the part played by nature in the formation of exchange value" (*ibid.*, p. 176); in other words, to remove the "secret", the deceptive, "fetish" (*ibid.*, p. 163 ff) character of the commodity, contained in exchange. Exchange seems to be a simple relationship between things, but behind this appearance lies a social relationship between people:

> "the use-value of a thing is realized without exchange, i.e. in the direct relation between the thing and man, while inversely, its value is realized only in exchange, i.e. in a social process." (*ibid.*, p. 177)

And as the general transformation of the products of labor into commodities is accomplished, as "exchange bursts its local bonds" and "the value of commodities accordingly expands more and more into the material embodiment of human labor" (I, II, p. 183), the transformation, through exchange, of a commodity into money is simultaneously accomplished.

After clarifying the first function of money, that of "measure of values"[1] (*i.e.* the unit of account), Marx discusses the exchange of commodities in the context of "partial money" in the sense of Hicks (see box), *i.e.* money as "measure of values" and "means of circulation" (*ibid.*, I, III, pp. 188–198; pp. 198–227, respectively, *i.e.* medium of exchange):

> "The process of exchange is therefore accomplished through two metamorphoses of opposite yet mutually complementary character – the conversion of the commodity into money, and the re-conversion of the money into a commodity. The two moments of this metamorphosis are at once distinct transactions by the weaver – selling or the exchange of the commodity for money, and buying, or the exchange of the money for a commodity – and the unity of the two acts: selling in order to buy." (*ibid.*, p. 200)

"Total money", "Partial money" in the sense of Hicks

Hicks (1935) proposes to go beyond the "simplifications" made, in his view, by Keynes ("In order to elucidate the relation between Mr. Keynes and the "Classics," we have invented a little apparatus [...] With that apparatus at our disposal, we are no longer obliged to make certain simplifications which Mr. Keynes makes in his exposition.", *ibid.*, p. 156) in order to truly integrate money into the theory of value. In this framework, the three functions of money ("unit of account", "medium of exchange" and "store of value") depend on individual choices regarding the demand for money in terms of transaction costs (which monetary exchange makes it possible to minimize) and the uncertainty affecting the profitability of investments. Depending on these choices, money is "partial" when it has the first two attributes (unit of account and medium of exchange) or "total" when it has all three attributes (the first two and the store of value). This analysis has its origins in that of Keynes (1933 in 2013, pp. 408–411) who differentiates between the "real-exchange economy" where money is exclusively a means of exchange ("neutral in its effects", *ibid.*, p. 408) and the "monetary economy" where money "affects motives and decisions and is, in short, one of the operative factors in the situation, so that the course of events cannot be predicted, either in the long period or in the short, without a knowledge of the behaviour of money" (*ibid.*, pp. 408–409). This conception was taken up by Keynes in *General Theory* (1936), notably when he set out "The postulates of Classical economics" (*ibid.*, chap. 2, pp. 4–22), based on the idea "that money makes no real difference except frictionally and that the theory of production and employment can be worked out (like Mill's) as being passed on "real" exchanges with money introduced perfunctorily in a later chapter [...] the modern version of the classical tradition." (*ibid.*, pp. 19–20), a kind of ideal barter economy through the artifice of a neutral currency that covers real values with a voile that does not alter them.

This exchange of goods in the context of "partial money" is represented by the formula ($C - M - C'$) where (C) and (C') are the goods exchanged and (M) is money, the simple neutral intermediary of exchanges ("commodity-form, stripping off of this form, and return to it", *ibid.*, p. 207), where money "appears in the first phase as a solid crystal of value into which the commodity has been transformed, but afterwards it dissolves into the mere equivalent-form of the commodity." (*ibidem*). In other words, an exchange is simply a correspondence of use values facilitated ("fluidified", *ibid.*, p. 217) by money, as "the medium of circulation" (*ibid.*, p. 212), which covers these values with a veil without influencing them. The introduction of money thus breaks down the spatial, temporal and relational constraints of barter (*i.e.* "the direct exchange of products", *ibid.*, p. 209), since in barter trade, no one can sell his product without someone else *simultaneously* selling theirs, whereas with money, "No one can sell unless someone else purchases. But no one directly needs to purchase because he has just sold." (*ibid.*, pp. 208–209) (see box).

The addition of money's third attribute, its function as a "store of value", makes it a "total money" in Hicks' sense (see above), money "as the only adequate form of existence of exchange value in the face of all the other commodities, here playing the role of use-values pure and simple" for Marx (*ibid.*, p. 227 ff). In this case, money can be held for its own sake, for hoarding purposes, where "the money is petrified into a hoard, and the seller of commodities becomes a hoarder of money", "social expressions for superfluity or wealth" (*ibid.*, p. 228), or transformed into *capital*: "The production of commodities and their circulation in its developed form, namely trade, for the historic presuppositions under which capital arises." (*ibid.*, I, IV, p. 247). In this case, the initial form of the circulation of commodities ($C - M - C'$), "selling in order to buy" (*ibid.*, p. 247), becomes the form of the circulation of money as capital ($M - C - M'$), "buying in order to sell" (*ibid.*, p. 248), wherein the first case money is definitively *spent*, while in the second it is simply *advanced*. In other words, in the first case, "this reflux of money to its starting-point does not depend on the commodity's being sold for more than was paid for it" (*ibid.*, p. 250), where the form ($C - M - C'$) "proceeds from the extreme constituted by one commodity, and ends with the extreme constituted by another, which falls out of circulation and into consumption. Consumption, the satisfaction of needs, in short use-value, is therefore its final goal." (*ibid.*, p. 250). On the contrary, the form ($M - C - M'$) "proceeds from the extreme of money and finally returns to that same extreme. Its driving and motivating force, its determining purpose, is therefore exchange-value." (*ibidem*). And in this second case, there is no qualitative difference between (M) and (M') but a quantitative difference, with ($M' = M + \Delta M$), *i.e.* the sum primitively advanced and a surplus that Marx calls "surplus-value" (*ibid.*, p. 251) (see box).

General Formula for Troc [Barter]:

$$\left(\frac{C}{a}\right) - \left(\frac{C'}{b}\right)$$

(a) and (b), owners of (C) and (C') respectively, meet (units of time and place) to exchange their commodities. The exchange is based on a simultaneous utility/disutility calculation. This simultaneity and, more generally, this exchange requires knowledge and even mutual trust between the two exchangers (a) and (b), *i.e.* "symmetrical" and "complete" information. Under these conditions, (a) performs the exchange if the utility it confers on acquiring (C') is greater than the disutility of discarding (C), and, symmetrically and instantaneously, (b) performs the exchange if the utility it confers on acquiring (C) is greater than the disutility of discarding (C').

General Formula for Commodity:

$$(C - M - C')$$

In the same context of use-value correspondence expressed in the troc formula, money (M) is simply introduced as a "facilitator", a neutral intermediary in exchanges, in order to loosen the geographical and temporal constraints inherent in troc, with agents (a) and (b) now undifferentiated ($\forall\ a, b$). This is Marx's "selling in order to buy" formula, where the equivalence of its two extremes shows the equality of the use values exchanged, and where (M) is a "partial money" in Hicks' sense, "money as the mere equivalent of commodities, money as means of circulation, money as means of payment" (*ibid.*, I, VI, pp. 273–274), that cannot be held for its own sake. For Keynes, this is "Classical economics", that of the principle of neutrality of money, where, since any prolonged hoarding of income is impossible, Say's law is always verified, hence the impossibility of any general crisis of overproduction (Gilles, 2009, pp. 16–19).

General Formula for Capital:

$$(M - C - M')\ \textit{with}\ (M' > M)$$

This is the Marxian formula of "buying in order to sell" or, better still, "buying in order to sell dearer" (*ibid.*, I, V, p. 266), whose motive is exchange value, where money is "total" in Hicks' sense, and can therefore be held for its own sake ("store of value" attribute); (M) is no longer simply *spent* (as in the commodity formula), but *advanced* in the form of *capital* that can be accumulated. The quantitative difference between (M') and (M), *i.e.* (ΔM), is "surplus value": "The value originally advanced [...] not only remains intact while in circulation, but increases its magnitude, adds to itself a surplus-value, or is valorized. And this movement converts it into capital." (*ibid.*, I, IV, p. 252)

This surplus value is produced by "labour-power" or "labour-capacity" (*ibid.*, I, VI, p. 270) which can only appear on the market "only if, and in so far as, its possessor, the individual whose labour-power it is, offers it for sale or sells it as a commodity" (*ibid.*, p. 271) to "the owner of money" (*i.e.* "l'homme aux écus", Marx, 1965, p. 714) in a "classical" relationship in which one buys and the other sells labor-power (*ibid.*, I, VI, p. 271). In this framework, for exchange to operate on the "labor market", the wage-earner must be "the free proprietor of his own labour-capacity, hence of his person" (*ibid.*, p. 272), a "free worker available on the commodity-market" (*ibid.*, p. 272)[2] who behaves like a "merchant": he "freely" sells his labor power (his physical and intellectual faculties) to a possessor of money who buys it, both being "equal in the eyes of the law" (*ibid.*, p. 271). This is not unrelated to a form of wage subjection, *i.e.* a particular form of domination, forced by nature, but "contracted" by the worker himself, of the "*Do ut des, do ut facias, facio ut des et facio ut facias*" type. While workers are socially obliged to work for a living, they are not legally obliged to work for a particular "owner of money" which for the transformation of "its shillings into capital, pays this value" (*ibid.*, p. 276). And the minimum value that must be paid refers to the "living wage", a condition for the reproduction of "labour-power":

> "The ultimate or minimum limit of the value of labour-power is formed by the value of the commodities which have to be supplied every day to the bearer of labour-power, the man, so that he can renew his life-process. That is to say, the limit is formed by the value of the physically indispensable means of subsistence. If the price of labour-power falls to this minimum, it falls below its value, since under such circumstances it can be maintained and developed only in a crippled state, and the value of every commodity is determined by the labour-time required to provide it in its normal quality." (*ibid.*, I, VI, pp. 276–277)

It is what distinguishes the worker from the slave or serf, and it is what contributes to the strength, the legitimacy, of a merchant system. But for this relationship of exchange of labor power between merchants to endure:

> "the proprietor of labour-power must always sell it for a limited period only, for if he were to sell it in a lump, once and for all, he would be selling himself, converting himself from a free man into a slave, from an owner of a commodity into a commodity. He must constantly treat his labour-power as

his own property, his own commodity, and he can do this only by placing it at the disposal of the buyer, i.e. handing it over to the buyer for him to consume, for a definite period of time, temporarily. In this way he manages both to alienate his labour-power and to avoid renouncing his rights of ownership over it." (*ibid.*, I, VI, p. 271)

Yet this relationship between possessors of money or commodities and possessors of their own labour power has no basis in "natural history", it is a social relationship that evolves in history, and when products and labour power take the form of commodities, where social production is entirely governed by exchange value, this characterizes a particular mode of production, "the capitalist one" (*ibid.*, p. 273). And, within this framework, "the capacity for labour is nothing unless it is sold" to quote Sismondi (*ibid.*, p. 277), and when it is sold, its value is then determined by "the labour-time necessary for the production" (*ibid.*, p. 274), *i.e.* the value of the means of subsistence that the owner of the labor-power needs for its maintenance or preservation, for the reproduction of his own labor power and that of his "worker's replacements", *i.e.* his family, including his children, "in order that this race of peculiar commodity-owners may perpetuate its presence on the market" (*ibid.*, p. 275) as demanded by the continual transformation of money into capital, to which are added, depending on the complexity of the labor force, when it requires "skill and dexterity", the inherent "costs of education" (*ibid.*, p. 276).

The exploitation of labour power as a condition for the extraction of surplus value and profit ["Hic Rhodus, hic salta !", ibid., I, V, p. 269]

Let us now follow the owner of money and the owner of labor-power into "the hidden abode of production, on whose threshold there hangs the notice "No admittance except on business"" where "surplus value", "the secret of profit-making" (*ibid.*, I, VI, p. 279), is generated, at the same time as "a certain change takes place, or so it appears, in the physiognomy of our *dramatis personae*" (*ibid.*, p. 280):

> "He who was previously the money-owner now strides out in front as a capitalist; the possessor of labour-power follows as his worker. The one smirks self-importantly and is intent on business; the other is timid and holds back, like someone wo has brought his own hide to market and now has nothing else to expect but – a tanning." (*ibid.*, p. 280)

In order to study this "hidden abode", Marx takes up Smith's distinction between "fixed capital and "circulating capital" (WON, II, I, pp. 211–214) as elements of "constant capital" (C) to which he associates "variable capital" (V) (*ibid.*, I, VIII, pp. 307–319).

(C) is the fraction of total capital invested (K) that is transformed into the means of production (instruments of labour (machinery, equipment, buildings), raw materials, energy, intermediate goods) which only transfer their own value to the product, without directly increasing it (*ibid.*, I, VIII, p. 317). (C) differs from value (c), which is the sum of capital depreciation and all productive consumption, when its turnover time (τ_C) is different from 1 (*i.e.* is not fully consumed during a period, or cycle, of production), since ($C = c\tau_C$). Variable capital (V) is the fraction of (K) converted into labour-power (*ibid.*) which alone allows an increase in the value of the capital engaged in production, in other words, labour-power is endowed with the specific virtue of creating a surplus, a surplus value (sv). (V) differs from (v), the periodic wage fund, when its turnover time (τ_V) is different from 1, since ($V = v\tau_V$).

Labour-time is made up of "necessary labour-time" (corresponding to the value of subsistence goods necessary for the reproduction of labour-power, *ibid.*, I, IX, p. 325, n. 5) and "surplus labour-time", or "surplus labour":

> "During the second period of the labour process, that in which labour is no longer necessary labour, the worker does indeed expend labour-power, he does work, but his labour is no longer necessary labour, and he creates no value for himself. He creates surplus-value which, for the capitalist, has all the charms of something created out of nothing. This part of the working day I call surplus labour-time, and to the labour expended during that that time I give the name of surplus labour." (*ibid.*, I, IX, p. 325)

In other words:

(*total labour − necessary labour = surplus labour*).

Hence the possibility of determining the rate or "degree" of exploitation or the rate of surplus value[3] (σ), or the ratio $\left(\frac{surplus\ labour}{necessary\ labour}\right)$ or $\left(\frac{surplus\ labour - time}{necessary\ labour - time}\right)$ (*ibid.*, I, IX, p. 326; I, X, p. 341), or $\left(\sigma = \frac{sv}{V}\right)$, if ($\tau_V = 1$). ($\sigma$) is therefore "an exact expression for the degree of exploitation of labour-power by capital, or of the worker by the capitalist" (*ibid.*, p. 326) and the mass of the surplus value (sv) is equal to "the amount of the variable capital advanced multiplied by the rate of surplus-value [*i.e.*] the product of the number of labour-powers simultaneously exploited by the same capitalist and the degree of exploitation of each individual labour-power." (*ibid.*, I, XI, p. 418), *i.e.*: ($sv = \sigma V$).

The extraction of (sv) represents, simultaneously, the condition and the motive for accumulation, and thus for the development of the CMP, (sv) appearing as the part of the value created by labour power that is not returned to it in the form of wages, thus "unpaid labour" (*ibid.*, I, XVIII, p. 672),[4] or "past labour as opposed to living labour" (*ibid.*, I, VII, p. 302) or "the uncompensated labour of the wage-labourer" (*ibid.*, I, XIX, p. 680):

> "Therefore the value of labour-power, and the value which that labour-power valorizes in the labour-process, are two entirely different magnitudes; and this

difference was what the capitalist had in mind when he was purchasing the labour-power [...] The owner of the money has paid the value of a day's labour-power; he therefore has the use of it for a day, a day's labour belongs to him. On the one hand the daily sustenance of labour-power costs only half a day's labour, while on the other hand the very same labour-power can remain effective, can work, during a whole day, and consequently the value which its use during one day creates is double what the capitalist pays for that use; this circumstance is a piece of good luck for the buyer, but by no means an injustice towards the seller." (*ibid.*, I, VII, pp. 300–301)

And Marx adds, with irony, that in capitalism, where the owner of the money becomes a capitalist, he "foresaw this situation, and was the cause of his laughter" (*ibid.*, p. 301):

"[In] the process of consuming labour-power, which was also the process of producing commodities [...] the capitalist, formerly a buyer, now returns to the market as a seller [...] This whole course of events, the transformation of money into capital [...] takes place through the mediation of circulation because it is conditioned by the purchase of the labour-power in the market; it does not take place in circulation because what happens there is only an introduction to the valorization process, which is entirely confined to the sphere of production. And so "everything is for the best in the best of all possible worlds."" (*ibid.*, p. 302)[5]

As we can see, this particular mode of surplus appropriation based on exploitation is not synonymous with robbery in the legal sense of the term, since it is not the product of his labour but his labour-power that is sold by the worker; but rather with "a barefaced though legalised robbery" in an "unjust and iniquitous system" or "a fraudulent system of unequal exchanges" according to John Francis Bray (1839, pp. 49–50)[6], an American chartist and radical socialist, from whom Marx drew inspiration here.

In a system characterized by capital feeding "the voracious appetite for surplus labour" (*ibid.*, I, X, p. 344), it is the production of surplus value or the extortion of surplus labour that constitutes its purpose, where (sv) thus represents the excess, in value, of gross receipts over fixed and variable costs, *i.e.* if (Y) is the gross national product expressed in value, ($Y = C + V + sv$), the part of (Y) that represents surplus value, ($sv = Y - (C + V)$), forms the "surplus product" (*ibid.*, I, IX, p. 338). The CMP dynamic is based on accumulation, *i.e.* the "production of capital on a progressively increasing scale" (*ibid.*, I, XXIV, p. 727), which requires a "transformation of a portion of the surplus product into capital" in "such articles as can be employed in the labour process", *i.e.* additional means of production and subsistence, beyond those needed to replace advanced capital in order to constitute "additional capital" (*ibid.*, p. 726). All in all, "surplus value can be transformed into capital only because the surplus product, whose value it is, already comprises the material components of a new quantity of capital." (*ibid.*, p. 727). Hence this famous passage from Capital, where, according to Classical economics, "the proletarian is merely a machine for the production of surplus-value, the capitalist too is merely a machine for the transformation of this surplus-value into surplus capital." (*ibid.*, p. 742):

> "Accumulate, accumulate! That is Moses and the prophets! "Industry furnishes the material which saving accumulates" [*dixit* Adam Smith]. Therefore, save, save, i.e. reconvert the greatest possible portion of surplus-value or surplus product into capital! Accumulation for the sake of accumulation, production for the sake of production: this was the formula in which classical economics expressed the historical mission of the bourgeoisie in the period of its domination." (*ibid.*, I, XXIV, p. 742)

One final element, the "most important factor" (*ibid.*, I, XXV, p. 762), is missing from the specification of "the General Law of Capitalist Accumulation", the "composition of capital" and the changes it undergoes as the accumulation progresses (*ibidem*). Marx's initial reasoning, as above, is based on the simplifying assumption that ($\tau_C = \tau_V = 1$), *i.e.* that the capital stock (constant and variable) is entirely consumed and reconstituted at each production cycle (*ibid.*, I, IX, pp. 321–322).[7] In this case, there is identity between the organic composition of expenditure ($k = c/v$) and what Marx calls the "organic composition of capital" ($k = C/V$), *i.e.* "the proportion in which it is divided into constant capital, or the value of the means of production, and variable capital, or the value of labour-power, the total sum of wages", either "the value-composition of capital", and "the relation between the mass of the means of production employed on the one hand, and the mass of labour necessary for their employment on the other", either "the technical composition of capital" (*ibid.*, I, XXV, p. 762). And the history of all discoveries and innovations, from manufacturing division with its "specialized worker" (*ibid.*, I, XIV, p. 458 ff) to machinery and large-scale industry (*ibid.*, I, XV, pp. 492–639), which occur as a result of the progress of accumulation, leads to a relative decrease in (V) compared to (C), or to "the increase of the constant constituent of capital at the expense of its variable constituent", and this trend is confirmed over the long term: "This law of the progressive growth of the constant part of capital in comparison with the variable part is confirmed at every step [...] whether we compare different economic epochs or different nations in the same epoch." (*ibid.*, I, XXV, pp. 773–774). The reason is to be found in the progress of accumulation, which means that the mass of material means of production increases more and more in comparison with the amount of labour-power required to put them into operation. In other words, as the growth of capital makes labour more productive, it reduces its demand in proportion to its own size. (*ibid.*, p. 773). This change in the organic composition of capital (*i.e.* an increase in (k)), while decreasing the *relative* magnitude of (V), nonetheless excludes its *absolute* increase, as the overall demand for labour increases with the progress of accumulation (*ibid.*, p. 774), even if, in capitalism, in order to maintain wages at a level compatible with the maximization of surplus "the working population always increases more rapidly than the valorization requirements of capital" (*ibid.*, I, XXV, p. 798). This necessarily results in structural unemployment (*i.e.* "industrial reserve army" or "a relative surplus population", *ibid.*, p. 781 ff, *cf. below*) coupled with increased worker pauperism,[8] from which it follows:

> "the law which always holds the relative surplus population or industrial reserve army in equilibrium with the extent and energy of accumulation rivets the worker to capital more firmly than the wedges of Hephaestus held Prometheus to the rock. It makes an accumulation of misery a necessary condition, corresponding to the accumulation of wealth. Accumulation of wealth at one pole is, therefore, at the same time accumulation of misery, the torment of labour, slavery, ignorance, brutalization and moral degradation at the opposite pole, i.e. on the side of the class that produces its own product as capital." (*ibid.*, p. 799)

Or, to quote J. Ch. L. Sismondi's criticism of J.-B. Say for failing to see "the new phenomenon" characteristic of "opulent nations", namely that "public misery never ceases to increase with material wealth", he concludes with this formula: "la classe qui produit tout, est chaque jour plus près d'être réduite à ne jouir de rien [the class that produces everything is each day closer to being reduced to enjoying nothing]" (Sismondi, 1827, II, p. 464).

It is therefore the increase in the rate of exploitation or rate of surplus value (σ), "the determining purpose of capitalist production" (*ibid.*, I, IX, p. 338), that is the aim of the action of the capitalist who has "advanced his money with the intention of making more money out of it" (*ibid.*, I, VII, p. 298). However, he does not judge the profitability of his capital by relating it exclusively to (*sv*), income from variable capital (V) alone in the "sphere of production", but evaluates it in relation to total capital (K), which refers to profit as income from total capital produced in the production process and then realized (*i.e.* sold) in the "sphere of circulation" (*i.e.* the market), the central object of Book III of Capital (Marx, 1991):

> "It makes no difference to the capitalist whether we see him as advancing the constant capital to make a profit out of his variable capital, or advancing the variable capital in order to valorize the constant; whether he lays out money on wages in order to give machines and raw material a higher value, or advances money in machinery and raw material in order to exploit labour. Even though it is only the variable part of capital that creates surplus-value, it does so only under the condition that the other parts are advanced as well, i.e. the conditions of production for labour [...] the actual degree of his profit is determined in relation not to his variable

capital but to his total capital; not by the rate of surplus-value but by the rate of profit" (*ibid.*, III, II, pp. 132–133)

It is therefore the search for a high rate of profit (ρ), the ratio of (sv) to (K), *i.e.* the rate of valorization of total capital (*ibid.*, pp. 133–134), that energizes the capitalist system:

$$\left(\rho = \frac{sv}{C+V} = \frac{\sigma V}{C+V} = \frac{\sigma}{C/V+1} = \frac{\sigma}{k+1}\right)$$

when ($\tau_C = \tau_V = 1$)

Considering that "the capitalist's profit, therefore, comes from the fact that he has something to sell for which he has not paid [...] The surplus-value or profits consists precisely in the excess of commodity value over its cost price, i.e. in the excess of the total sum of labour contained in the commodity over the sum of labour that is actually paid for. The surplus-value, from wherever it may derive, is consequently an excess over and above the total capital advanced. This excess then stands in a certain ratio to the total capital [i.e.] the rate of profit distinct from the rate of surplus-value." (*ibid.*, p. 133). It is therefore from the conversion of (σ) into (ρ) that we must deduce the conversion of capital gain into profit, and not the other way round: "profit is still for all that a transformed form of surplus-value, a form in which its origin and the secret of its existence are veiled and obliterated" (*ibid.*, III, II, p. 139). And this conversion becomes a reality when surplus value is realized. In other words, the capitalist's appropriation of the surplus-value contained in the commodity requires that it be sold, *i.e.* that it be realized on the market (*i.e.* the sphere of circulation), with profit appearing as the realized surplus-value (expression of the exploitation of labor in the production process realized in the circulation process) possibly accompanied by "commercial profit" ("from the mutual cheating of the dealers in the circulation process", *ibid.*, p. 138). Therefore, (ρ) is always less than (σ), because (V) is always less than (K) (*ibid.*, III, III, p. 142).

On this basis, taking up Smith's argument on the sectoral compensation of working conditions (*cf.* Part I), Marx assumes that "the degree of exploitation of labour, i.e. the rate of surplus-value, and the length of the working day, is the same in all the spheres of production" (*ibid.*, III, VIII, p. 241). In other words, all branches of "social capital" record identical wages and working hours. Consequently, if (k) differs from branch to branch, with (ρ) varying inversely with capitalistic intensity (*cf.* above, for a given (σ) donné, if (k) increases [high] then (ρ) decreases [low]), this creates a *theoretical problem* (the multiplicity of (ρ), for a given economy and period) and a *contradiction*, since the Marxian thesis of accumulation shows that the development of CMP leads, through capital/labour substitution (*cf. supra*), to a rise in (k) and, consequently, a fall in (ρ), which is precisely the motive for accumulation.

The *problem* refers to the construction of "a general rate of profit" and the transformation of values into prices. To resolve it, Marx mobilizes Ricardo's analysis (1817, IV, p. 83; V, p. 131), basing the tendency of profit rates to equalize on[9], in other words, in a situation of competition between capitalists, maximization of (ρ) leads to capital mobility between sectors according to their respective profitability, which ultimately results in the equalization of sectoral profit rates into a general profit rate, *i.e.*: (*mobility* + *maximization* = *equalization*)[10]:

> "if commodities were sold at their values [...] this would mean very different rates of profit in the different spheres of production, as we have already explained, according to the different organic composition of the masses of capital applied. Capital withdraws from a sphere with a low rate of profit and wends its way to others that yield higher profit. This constant migration, the distribution of capital between the different spheres according to where the profit rate is rising and where it is falling, is what produces a relationship between supply and demand such that the average profit is the same in the various different spheres, and values are therefore transformed into prices of production." (*ibid.*, III, X, p. 297)

Therefore, if (ρ) is the single general rate of profit and (k) differs from sphere of production to sphere of production, (σ) cannot be identical for all spheres. In other words, the factors that equalize (ρ) generate, simultaneously, different rates of surplus value from one branch to another, hence the need to move from "value" to "prices of production"[11] to resolve this problem.

Note, first, that "values" ($C + V + sv = C + V + \sigma V$) differ from "prices of production" ($C + V + \rho(C + V)$), under the hypothesis that ($\tau_C = \tau_V = 1$). Posing (P), the total profit for (n) spheres, *i.e.* $\left(P = \sum_{i=1}^{n} \rho_i\right)$, and ($\sum_{i=1}^{n} \sigma_i$) the total surplus value, posing ($P = \sum_{i=1}^{n} \sigma_i$) and ($k$) the average organic composition of capital, profit is higher than surplus-value in sectors (x) for which ($k_x > k$), is capital-intensive, and therefore "low" in surplus-value productions. Conversely, profit is lower than the added value in sectors (y) where $\left(k_y < k\right)$, spheres with low capital intensity (or high human concentration), and therefore high added value production. At the macroeconomic level, the equalization of profit rates ultimately reflects the "redistribution" of surplus value from spheres (y) to spheres (x) which will sell their products at prices higher than their value, "appropriating" the surplus value generated by spheres (y) whose profits are lower than the surplus value they produce.

To resolve the *contradiction* (see above), we need to explain the dynamics of surplus value and profit, which in turn relates to capital accumulation.

Notes

1 "The first main function [of gold in Marx's example] is to supply commodities with the material for the expression of their values, or to represent their values as magnitudes of the same dénomination, qualitatively equal and quantitatively comparable. It thus acts as a universal measure of value." (*ibid.*, I, III, p. 188).
2 "This worker must be free in the double sense that as a free individual, he can dispose of his labour-power as his own commodity, and that, on the other hand, he has no other commodity for sale, i.e. he is rid of them, he is free of all the objects needed for the realization of his labour-ower." (*ibid.*, pp. 272–273).
3 "Although the rate of surplus-value is an exact expression for the degree of exploitation of labour-power, it is in no sense an expression for the absolute magnitude of the exploitation." (*ibid.*, p. 326, n. 7).
4 "Capital, therefore, is not only the command over labour, as Adam Smith thought. It is essentially the command over unpaid labour. All surplus-value, whatever particular for (profit, interest or rent) it may subsequently crystallize into, is in substance the materialization of unpaid labour-time. The secret of the self-valorization of capital resolves itself into the fact that it has at its disposal a definite quantity of the unpaid labour of other people." (*ibid.*, p. 672).
5 For Smith's "best of all possible worlds", see below, chap. 2, and Keynes', see Part 3, Introduction.
6 "The whole transaction, therefore, between the producer and the capitalist, is a palpable deception, a mere farce: it is, in fact, in thousands of instances, no other than a barefaced though legalised robbery, by means of which the capitalists and proprietors contrive to fasten themselves upon the productive classes, and suck from them their whole substance." (*ibid.*, p. 50).
7 This simplifying assumption will be lifted (*cf.* chap. 6) when Marx divides (C) into its fixed elements, subject to wear and tear and obsolescence, which transmit only part of their value to the product during the production cycle, and its circulating elements (raw materials, energy, *etc.*), which are entirely consumed during this cycle, except for inventories.
8 "The same causes which develop the expansive power of capital, also develop the labour-power at its disposal. The relative mass of the industrial reserve army thus increases with the potential energy of wealth. But the greater this reserve army in proportion to the active labour-army, the greater is the mass of a consolidated surplus population [long-term unemployed], whose misery is in inverse ratio to the amount of torture it has to undergo in the form of labour. The more extensive, finally, the pauperized sections of the working class and the industrial reserve army, the greater is official pauperism. *This is the absolute general law of capitalist accumulation.*" (*ibid.*, I, XXV, p. 798, Marx emphasises).
9 "With the rise or fall of price, profits are elevated above, or depressed below their general level, and capital is either encouraged to enter into, or is warned to depart from the particular employment in which the variation has taken place. Whilst every man is free to employ his capital where he pleases, he will naturally seek for it that employment which is most advantageous [...] This restless desire on the part of all the employers of stock, to quit a less profitable for a more advantageous business, has a strong tendency to equalize the rate of profits of all" (Ricardo, 1817, IV, p. 83).
10 The same reasoning applies to the "general movements of wages" (I, XXV, p. 790–791).
11 "competition equalizes profit rates between the different spheres of production to produce an average rate of profit, and that this is precisely the way in which the values of products from these various spheres are transformed into prices of production." (*ibid.*, III, XII, p. 310).

Bibliography

Blaug, Mark (1985). *Economic theory in retrospect* (1962). Cambridge: Cambridge University Press, fourth edition.

Bray, John Francis (1839). *Labour's wrongs and labour's remedy; or the age of might and the age of right*, Leeds, Published by David Green, Briggate.

Gilles, Philippe (2009). *Histoire des crises et des cycles économiques. Des crises industrielles du 19ème siècle aux crises actuelles*. Paris: A. Colin, coll. "U", 2ème édition.

Hicks, John Richard (1935). A suggestion for symplifying the theory of money. *Economica*, *2*(5), february, 1–19.

Hippocrates from Cos (1983). *Hippocratic writings*, edited by G.E.R. Lloyd, translated by J. Chadwick & W.N. Mann. London: Penguin Books Ldt, "Penguin Classics".

Keynes, John Maynard (1936). *The general theory of employment interest and money*. London: MacMillan and Co, Limited, S Martin's Street.

Keynes, John Maynard (2013). A monetary theory of production (1933). In D. Moggridge (Ed.), *The collected writings of John Maynard Keynes*, vol. XIII "*The General Theory and after: Part I, Preparation*" (pp. 408–411). Cambridge: Cambridge University Press for the Royal Economic Society.

Marx, Karl (1965). *Œuvres Economie*, Tome I, Paris, Edition établie et annotée par Maximilien Rubel, Editions Gallimard, NRF, coll. "Bibliothèque de la Pléiade".

Marx, Karl (1969). *Theories of surplus value*, Part II (1862–3). London: Lawrence & Wishart; Moscow, Progress Publishers, 1968.

Marx, Karl (1990). *Capital. A critique of political economy*, Volume I (1867), Translated by Ben Fowkes. London, Penguin Books in association with New Left Review, Penguin Classics.

Marx, Karl (1991). *Capital. A critique of political economy*, Volume III (1864–75), Translated by David Fernbach. London, Penguin Books in association with New Left Review, Penguin Classics.

Schumpeter, Joseph Alois (1966). *History of economic analysis* (1954). New York: Oxford Universty Press, sixth printing.

Sismondi, Jean-Charles Léonard Simonde de (1827). *Nouveaux Principes d'Economie politique, ou De la Richesse dans ses rapports avec la Population* (1819). Paris, Delaunay Libraire, 2 Tomes, 2ème édition.

Smith, Adam (1913). *An inquiry into the nature and causes of the wealth of nations* (1776), London: George Routledge & Sons, Limited; New York, E.P. Dutton and Co.

5 Accumulation of "individual capital" and accumulation of "total social capital"

Conditions and mechanisms of "simple reproduction" and "reproduction on an extended scale"

Marx's analysis of capital accumulation is first dealt with in the "production process", in Book I, Chapter XXV, of Capital ("The General Law of Capitalist Accumulation", 1990, I, pp. 762–870), then extended to "money circulation" in Book II of Capital on "The Process of Circulation of Capital" (Marx, 1992). Marx proceeds in two stages: i) the accumulation of "individual capital", "autonomous part of the social capital" (*ibid.*, II, XVIII, p. 429), centred on the microeconomics of production decisions "intertwined with the others and conditioned by them" (*ibid.*, II, III, p. 177) to form ii) the macroeconomic dynamics of "total social capital":

> "each individual capital forms only a fraction of the total social capital, a fraction that has acquired independence and been endowed with individual life, so to speak, just as each individual capitalist is no more than an element of the capitalist class. The movement of the social capital is made up of the totality of movements of these autonomous fractions, the turnovers of the individual capitals [...] the metamorphosis of the individual capital, its turnover, is a single term in the circuit of the social capital." (*ibid.*, II, XVIII, pp. 427–428)

The microeconomic foundations of capital accumulation: the reproduction of "individual capital"

The reproduction of "individual capital" refers to the behaviour of an entrepreneur (γ), undifferentiated ($\forall\ \gamma$), who aims to reproduce and increase his capital by transforming money capital into "productive capital" (*ibid.*, II, I, p. 118), with the aim of appropriating unpaid labour, in order to maximize his surplus value and then his profit on the sale of what has once again become a "commodity" that is shedding its form of utility to resume the form of an independent exchange value, "commodities becom[ing] commodity capital" (*ibid.*, II, I, p. 121). All these micro-decisions feed into the reproduction of "social capital", but this raises additional problems. Whereas the reproduction of "individual capital" mainly takes the form of a capitalist/worker opposition, the "relation between the unpaid labour which has been transformed into

DOI: 10.4324/9781032649054-10

capital and the additional paid labour necessary to set in motion this additional capital [or simply] the relation between the unpaid and the paid labour" (*ibid.*, I, XXV, p. 771), synthesized in (σ), the reproduction of "social capital" adds to this antagonism, the struggles between capitalists for the sharing of surplus value and profit, where at the mercy of the "vicissitudes of circulation", "one capitalist seizes for himself a piece of another's surplus-value" which produces "a one-sided accumulation and centralization of both money capital and productive capital" (*ibid.*, II, XVII, p. 424).

Let a capitalist (γ), ($\forall\ \gamma$), be endowed with an initial capital (K) consisting of a wage fund (v) and means of production (c). With ($\tau_C = \tau_V = 1$), according to a given proportion (k), production (Y_γ) then has the value:

$$(Y_\gamma = C + V + \sigma V = C + (1 + \sigma)V)$$

Since, by hypothesis, (Y_γ) is fully realized at its value (*cf.* above), the capitalist (γ) must, in order to maintain his production capacity, renew, in the following period, the (constant and variable) capital consumed, *i.e.* here, ($c + v$) or ($C + V$), if ($\tau_C = \tau_V = 1$). This leaves him with his surplus-value ($sv_\gamma = \sigma V$). If this surplus-value is entirely consumed by (γ), "if it is consumed as periodically as it is gained", we are dealing, *mutatis mutandis* (*i.e.* with strict maintenance of its productive capacities) with a simple reproduction of "individual capital" (*ibid.*, I, XXIII, p. 712).[1] If, instead of being entirely consumed, (sv_γ) is totally or partially advanced and employed as additional capital, (γ) performs "his function as a capitalist and enriches himself" (*ibid.*, I, XXIV, p. 739), and a new capital (K') is formed and added to the old one, thus ($K' > K$). As Marx points out (*ibid.*, p. 725), "the employment of surplus-value as capital, or its reconversion into capital, is called accumulation of capital". And this accumulation is part of an overall dynamic:

> "Accumulation requires the transformation of a portion of the surplus product into capital. But we cannot, except by a miracle, transform into capital anything but such articles as can be employed in the labour process (i.e. means of production), and such further articles as are suitable for the sustenance of the worker (i.e. means of subsistence). Consequently, a part of the annual surplus labour must have been applied to the production of additional means of production and subsistence, over and above the quantity of these things required to replace the capital advanced. In a word, surplus-value can be transformed into capital only because the surplus product, whose value it is, already comprises the material components of a new quantity of capital." (*ibid.*, I, XXIV, pp. 726–727)

This context of "reproduction on an expanded scale" of "individual capital" is that of capitalism, a dynamic system in which "the ownership of past unpaid labour is thenceforth the sole condition for the appropriation of living unpaid labour on a constantly increasing scale. The more the capitalist has accumulated, the more is he able to accumulate" (*ibid.*, I, XXIV, p. 729), "and so on" (*ibid.*, p. 737). It is competition between capitalists, which imposes "the immanent laws of capitalist production, as external and coercive laws" (*ibid.*, p. 739), that conditions this necessity: to be competitive and to exist, each capitalist as the "personification of capital" (*ibidem*) must produce at lower cost, increase labour productivity, introduce new machines and production methods. At the same time, the need for profitability leads the capitalist to spread the costs of technical transformations and production tools over a larger number of products, with the profitability of investments ensured by increasing returns. So every capitalist, ($\forall \gamma$), is placed before this alternative, to increase his production or disappear, becoming, thereby "fanatically intent on the valorization of value; consequently, he ruthlessly forces the human race to produce for production's sake" (*ibid.*, p. 739). In this framework, (γ) functions as "capital personified" (*ibidem*), a product of the CMP of which it is only a component, and (Y_γ) must now be assigned:

- on the one hand, the renewal of (K) consumed productively, since ($\tau_C = \tau_V = 1$), condition of simple reproduction;
- secondly, to an additional investment ($\Delta I = \Delta C + \Delta V$), in proportion to ($k$), coming from the fraction saved and reinvested of its surplus value ($\alpha(\sigma V)$), with ($0 < \alpha < 1$), that is ($\Delta I = \alpha(\sigma V)$), condition of extended reproduction;
- finally, his final consumption for the remaining amount of his surplus value, *i.e.* ($(1 - \alpha)\sigma V$).

In this framework, assuming by simplification (σ, α, k) constant, the fractions (C, V, sv) as well as the product (Y_γ) follow a geometric progression of reason ($1 + \alpha\sigma/k + 1$), where ($\alpha\sigma/k + 1 = \alpha\rho = g$), with ($\rho$) the rate of profit, and (g) the rate of accumulation (here, constant, by the set of assumptions), which is all the stronger the higher the savings, and therefore investment, capacity of (γ), *i.e.* (α *and* σ), for a given (V), and the lower the capital intensity (k). (α), the savings rate, and (k), the organic composition of capital, depending on the capitalist's (γ) decision as a function of technical progress and the desired level of investment given competition, the rate of accumulation (g) ultimately depends on the rate of surplus value (σ). Hence, if the additional value created during a working day by the average worker (abstract labour) is (T) hours of labour, and if each worker receives a daily wage for the reproduction of his labour-power (living, paid labour), which enables him to buy (B_i) quantities of subsistence goods of unit value (δ_i), the amount of labour necessary to reproduce the daily labour-power made up of (n) workers is equal to:

$$\left(V = \sum_{i=1}^{n} \delta_i B_i\right),$$

surplus value at:

$$\left(sv = Tn - \sum_{i=1}^{n} \delta_i B_i\right),$$

hence the surplus value rate:

$$\left(\sigma = Tn - \sum_{i=1}^{n} \delta_i B_i / \textstyle\sum_{i=1}^{n} \delta_i B_i\right).$$

Therefore, the rate of exploitation or rate of surplus value (σ) is a function of three parameters that can be combined:

- the size of (B_i), for a given unit price (δ_i), which results from the balance of power between capitalists and workers, which is "regulated by the expansion and contraction of the industrial reserve army, and this in turn corresponds to the periodic alternations of the industrial cycle [and] by the varying proportions in which the working class is divided into an active army and a reserve army, by the increase or diminution in the relative amount of the surplus population, by the extent to which it is alternately absorbed and set free." (ibid., I, XXV, p. 790, cf. chap. 6). So, mutatis mutandis, (σ) decreases if (B_i) and/or (δ_i) increase, and vice versa.
- the value of (T): for ($T' > T$), *i.e.* an increase in working hours (extensive scheme), for a given wage rate ($\delta_i B_i$), we have, for (n) workers: ($\sigma' = T'n - \sum_{i=1}^{n} \delta_i B_i / \sum_{i=1}^{n} \delta_i B_i > \sigma$), which Marx calls the extraction of absolute surplus value: "The working day is not a constant, but a variable quantity. One of its parts, certainly, is determined by the labour-time required for the reproduction of the labour-power of the worker himself [($\delta_i B_i$)]. But its total amount varies with the duration of the surplus labour. The working day is therefore capable of being determined, but in and for itself indeterminate [...] I call that surplus-value which is produced by the lengthening of the working day, *absolute surplus-value*." (*ibid.*, I, X, p. 341; I, XII p. 432, Marx emphasises).
- the increase in "productive force" or "productivity of labour" (*ibid.*, I, XII, p. 431), *i.e.* "an alteration in the labour process of such a kind as to shorten the labour-time socially necessary for the production of a commodity, and to endow a given quantity of labour with the power of producing a greater quantity of use-value." (intensive scheme with the extraction of *relative surplus value*). In this case, it concerns (γ)'s own production, in particular

by incorporating technical progress into (Y_γ), resulting in an increase in (k_γ) and (T), according to the same pattern as above, with ($T' > T$) where the "conversion of necessary labour into surplus labour" requires, from now on, that "the technical and social conditions of the process and consequently the mode of production itself must be revolutionized before the productivity of labour can be increased" (*ibid.*, p. 432), compared to the situation of absolute surplus value, which left the mode of production unchanged: "when surplus-value has to be produced by the conversion of necessary labour into surplus labour, it by no means suffices for capital take over the labour process in its given or historically transmitted shape and then simply to prolong its duration." (*ibidem*).

The other increase in labour productivity likely to lower the value of labour power and thus shorten the time required for its reproduction concerns the production of subsistence goods that make up wage levels (B_i):

> "In order to make the value of labour-power go down, the rise in the productivity of labour must seize upon those branches of industry whose products determine the value of labour-power, and consequently either belong to the category of normal means of subsistence, or are capable of replacing him [...] But an increase in the productivity of labour in those branches of industry which supply neither the necessary means of subsistence nor the means by which they are produced leaves the value of labour-power undisturbed. The cheapening of the commodity [δ_i], of course, causes only a relative fall in the value of labour-power, a fall proportional to the extent to which that commodity enters into the reproduction of labour-power." (*ibid.*, I, XII, pp. 432–433)

For Marx, this increase in surplus labour (or decrease in necessary labour time) through a change in the instruments or method of work refers to relative surplus value: "I call that surplus-value which arises from the curtailment of the necessary labour-time, and from the corresponding alteration in the respective lengths of the two components of the working day, *relative surplus-value*." (*ibid.*, p. 432, Marx emphasises).

This "general law of capitalist accumulation" results in:

i A structural increase in the organic composition of capital (k). Capitalists more than proportionally replace (V) with (C), particularly in periods marked by major scientific and technical discoveries:

> "the development of the capitalist mode of production, and of the productivity of labour – which is at once the cause and the effect of accumulation – enables the capitalist, with the same outlay of variable capital, to set in motion more labour by greater exploitation (extensive or intensive) of each individual labour-power. We have further seen that the

capitalist buys with the same capital a greater mass of labour-power, as he progressively replaces skilled workers by less skilled, mature labour-power by immature, male by female, that of adults by that of young persons or children. On the one hand, therefore, with the progress of accumulation a larger variable capital sets more labour in motion without enlisting more workers; on the other, a variable capital of the same magnitude sets in motion more labour with the same mass of labour-power; and, finally, a greater number of inferior labour-powers is set in motion by the displacement of more skilled labour-powers" (*ibid.*, I, XXV, p. 788)

ii The endemic existence of "relative surplus population". This proportional decrease in (*V*), thanks to the development of "modern and mechanical industry" (*ibid.*, p. 785, 786 n.), generates a workforce that finds little or no employment, condemned to "idleness" (*ibid.*, p. 789). This "part of the working class to enforce idleness" constitutes the "surplus population of workers" or "industrial reserve army" (*ibid.*, I, XXV, p. 784) (*i.e.* the unemployed, "a mass of human material always ready for exploitation by capital in the interests of capital's own changing valorization requirements" (*ibid.*, p. 784)). This surplus population is relative, as it is not the result of a demographic increase, but of the relative decrease in the need for labour required to develop (*C*) as it evolves:

"This accelerated relative diminution of the variable component, which accompanies the accelerated increase of the total capital and moves more rapidly than this increase, takes the inverse form, at the other pole, of an apparently absolute increase in the working population, an increase which always moves rapidly than that of the variable capital or the means of employment. But in fact it is capitalist accumulation itself that constantly produces, and produces indeed in direct relation with its own energy and extent, a relatively redundant working population, i.e. a population which is superfluous to capital's average requirements for its own valorization, and is therefore a surplus population." (*ibid.*, I, XXV, p. 782)

And this unemployment facilitates the accumulation of each "individual capital", this "disposal human material", becoming "the lever of capitalist accumulation", "which belongs to capital just as absolutely as if the latter had bred it at its own cost" (*ibid.*, pp. 784, 785–786):

- by giving (*V*), the mobility necessary for the development of existing industries and the emergence of new ones, making the labour supply highly elastic, "by the simple process that constantly 'sets free' a part of the working class" (*ibid.*, p. 786);
- by reducing the risk, for the capitalist, of an increase in the "general movements of wages", and therefore of a reduction in appropriable surplus labour (*ibid.*, p. 790 ff);

- by allowing capitalists to increase the proportion of surplus labour compared to necessary labour, "a means of enriching the individual capitalists" by maintaining "the production of the industrial reserve army on a scale corresponding with the progress of social accumulation" (*ibid.*, pp. 789–790), and thus remunerating the worker at the simple value (or even below) of reconstituting his labour-power:

> "Increase of variable capital, in this case, becomes an index of more labour, but not of more workers employed. It is the absolute interest of every capitalist to extort a given quantity of labour out of a smaller rather than a greater number of workers, if the cost is about the same. In the latter case, the outlay of constant capital increases in proportion to the mass of labour set in motion; in the former that increase is much smaller. The more extended the scale of production, the more decisive is this motive. Its force increases with the accumulation of capital." (*ibid.*, I, XXV, p. 788)

It is on this endemic "relative surplus population" that Marx constructs his "General Law of Capitalist Accumulation", one of capitalism's fundamental contradictions between the accumulation of capital and the misery of the proletariat:

> "The same causes which develop the expansive power of capital, also develop the labour-power at its disposal. The relative mass of the industrial reserve army thus increases with the potential energy of wealth. But the greater this reserve army in proportion to the active labour-army, the greater is the mass of a consolidated surplus population, whose misery is in inverse ratio to the amount of torture it has to undergo in the form of labour. The more extensive, finally, the pauperized sections of the working class and the industrial reserve army, the greater is official pauperism. *This is the absolute general law of capitalist accumulation.*" (*ibid.*, I, XXV, p. 798, Marx emphasises)

A proletariat made up of a large proportion of women, children, adolescents and young people, accustomed to chronic misery, and to totally precarious living conditions, "characterized by a maximum of working time and a minimum of wages" (*ibid.*, p. 796), where "the worker has already more or less completely lived himself out when he is only half-way through his life" (*ibid.*, p. 795), with the shortest average lifespan, living, in his "lowest sediment of the relative surplus population", *i.e.* an extreme category (children of the poor on assistance, orphans, sick, crippled, *etc.*, direct victims of industry), in "the sphere of pauperism" (*ibid.*, p. 797), which we will develop below (*cf.* chap. 6). This situation, and the resulting antagonistic polarizations (class struggle), complicates the realization (*i.e.* consumption) of part of the global product (Y) (*i.e.* subsistence goods

(B_i)), and therefore, at the aggregate (macroeconomic) level, threatens the equilibrium of "social capital", which requires taking into account the nature of the commodity (final consumption goods, productive goods, investment goods, *etc.*):

> "As long as we were dealing with capital's value production and the value of its product individually, the natural form of the commodity product was a matter of complete indifference for the analysis, whether it was machines or corn or mirrors. This was always simply an example, and any branch of production whatever could equally serve as illustration [...] But this purely formal manner of presentation is no longer sufficient once we consider the total social capital and the value of its product." (Marx, 1992, II, XX, p. 470)

Macroeconomic analysis of capital accumulation: schemes of reproduction

The study of the accumulation and reproduction of social capital requires a distinction to be made between goods consumed productively and those that form the final consumption of agents, hence the breakdown of "society's total product" or "total production process" into "two great departments" (*ibid.*, II, XX, p. 471) :

- department (or Section) I (D.I) "means of production";
- department (or Section) II (D.II) "means of consumption" (*ibidem*).

The "means of production" are commodities intended for the production of other commodities (production and/or consumption), *i.e.* consumed productively in the production process; the "means of consumption" are commodities that enter directly into the final consumption of workers and capitalists alike. Productive consumption (outlets of (D.I)) is, by definition in the CMP, provided only by the owners of the means of production. Final consumption (outlets of (D.II)) concerns both social classes, grouping together subsistence and luxury goods. The operation of each of these two sections requires constant capital (fixed and circulating elements) and variable capital. With the simplifying assumption that ($\tau_C = \tau_V = 1$), and considering, initially, that the organic composition of the capital of the different branches aggregated in each of the two sections is identical, we obtain:

$(\gamma_I = C_I + V_I + sv_I)$, for(D.I);

$(\gamma_{II} = C_{II} + V_{II} + sv_{II})$, for(D.II);

Hence

$(\gamma = C + V + sv)$, the total product.

To study the reproduction of "social capital", both "simple" and "extended" (*i.e.* "on an expanded scale"), Marx uses numerical examples that he calls "schema" (*ibid.*, II, XX, p. 473), the "schemes of reproduction" that, for Morishima (1973, p. 3), form "a two-departmental macro-economic model", "a macro-dynamic model rigorously constructed in a scientific way":

> "Marx's theory of reproduction and Walras' theory of capital accumulation should be honoured together as the parents of the modern, dynamic theory of general economic equilibrium [...] It is no exaggeration to say that before Kalecki, Frisch and Tinbergen, no economist except Marx, had obtained a macro-dynamic model rigorously constructed in a scientific way [...] Marx's theory of reproduction is very similar to Leontief's input—output analysis. (Or more correctly, we should say conversely that Leontief reproduced Marx as well as Walras in a pragmatic way.) [and] Marx's theory contains in itself a way to the von Neumann Revolution" (*ibid.*, pp. 2–3).

For the simple reproduction of "social capital", Marx takes a numerical example, with simplification $(\sigma = sv/V = 100\% = 1)$, the figures being able to indicate, indifferently, "millions of marks, francs or pounds sterling" (*ibid.*, II, XX, p. 473).

Value of initial social capital in a "closed" economy (*i.e.* with no external relations):

(D.I): $4000C_I + 1000V_I$
(D.II): $2000C_{II} + 500V_{II}$

Therefore, given that $(\sigma = 1)$, then, at the end of the production period, $(sv = \sigma V = V)$, the total annual commodity product is thus:

$(\gamma_I = 4000C_I + 1000V_I + 1000plv_I)$
$(\gamma_{II} = 2000C_{II} + 500V_{II} + 500plv_{II})$

The value of the total product (γ) increases from 7500 to 9000 (*i.e.* $(\gamma = \gamma_I + \gamma_{II})$ at the end of the production process. However, this growth does not allow for the possibility of "extended reproduction". Only "simple reproduction" remains possible in this case. Why is this?

To reproduce (C_{II}), which is fully consumed since ($\tau_C = 1$), the capitalists of (D.II) need material means of production worth 2000, and identically, the capitalists of (D.I) need 4000 to reproduce (C_I), *i.e.*:

$$(C_I + C_{II} = 6000)$$

Yet (γ_I), *i.e.* the overall supply of production goods expressed in value, is precisely equal to 6000. It is therefore not possible for the capitalists of (D.I) and (D.II) to reproduce, in a closed economy, their constant capital on an expanded basis, the available means of production being quantitatively limited to (γ_I) which is, here, equivalent to the constant capital productively consumed in the two departments. The material conditions for expanded reproduction (*i.e.* the production of production commodities additional to primary needs) do not exist.

Therefore, the first formula of the "simple reproduction" of social capital is as follows: the product of (D.I), (γ_I), is equal to the sum of the means of production consumed in the production process, ($C_I + C_{II}$), since ($\tau_C = \tau_V = 1$) by hypothesis, *i.e.*:

$$(\gamma_I = C_I + C_{II})$$

Concerning inter-sectoral flows, the capitalists of (D.I), out of a global product of 6000, keep 4000 for their own productive consumption (reconstitution of (C_I)), and sell to the capitalists of (D.II) means of production worth 2000 (*i.e.* (C_{II})). The latter exchange them for means of consumption of the same value (2000), which the capitalists of (D.I) devote to reconstituting the labour power of their employees (paid labour, *i.e.* (V_I)) and to their own consumption (sv_I), consuming their entire income (($\alpha = 0$), *cf. supra*). Thus, the productive consumption needs of the capitalists of (D.II), (C_{II}), are financed by the final consumption needs expressed by the capitalists and workers of (D.I), respectively (sv_I) et (V_I), *i.e.* the second formula of simple reproduction:

$$(C_{II} = V_I + sv_I)$$

From this second formula, we can immediately deduce a third:

$$(\gamma_{II} = V_I + sv_I + V_{II} + sv_{II})$$

In other words, the total production of the means of consumption of (D.II), (γ_{II}), is entirely allocated to the final consumption of the workers and capitalists of the two departments, respectively ($V_I + V_{II}$) et ($sv_I + sv_{II}$).

Marx gives this example of "simple reproduction" to theoretically present the functioning and interdependence of the two departments; it is therefore a hypothetical framework, "the necessary starting point for all scientific exposition of enlarged reproduction" for Rosa Luxemburg (2003, p. 79), which does not correspond to the reality of capitalism, but to the initial state of accumulation (*in statu nascendi*). As Marx points out:

> "Simple reproduction on the same scale seems to be an abstraction, both in the sense that the absence of any accumulation or reproduction on an expanded scale is an assumption foreign to the capitalist basis, and in the sense that the conditions in which production takes place do not remain absolutely the same in different years (which is what is assumed here). The supposition is that a social capital of a given value supplies the same mass of commodity values and satisfies the same quantity of needs in both the current year and the previous year, even if the forms of the commodities may change in the reproduction process. But since, when accumulation takes place, simple reproduction still remains a part of this, and is a real factor in accumulation, this can also be considered by itself." (*ibid.*, II, XX, pp. 470–471)

argument taken up by R. Luxemburg (*ibid.*, p. 79):

> "The shortcomings of the diagram of simple reproduction are obvious: it explains the laws of a form of reproduction which is possible only as an occasional exception in a capitalist economy. It is not simple but enlarged reproduction which is the rule in every capitalist economic system, even more so than in any other. Nevertheless, this diagram is of real scientific importance."

As we have seen, in capitalist reality, only "enlarged reproduction" is conceivable, since to sustain competition, capitalists in (D.I) and (D.II) are constantly obliged to broaden the base of their production (*cf. above*). Instead of consuming all their surplus values ($\alpha = 0$), they reinvest part of it ($0 < \alpha < 1$) in constant and variable capital in proportion to their organic compositions of capital, the basis of accumulation on a progressive scale, the capitalist expression of the effects of the increasing productivity of the means of production, and, with technical progress, "living or paid labor" is able to transform into commodities, in an ever shorter time, increasingly considerable masses of means of production, hence ($\alpha \rightarrow 1$).

"Extended reproduction" therefore requires an additional quantity of means of production supplied in the previous period: "The surplus-value that is transformed into money in this way is then transformed back by the capitalist into additional natural elements of his productive capital" (*ibid.*, II, XXI, p. 565), *i.e.* "for the extension of the constant capital already functioning, or for the installation of a new industrial business" (*ibidem*). In other words, it finds its material basis only in a relative overproduction of (D.I) compared to (D.II). Consequently, there must be a permanent disproportion between the two departments for the accumulation of social capital to take place by means of the capitalization of the part (α) of (sv_I) and (sv_{II}), respectively ($\alpha\sigma V_I$) and ($\alpha\sigma V_{II}$). This conversion of a fraction of surplus value into additional capital necessarily translates into a drop in the effective demand for capitalists' means of consumption, and therefore a drop in outlets for (D.II); the now capitalized (*i.e.* unconsumed) part of the surplus value exceeding any increase in paid labour (*i.e.* "the additional variable capital", *ibid.*, p. 577 ff) linked to the implementation of the additional production capacities, *i.e.* ($[(\alpha\sigma V_I) + (\alpha\sigma V_{II})] > [(\Delta V_I) + (\Delta V_{II})]$). The resulting relative and secondary overproduction of (D.II) is then conditioned by the effective and prior overproduction of (D.I).

In order to illustrate the conditions and process of "enlarged reproduction" of "social capital", Marx proposes a new numerical example (*ibid.*, II, XXI, p. 586 ff) which contains the possibility of an accumulation of social capital, with no change, compared to the previous example, in the distribution of (γ_I) and with the same overall values of (γ_I) and (γ_{II}), hence of total capital (γ), *i.e.* ($\gamma_I + \gamma_{II} = 9000$), with ($\sigma = 1$), or at the end of the production process:

$$(\gamma_I = 4000C_I + 1000V_I + 1000sv_I) = 6000$$
$$(\gamma_{II} = 1500C_{II} + 750V_{II} + 750sv_{II}) = 3000$$

In this scheme, the product of (D.I), *i.e.* the total value of production commodities produced, is greater than the sum of the means of production of the two departments used in their respective production cycles, ($6000 > (4000 + 1500)$), *i.e.*:

$$(\gamma_I > C_I + C_{II})$$

This is the first formula of "extended reproduction", which enables the accumulation of social capital on a progressive scale. This disproportion shows the effective overproduction of the means of production and, simultaneously, the predominance of (D.I) in the dynamics of the capitalist system.

Moreover, (γ_{II}), *i.e.* (3000), the total value of consumer commodities produced, is less than the sum of the potential (*i.e.* solvent) final consumption of the workers and capitalists of the two departments (3500), *i.e.*:

$$(\gamma_{II} < V_I + sv_I + V_{II} + sv_{II})$$

second formula of "expanded reproduction", which illustrates that the total value of solvent consumption does not translate into effective consumption, since ($\alpha \neq 0$), part (α) of the capitalists' surplus-value being capitalized, only the other part ($1 - \alpha$) is, henceforth, consumed.

Assume, here, writes Marx (*ibid.*, p. 586), that half of (sv_I), is accumulated, *i.e.* ($\alpha\sigma V_I = \alpha sv_I = 500$). The capitalists of (D.I) supply the capitalists of

(D.II) ($1500C_{II}$), in exchange for which they reconstitute their labour power ($1000V_I$) and satisfy their own final consumption ($500sv_I = (1 - \alpha)\sigma V_I$), their share of productively consumed surplus-value equal to ($500sv_I = \alpha\sigma V_I$), or surplus-product, constituting the basis of accumulation. The resulting additional capital, *i.e.* ($\Delta I = \alpha\sigma V_I = 500 = \Delta(C_I + V_I)$), must be made up, for its valuation, of constant and variable capital, according to a proportion (k_I). With, here, ($k_I = C_I/V_I = 4$), the capitalists of (D.I) allocate ($400 = 500 \times 4/5$) to (ΔC_I), and ($100 = 500 \times 1/5$) to (ΔV_I). (ΔV_I) leads the capitalists of (D.I) to sell (100) means of production to the capitalists of (D.II). The latter then, in turn, accumulate this additional product in constant (ΔC_{II}) and variable (ΔV_{II}) capital in proportion to (k_{II}), *i.e.* ($k_{II} = C_{II}/V_{II} = 2$), with ($\Delta C_{II} = 100 \times 2/3 \approx 67$) and ($\Delta V_I = 100 \times 1/3 \approx 33$).

The new repartition of the "social capital" is then as follows:

$$(\gamma_I = 4400C_I + 1100V_I \textit{ remain } 500[sv_I = 1 - \alpha\sigma V_I])$$
$$(\gamma_{II} = 1567C_{II} + 783V_{II} \textit{ remain } 650[sv_{II} = 1 - \alpha\sigma V_{II}])$$

The social product is still (9000), but the social capital ($C_{I+II} + V_{I+II}$) increases from 7250 to 7850. If, as before, ($\sigma = 1$), the social capital becomes, at the end of the period:

$$(\gamma_I = 4400C_I + 1100V_I + 1100sv_I = 6600)$$
$$(\gamma_{II} = 1567C_{II} + 783V_{II} + 783sv_{II} = 3133)$$

The social product has thus risen from 9000 to 9733, with the maintenance of the initial double disproportion ($\gamma_I > C_I + C_{II}$) and ($\gamma_{II} < V_I + sv_I + V_{II} + sv_{II}$) characteristic of "expanded reproduction", which seems to show the possibility of an indefinite development of capitalism, of accumulation without hindrances or limits espousing a regime of steady growth. However, the Marxian schemes of expanded reproduction of "social capital" in Book II of Capital can only constitute a mathematical demonstration of the indefinite possibility of capitalist accumulation, if the initial disproportions between (D.I) and (D.II); in other words, as R. Luxemburg points out (*ibid.*, pp. 99–100), that these "the few easy rules", resulting from a "certain fool-proof mathematical exercise in addition and subtraction" presenting without "any surprise" an accumulation continuing "smoothly, ad infinitum", are verified in reality, whereas "the concrete social conditions of accumulation" show us the contrary:

> "But now it is time to take care lest we should only have achieved these surprisingly smooth results through simply working out certain fool-proof mathematical exercises in addition and subtraction, and we must further inquire whether it is not merely because mathematical equations are easily put on paper that accumulation will continue ad infinitum without any friction. In other words: the time has come to look for the concrete social conditions of accumulation." (Luxemburg, 2003, p. 91)

Such is the case with the hypothetical invariance of (k), the absence of subdivision in terms of "circulation time" between the fixed and circulating elements of (C), or the fact that "it is quite obvious that Department I has taken the initiative and actively carries out the whole process of accumulation, while Department II is merely a passive appendage" (*ibid.*, p. 99), or that the capitalists of (D.II) are ill-treated ("the capitalists of the provisions department get just as rough a deal", *ibid.*, p. 94), dependent or even submissive to (D.I) (*ibid.*, pp. 97–98), or that demography is not taken into account (*ibid.*, p. 105), as is "demo-economics" since:

> "Even under the sway of capitalism, society does not consist exclusively of capitalists and wage labourers. Apart from these two classes, there are a host of other people: the landowners, the salaried employees, the liberal professions such as doctors, lawyers, artists and scientists. Moreover, there is the Church and its servants, the Clergy, and finally the State with its officials and armed forces. All these strata of the population can be counted, strictly speaking, neither among the capitalist nor among the working class." (Luxemburg, *ibid.*, p. 106)

The debate on the "decline" *vs.* "perpetuation" of capitalism is far from over, and we will come back to it in the next chapter 6. In the meantime, let us note that these patterns of reproduction allow for three theoretical advances:

- the dynamics of social capital are first ensured by the means of production: accumulation takes place in (D.I) then its volume quantitatively sets the conditions for expanded reproduction in (D.II);
- a permanent double disproportion forms the structure of the extended reproduction of social capital. Situations of actual and relative overproduction, and therefore of relative disequilibrium, far from being dysfunctions of the system, condition and enable the accumulation of capital, thereby exercising a regulatory function;
- the organic composition of capital is very different between the two sections, with the relative share of (C_I), and therefore the capital intensity of (D.I), being greater than that of (C_{II}), *i.e.* $(k_I > k_{II})$. It follows that the mass of profit and the mass of surplus value are not interchangeable quantities. Marx's initial model can then be modified by substituting profit for surplus value:

$$(\gamma_I = 4000C_I + 1000V_I + 1000sv_I) = 6000$$
$$(\gamma_{II} = 1500C_{II} + 750V_{II} + 750sv_{II}) = 3000$$

Using Ricardo's law of equalization (see above), the average rate of profit for this economy is:

$$(\rho = sv_I + sv_{II}/C_I + C_{II} + V_I + V_{II}) = (1750/7250), \text{ soit } \approx 24\%.$$

The mass of profit (P), equivalent to that of the surplus value (SV) (*cf. supra*), (see above), *i.e.* here (1750), is then distributed between the two departments as follows:

$(P_I = [4000C_I + 1000V_I] \times 24\%) = 1207;$
$(P_{II} = [1500C_{II} + 750V_{II}] \times 24\%) = 543;$

instead of ($sv_I = 1000$) and ($sv_{II} = 750$).

As we have seen, the realization of (sv), *i.e.* the transition to (ρ), is to the advantage of (D.I), characterized by high (k_I), to the detriment of (D.II), with low (k_{II}). Here again, the means of production, *via* capital intensity, exert a drag effect on the social product, amplified by the attraction exerted by (D.I) as a function of high levels of profitability. The emergence of new branches of production in (D.I), due in particular to technical progress, is likely to counteract Ricardian trend equalization.

However, the highly hypothetical nature of the conditions for the realization of reproduction schemes makes it impossible to answer the problem of regulating a system subject to the individual decisions of isolated entrepreneurs, *i.e.* in the absence of *ex ante* coordination of economic decisions. Marx (1991, III, Part Three) confers on (ρ) the role of regulator as the driving force, the stimulant of capitalist production, the condition and motive of accumulation, universally adopted by all capitalists and, in so doing, homogenizing their behaviour and decision-making:

> "it is the appropriation of unpaid labour, and the proportion between this unpaid labour and objectified labour in general – to put it in capitalist terms, profit and the proportion between this profit and the capital applied, *i.e.* a certain rate of profit - it is this that determines the expansion or contraction of production, instead of the proportion between production and social needs, the needs of socially developed human beings [...] It is the rate of profit that is the driving force in capitalist production, and nothing is produced save what can be produced at a profit." (*ibid.*, III, XV, pp. 367–368)

Now, this accumulation of capital implies a rise in (k) and an induced increase in labour productivity, all mechanisms likely to cause the failure, or even the inversion, of the dynamics of (ρ), which Marx (*ibid.*, III, Part Three, pp. 315–375) summarizes in "the law of the tendential fall in the rate of profit". Demonstrating this close link between (ρ) and (k) is straightforward: if, when ($\tau_C = \tau_V = 1$), ($\rho = \sigma / k + 1$) (see above), then any increase in (k), for (σ) constant, decreases (ρ); in other words, ($\rho \downarrow$ *when* $\sigma \rightarrow / k \uparrow + 1$):

> "this gradual growth in the constant capital, in relation to the variable, must necessarily result in a *gradual fall in the general rate of profit*, given

that the rate of surplus-value, or the level of exploitation of labour by capital, remains the same. Moreover, it has been shown to be a law of the capitalist mode of production that its development does in fact involve a relative decline in the relation of variable capital to constant, and hence also to the total capital set in motion [...] This progressive decline in variable capital in relation to the constant capital, and hence in relation to the total capital as well, is identical with the progressively rising organic composition, on average, of the social capital as a whole. It is just another expression for the progressive development of the social productivity of labour, which is shown by the way that the growing use of machinery and fixed capital generally enables more raw and ancillary materials to be transformed into products in the same time by the same number of workers, i.e. with less labour." (*ibid.*, III, XIII, p. 318, Marx emphasises)

As we have seen, the rate of surplus value can only vary if the wages, and/or the length of the working day, and/or the intensity of labour varies (*ibid.*, III, III, p. 143), in the sense that "wages affect the size and the rate of surplus-value in the opposite direction to the length of the working day and the intensity of labour; a rise in wages reduces surplus-value, while an extension of the working day and a greater intensity of labour both increase it." (*ibidem*). Henceforth, the relative constancy of (σ) (see above) reflects the limits of exploitation linked to transformations in the relationship between capital and labour. These limits arise, firstly, "mechanically" as the industry becomes increasingly capital-intensive, since labour is the source of value:

"the mass of living labour applied continuously declines in relation to the mass of objectified labour that it sets in motion, i.e. the productively consumed means of production, the part of this living labour that is unpaid and objectified in surplus-value must also stand in an ever-decreasing ratio to the value of the total capital applied." (*ibid.*, III, XIII, p. 319)

The constancy of (σ) can also be explained by the degree of resistance of the working class, whether legal (legislation and labour law), organized (unions), linked to the degree of qualification (which reduces the substitutability of "labour power"), to the growing importance of working-class consumption in global outlets, and/or cyclical (the level of "relative surplus-population", *cf. above*). Finally, (σ), in its "extensive" version (*i.e.* the extortion of absolute "surplus-value", *cf. above*), is "naturally" limited by the 24-hour day and by the minimum wage below which the simple reproduction of labour power is no longer assured.

Unlike Ricardo's "the natural tendency of profits then is to fall", *i.e.* the "gravitation of profits" (1817, p. 133), which is the result of diminishing returns in agriculture linked to demographic change, and therefore insufficient technical progress,[2] Marx's "law of the tendency fall in the rate of profit" is the CMP's own expression of "the progressive development of the social productivity of labour" (*ibid.*, III, XIII, p. 319). However, this "law" is relative in the sense that the downward trend in (ρ) can and must (*ibid.*, p. 324) be accompanied, in capitalism, by an increase in the absolute mass of surplus labour, and thus in the "absolute quantity of profit", *i.e.* the rate of profit is not synonymous with the mass of profit, as capitalists increase the volume of advanced capital and, hence, the mass of appropriable surplus-value:

> "The decline is relative, not absolute, and it has in fact nothing whatsoever to do with the absolute amount of the labour and surplus labour set in motion [...] The number of workers employed by capital, i.e. the absolute mass of labour it sets in motion, and hence the absolute mass of surplus labour it absorbs, the mass of surplus-value it produces, and the absolute mass of profit it produces, *can* therefore grow, and progressively so, despite the progressive fall in the rate of profit. This is not only *can* but *must* be the case – discounting transient fluctuations – on the basis of capitalist production." (*ibid.*, III, XIII, pp. 323, 324, Marx emphasises)

In addition, three main types of "counteracting factors" (*ibid.*, III, XIV, pp. 339–348) "checking and cancelling" (*ibid.*, p. 339) certain effects of the "general law", reducing it to "a tendential fall":

- those that raise (σ) by the intensification of work (relative surplus-value) and the extension of the working day (absolute surplus-value), "this discovery of modern industry" (*ibid.*, p. 340), *i.e.* (ΔT) (see above), and/or by the fall in wages made possible by the rise of the "industrial reserve army", with all the limits noted above. At constant productivity, (ρ) is for Marx, as for Ricardo, a decreasing function of the real wage rate.
- those that decrease (k) due to the depreciation of (C) caused by rising labour productivity, the technological and scientific environment, and, more generally, the "development of industry" (*ibid.*, p. 343). In addition, "relative surplus population", which results from capital/labour substitution, can also drive down (k) insofar as it encourages capitalists to invest in less capital-intensive industries or those that "oppose the transformation of manual work into machine production", and/or new branches of production such as "luxury consumption", for example (*ibid.*, p. 344).
- finally, foreign trade enables capitalists to make their element of constant capital (C) and their "necessary means of subsistence" ($\delta_i B_i$) needed to reconstitute the workforce "cheap". In addition, foreign markets widen the outlets for domestic products that can be sold above their value ("unequal exchange" theory):

> "Capital invested in foreign trade can yield a higher rate of profit, firstly, because it competes with the commodities produced by other countries with less developed production facilities, so that the more advanced country sells its goods above their value, even though still more cheaply

than its competitors. In so far as the labour of the more advanced country is valorized here as labour of a higher specific weight, the profit rate rises, since labour that is not paid as qualitatively higher is nevertheless sold as such. [A manufacturer] thus realizes a surplus profit." (*ibid.*, pp. 344–345)

Despite these "counteracting factors", Marx concludes that there is a strong downward trend in (ρ) which, as a "spur to capitalist production", acts "as a threat to the development of the capitalist production process" (*ibid.*, III, XV, pp. 349–350), promoting "overproduction, speculation and crises, and leads to the existence of excess capital alongside a surplus population" (*ibid.*, p. 350). At the same time, however:

"If a falling rate of profit coincides with a rise in the mass of profit [...] then a greater part of the annual product of labour is appropriated by the capitalist under the heading of capital (as replacement for the capital used up) and a relatively smaller part is appropriated under the heading of profit. Hence the fantasy of Reverend Chalmers to the effect that the smaller the mass of the annual product the capitalists spend as capital, the greater the profits they pocket." (*ibid.*, III, XV, p. 354).

As a result, the terms of the "withering away" *vs.* "perpetuation" of capitalism debate differ according to whether or not the first (rate) effect takes precedence over the second (mass) effect. A similar dialectic can be found in the ambivalent status of the crises discussed here, which can also be interpreted as capitalism's ability to temporarily but periodically overcome its contradictions. Crises are not merely possible, endowed with an "accidental" or "matter of chance" occurrence (Marx, 1969, XVII, p. 512), but become necessary, regular and inherent to its regulation:

"The world trade crises must be regarded as the real concentration and forcible adjustment of all the contradictions of bourgeois economy [...] In world market crises, all the contradictions of bourgeois production erupt collectively; in particular crises (particular in their content and in extent) the eruptions are only sporadical, isolated and one-sided." (*ibid.*, XVII, p. 510, 534)

It is the physiognomy of this regulation through the recurrence of crises, as a "moment" in the cycle, that is the subject of the following developments.

Notes

1 "Simple reproduction is only the periodic repetition of this first operation; each time, money is freshly transformed into capital." (*ibid.*, I, XXIV, p. 731).

2 "The natural tendency of profits then is to fall; for, in the progress of society and wealth, the additional quantity of food required is obtained by the sacrifice of more

and more labour. This tendency, this gravitation as it were of profits, is happily checked at repeated intervals by the improvements in machinery, connected with the production of necessaries, as well as by discoveries in the science of agriculture which enable us to relinquish a portion of labour before required, and therefore to lower the price of the prime necessary of the labourer." (Ricardo, 1817, pp. 133–134).

Bibliography

Luxemburg, Rosa (2003). *The accumulation of capital*, (1913), Translated by Agnes Schwarzschild. London and New York: Routledge "Classics".

Marx, Karl (1969). *Theories of surplus value*, Part II (1862–3). London: Lawrence & Wishart; Moscow, Progress Publishers, 1968.

Marx, Karl (1990). *Capital. A critique of political economy*, Volume I (1867), Translated by Ben Fowkes. London, Penguin Books in association with New Left Review, Penguin Classics.

Marx, Karl (1991). *Capital. A critique of political economy*, Volume III (1864–75), Translated by David Fernbach. London, Penguin Books in association with New Left Review, Penguin Classics.

Marx, Karl (1992). *Capital. A critique of political economy*, Volume II (1869–79), Translated by David Fernbach. London: Penguin Books in association with New Left Review, Penguin Classics.

Morishima, Michio (1973). *Marx's economics, A dual theory of value and growth*. Cambridge, London, New York, Melbourne: Cambridge University Press.

Ricardo, David (1817). *On the principles of political economy, and taxation*. London: John Murray, Albemarle-Street.

6 Business cycles and the dynamics of capitalism

Marx's thought, particularly that contained in Capital, constitutes a major epistemological advance in the specification of the paradigm of economic crises, through a triple demonstration: i) that of the conditions of equilibrium in connection with the accumulation of capital (*cf. supra*); ii) that of the processes of disequilibrium and crisis as phenomena *inherent* to the system; iii) that of the necessity of crises in the capitalist system as a means (*i.e.* as a propitious moment) of temporarily and brutally overcoming some of the contradictions generated by the dynamics of the capitalist mode of production (*i.e.* "The mechanism of the capitalist production process removes the very obstacles it temporarily creates", 1990, I, XXV, p. 770):

> "Capitalist production constantly strives to overcome these immanent barriers, but it overcomes them only by means that set up the barriers afresh and on a more powerful scale [Thus] Crises are never more than momentary, violent solutions for the existing contradictions, violent eruptions that re-establish the disturbed balance for the time being." (1991, III, XV, p. 358, 357)

In this context, the economic crisis is at once the end and the beginning, the breakdown of equilibrium and sudden rebalancing, and becomes the essential element of a dynamic understood as the capitalist system's ability to overcome its contradictions temporarily but periodically. In this way, Marx constructs the concept of "crisis" and, by virtue of its regulatory role—and hence its necessity—provides the conceptual material for the construction of a theory of the economic cycle (Hansen & Clemence, 1953, p. 129; Leontief, 1938, p. 3). Nevertheless, there is nowhere to be found anything approaching a complete or systematic treatment of the subject in Marx's writings, "the great 'unwritten chapter' of his work" for Schumpeter (1966, p. 747, 1131).

By grasping the crisis as a moment in a cycle, Marx makes it possible to grasp the dynamics of capitalism characterized by "the almost regular periodicity of crises on the world market" (Marx, 1969, XVII, p. 498), and thus, in the first place, to abstain from the "allegedly theoretical twaddle" (*ibid.*, p. 500), emanating from the "apologists" of capitalism,[1] relating to the

DOI: 10.4324/9781032649054-11

impossibility of general crises of overproduction. Marx thus opposes classical representations of the capitalist economy, which preclude the possibility of a theory of crises, or allow at best the formal possibilities of crises *via* the problem of demand insufficiency with the questions of "purchasing power" (Sismondi) and "willingness to buy" related to the dependence of investment on consumption (Malthus), where the weakness of "effective demand" explains macroeconomic imbalances and crises. Marx breaks with this "dogma of impossibility" (Sweezy, 1952, p. 137) and reverses the terms of this debate around "Say's Law"[2] by explaining what makes crises necessary. This structural need for regulation is part of the dynamics of capital accumulation, the expression of a contradiction between the social character of production and the private character of the ownership of the means of production and of economic decisions, this need being asserted in a framework which enables the use of money as capital.

Thus, despite the incompleteness and scattered nature of these developments relating to business cycles,[3] readings of Capital and theories of surplus value enable us to piece together the puzzle, *i.e.* to outline the contours of a Marxian conception of cyclical and periodic movements, hence the recourse to secondary literature in this chapter. For Marx, these cyclical movements and the recurrence of crises are consubstantial with the capitalist mode of production and, consequently, obey intrinsic rationality linked to specific laws of change:[4]

> "The constant recurrence of crises had in fact reduced the rigmarole of Say and others to a phraseology which is now only used in times of prosperity but is cast aside in times of crises. In the crises of the world market, the contradictions and antagonisms of bourgeois production are strikingly revealed [hence the need] of investigating the nature of the conflicting elements which errupt in the catastrophe [...] *Over-production* is specifically conditioned by the general law of the production of capital: to produce to the limit set by the productive forces, that is to say, to exploit the maximum amount of labour with the given amount of capital, without any consideration for the actual limits of the market or the needs backed by the ability to pay; and this is carried out through continuous expansion of reproduction and accumulation, and therefore constant reconversion of revenue to capital, while on the other hand, the mass of the producers remain tied to the average level of needs, and must remain tied to it according to the nature of capitalist production." (Marx, 1969, XVII, pp. 500, 534–535)

Or else:

> "Modern industry's whole form of motion therefore depends on the constant transformation of a part of the working population into unemployed or semi-employed "hands". The superficiality of political economy shows itself in the fact that it views the expansion and

contraction of credit as the cause of the periodic alternations in the industrial cycle, whereas it is a mere symptom of them [...] Effects become causes in their turn, and the various vicissitudes of the whole process, which always reproduces its own conditions, take on the form of periodicity. When this periodicity has once become consolidated, even political economy sees that the production of a relative surplus population [...] is a necessary condition for modern industry." (Marx, 1990, I, XXV, p. 786)

And these "eruptions of all the contradictions of bourgeois production", which manifest themselves in and through crises, occur at almost decennial intervals[5], according to the following three-dimensional configuration: i) the evolution of the "industrial reserve army" which refers to the labour dimension which determines the evolution of wage rates and thus the exploitation rate; ii) the dynamics of the rate of profit and the interest rate which give rhythm to the financial dimension which sets the trade-off between profit rate and interest rate; iii) the rotation of fixed capital which marks out the technological dimension that determines the accumulation of capital and thus the organic composition of capital. The interrelation of these three dimensions allows us to specify the duration and amplitude of cycles and thus the conditions for restoring the profitability of production and allowing the resumption of accumulation and, in the long term, the modalities of the dynamics of the capitalist system (*i.e.* the "withering away" *vs.* "perpetuation" of capitalism debate, see above).

The cyclicality of the "industrial reserve army": the labour dimension

The general law of capitalist accumulation (see above, I, XXV, pp. 762–870) concerns the conditions of extraction of surplus value, which are more or less favourable according to the size of the "industrial reserve army". This tends to increase under the combined effects of "changes in the technical composition of capital" (*ibid.*, p. 773),[6] the "concentration of means of production" (*ibid.*, p. 776) and the "centralization of capitals" *i.e.* "the attraction of capital by capital" (*ibid.*, p. 777). Within this long-run tendency, the cyclicality of the "relative surplus population" and "the constant and daily transformations in the mode of production" (*ibid.*, III, XV, p. 372) set wage rates and, implicitly, the appropriable surplus labour, the origin of surplus value and profit, which in turn marks out economic cycles:

"if a surplus population of workers is a necessary product of accumulation or of the development of wealth on a capitalist basis, this surplus population also becomes, conversely, the lever of capitalist accumulation, indeed it becomes a condition for the existence of the capitalist mode of production. It forms a disposable industrial reserve army, which belongs to capital just as absolutely as if the latter had bred it as its own cost.

> Independently of the limits of the actual increase of population, it creates a mass of human material always ready for exploitation by capital in the interests of capital's own changing valorization requirements [...] The path characteristically described by modern industry, which takes the form of a decennial cycle [...] depends on the constant formation, the greater or less absorption, and the re-formation of the industrial reserve army or surplus population. In their turn, the varying phases of the industrial cycle recruit the surplus population, and become one of the most energetic agencies for its reproduction." (*ibid.*, I, XXV, pp. 784–785)

Variations in wage rates thus depend on the evolution of surplus population, *i.e.* the proportion in which the working class is divided into an "active army" and a "reserve army" (*ibid.*, p. 790), linked to the phase of the cycle, but according to a non-linear dynamics since the rise, during phases of expansion, remains contained within limits imposed by capitalist accumulation, which "not only leave intact the foundations of the capitalist system, but also secure its reproduction on an increasing scale" (*ibid.*, p. 771). This configuration depends on "the relation between the unpaid and the paid labour for the same working population":

> "If the quantity of unpaid labour supplied by the working class and accumulated by the capitalist class increases so rapidly that its transformation into capital requires an extraordinary addition of paid labour, then wages rise and [...] the unpaid labour diminishes in proportion. But as soon as this diminution touches the point at which the surplus labour that nourishes capital is no longer supplied in normal quantity, a reaction sets in: a smaller part of revenue is capitalized, accumulation slows down, and the rising movement of wages comes up against an obstacle." (*Ibidem*).

In other words, the capitalist system is able to overcome this contradiction by constantly maintaining a certain level of the relative surplus population dictated by the requirements of capital accumulation (see above), keeping wage levels more or less constant when "the working population [...] increases more rapidly than the valorization requirements of capital" (*ibid.*, p. 798) *via* "an artificial surplus population" (*ibid.*, III, XV, p. 358), by modifying the composition of the productive population through recourse, if necessary, to forced labour (prolongation of the working day, *ibid.*, I, XV, pp. 526–533), to women's and children's labour (*ibid.*, pp. 517–526, 799).

Here, the movements of the level of wages depend upon the relative bargaining strength of capitalists and workers and on "the political balance of power" (Robinson, 1966, p. ix). At the same time, the rate of surplus value or of exploitation can remain at a high level by developing the production of relative surplus value through technical progress (the intensification of labour, *ibid.*, I, XV, pp. 533–543), a manifestation of the technological dimension (see further), which favours the increase of productivity and the organic composition of capital, thus the substitution of capital for labour; as incorporated science in the labour process, making the individual worker "an appendage of a machine" or the "machine-worker" (*ibid.*, I, XXV, p. 799; I, XV, p. 533). Capitalists mobilize machinery according to the joint evolution of wage rates and "relative surplus population" according to the Volterra case of "prey and predator" specified by Goodwin (1967, p. 55); this mobilization is, mainly, motivated by the relative increase in the wage rate (*i.e.* low level of the relative surplus population) during expansion phases, and facilitated during depression phases, when the industrial reserve army is larger and therefore more easily "submit[ed] to the dictates of capital" (*ibid.*, I, XV, p. 532). The capitalist system then resembles "a system of piracy, preying upon the very life of the workers" in the words of Joan Robinson (1966, p. 22). Thus, the activation of this technological dimension (see further) impacts on labour productivity, favoured by the dispossession of workers' knowledge[7] and the parcelization of tasks "with labour repeated day after day with unvarying uniformity" (*ibid.*, I, XV, p. 533),[8] an increase in the substitutability of the labour factor, an increase in working time "as far as possible" (*ibid.*, p. 530), and an impoverishment of the content of work; all elements which enable to restore, on an enlarged basis, the motives of accumulation by subjecting the active population, henceforth extended to every member of the worker's family,[9] without distinction of age or sex, under "the direct sway of capital" (*ibid.*, p. 517). Consequently, it is the superabundance of the available working population, particularly during the phases of depression, which allows the transformation of the mode of labour and "the character of the social working organism" (*ibid.*, p. 531) so as to break all resistance to the renewed accumulation and valorization of capital, where "the overseer's book of penalties replaces the slave-driver's lash" (*ibid.*, p. 550).

This framework illustrates the opposition between the dimensions of labour and technology, *i.e.* the opposition between the rate of exploitation and the rate of accumulation; and these responses of capital radically transform material conditions and social realities: from the rural exodus (*ibid.*, I, XXV, pp. 795–796) to the phenomena of urbanization (the habitat of the "sphere of pauperism", *ibid.*, p. 797), from the emigration of workers to other branches of industry (*ibid.*, p. 792) to "domestic industry" (*ibid.*, p. 796), from the reduction of life expectancy to the exploitation of children and the "early marriages" necessary for the docility of the new generations (*ibid.*, p. 795; *ibid.*, III,, XV, p. 363).

The inverse relationship between the real wage rate and the rate of profit is part of the usual framework of this dimension of labour, where the process of capital accumulation in a context where the technological dimension is very active leads to a downward trend in the rate of profit; where crises are the manifestation of a temporary disequilibrium in the value system that can be corrected by a population surplus or an increase in productivity, which are the preconditions for the recovery (or the slowing of the decline) of the rate of profit. However, if one leaves this framework (by considering the technological dimension as not very active) and abandons the hypothesis that all goods "naturally" sell at their equilibrium value[10] (which is implicit in the theory of value), the inverse relation between the real wage rate and the rate of profit is no longer fully verified. The essential difficulty is to realize the value that is already, in the physical sense, embodied in the finished products, the expression of realization crises. Both cases illustrate a fall in the rate of profit, but according to two different logics (*i.e.* two different roles for the rate of exploitation and the level of the real wage rate, and thus for the labour dimension): "In the one case we have to do with movements in the rate of surplus value and the composition of capital, with the value system remaining intact; in the other case we have to do with as yet unspecified forces tending to create a general shortage in effective demand for commodities, not indeed in the sense that the demand is insufficient to buy all the commodities offered, but that it is insufficient to buy them all at a satisfactory rate of profit." (Sweezy, 1952, p. 146).

The cyclicality of profit rates and interest rates: the financial dimension

The financial dimension refers to the capacity of financial markets to accelerate time (*ibid.*, III, XXVII, p. 567, 572),[11] that is, to transform a hypothetical future into a tangible reality made possible by unqualified confidence in the future nourished by a form of amnesia, a "disaster myopia" in Minsky's sense (*i.e.* "over time the memory of the past disaster is eroded", Minsky, 1975, p. 125).

This vision is consubstantial with the financial markets and leads to speculative euphoria, the illusion of real capital (*ibid.*, III, XXIX, p. 598) and financial fragility, which are constantly renewed but never anticipated, because investors always prefer to choose the opinion that tells them everything is (and will be) fine (*i.e.* unqualified confidence in the future): "[t]his is why business always seems almost exaggeratedly healthy immediately before a collapse" (*ibid.*, III, XXX, p. 616). Hence, surprisingly, the crisis occurs while it obeys recurrent and well-known mechanisms; in other words, financial markets are oblivious to past crises, hence their recurrence and, consequently, their cyclicality.

This financial dimension based on the logic of the short term, the appetite for risk and the decision-making urgency of financial profitability is likely to enter into contradiction with that of the productive organization and accumulation of productive capital centred on the calculation of economic profitability, the product of the relationship between the dimensions of work and technology.

It is this contradiction that is at the centre of the financial dimension, the second Marxian explanation of the ten-year cycles (*ibid.*, III, chapters 28–32, pp. 574–652), taking the form of an opposition between interest-producing capital and capital accumulation, *i.e.* the respective dynamics of the rate of profit and the rate of interest. Marx makes a "qualitative distinction" between the "financial or money capitalist" (*Geldkapitalisten*) and the "industrial capitalist" (or "functioning capitalist", *ibid.*, III, XXIII, p. 498) who respectively embody the two constituent parts of profit:

"Both for the industrial capitalist in so far as he works with borrowed capital, and for the money capitalist in so far as he does not apply his capital himself, the merely quantitative division of gross profit between two different persons, with different legal titles to the same capital and hence to the profit it produces, turns into a qualitative distinction. One part of the profit now appears in and of itself as the fruit that accrues to capital in *one* capacity, as interest; the other part appears as a specific fruit of capital in an opposite capacity, and hence as profit of enterprise: one as the simple fruit of property in capital, the other as the fruit of merely functioning with capital, as the fruit of capital as capital in process, or of the functions that the active capitalist exercises." (Marx, 1991, III, XXIII, p. 498, Marx emphasises).

In other words, "the capitalist who works with his own capital, as well as the one working with borrowed capital, divides his gross profit into interest that accrues to him as owner, as lender of his own capital to himself, and profit of enterprise, which accrues to him as an active, functioning capitalist" (*ibidem*).

It is therefore the coexistence of industrial capitalists (*i.e.* in the production process) and financial or money capitalists (*i.e.* outside the production process) that transforms part of the profit into interest. Consequently, capital must be in the process of reproduction in order to produce profit, and therefore interest, as the "variations in the rate of interest [...] taking place over longer periods [are] conditioned by variations in the general rate of profit" (*ibid.*, III, XXXI, p. 631). There is therefore no "natural rate of interest" and the average or middling rate of interest, as distinct from the constantly fluctuating market rate (*i.e.* "*Marktrate des Zinses*"), "cannot be given limits by a general law, since what is involved is simply a distribution of the gross profit between two persons who possess capital under different titles" (*ibid.*, III, XXII, p. 487), the capitalist lender and the capitalist entrepreneur. There is thus a necessary and close link between the rate of profit and the rate of interest, the problem being they are opposed or even clash as regards this sharing:

"it is the capitalist actually functioning in the reproduction process whom the lending capitalist directly confronts [...] Interest-bearing capital is capital *as property* as against capital *as function*. [So] profit of enterprise does not form an antithesis with wage-labour but rather with interest. [T] aking the average profit as given, the rate of profit of enterprise is determined not by wages but rather by the rate of interest. It is either high or low in inverse proportion to the latter [...] From the fact that interest confronts profit of enterprise, and vice versa [...] it seems to follow that profit of enterprise plus interest, *i.e.* profit and consequently surplus-value, is derived from what ? From the antithetical form of its two parts!" (*ibid.*, III, XXIII, pp. 503–505, Marx emphasises)

The dynamics of the interest rate and the corporate profit rate follow this inverse relationship during all phases of the industrial cycle:[12]

> "If we consider the turnover cycles in which modern industry moves - inactivity, growing animation, prosperity, overproduction, crash, stagnation, inactivity, etc. – [...] we find that a low level of interest generally corresponds to periods of prosperity or especially high profit, a rise in interest comes between prosperity and its collapse, while maximum interest up to extreme usury corresponds to a period of crisis [...] The rate of interest reaches its highest level during crisis, when people have to borrow in order to pay, no matter what the cost" (*ibid.*, III, XXII, pp. 482–483)

Expansionary phases, when the reproduction process intensifies on a broad basis with a very active technological dimension, are the periods when credit is the most flexible and easy (abundance of interest-bearing capital with low-interest rates). More precisely, this available money capital is converted into productive capital, *i.e.* means of production and labour power, which in turn feed accumulation and consumption, and as long as this process of expanded reproduction continues, the supply and demand for credit is maintained or even expanded, but any disruption (delayed returns, overstocked markets, fallen prices, *etc.*, *ibid.*, p. 614), however marginal, diminishes the financial absorption capacity of the economy (*ibid.*, pp. 358–362).

Therefore, the appearance of a relative over-abundance of available money capital (excess liquidity) generates two processes at the end of the expansion phase: on the one hand, a rise in speculation ("the fraudulent businesses and speculative dealings that the credit system fosters", *ibid.*, p. 615; "this fictitious money", *ibid.*, p. 625; "floating capital", *ibid.*, pp. 627–628; "extensive fictitious credits", *ibid.*, pp. 629, 635–636; "periods of speculation", *ibid.*, p. 645), *i.e.* a relative eviction of the financing of productive capital towards financial investments (*ibid.*, p. 622), with an "all-engrossing capital at compound interest" (*ibid.*, p. 523), which makes interest rise to the detriment of the profit of enterprise in a context of still high rate of profit (*ibid.*, p. 645); on the other hand, an under-assessment of "borrower risks" by the "class of money capitalists" (bankers, money-lenders, financiers, *ibid.*, pp. 642–643) which increases their vulnerabilities with regard to the risk of runs (*ibid.*, pp. 599–603),[13] "put the public's money capital at the disposal of this gang of dealers on a massive scale, and so the brood of gamblers multiplies" (*ibid.*, p. 644) and favors distrust of the financial system ("a lack of credit", "the demand for cash payment and distrust of credit selling", *ibid.*, p. 614), the sudden return to a preference for liquidity (*ibid.*, p. 598, 614, 648, 661, 708), which can take the form of a race to withdraw money, a banking run, thereby precipitating the crisis:[14]

> "In a system of production where the entire interconnection of the reproduction process rests on credit, a crisis must evidently break out if credit is suddenly withdrawn and only cash payment is accepted, in the

form of a violent scramble for means of payment. At first glance, therefore, the entire crisis presents itself as simply a credit and monetary crisis. And, in fact all it does involve is simply the convertibility of bills of exchange into money. The majority of these bills represent actual purchases and sales, the ultimate basis of the entire crisis being the expansion of these far beyond the social need. On top of this, however, a tremendous number of these bills represent purely fraudulent deals, which now come to light and explode; as well as unsuccessful speculations ..." (*ibid.*, III, XXX, p. 621)

In these conditions, the rescue of the banking and financial sector requires the action of the central banker, through its function of lender of last resort and its policy of repurchasing securities, which is not without a moral hazard problem:[15]

"It is clear that this entire artificial system of forced expansion of the reproduction process cannot be cured by now allowing one bank, e.g. the Bank of England, to give all the swindlers the capital they lack in paper money and to buy all the depreciated commodities at their old nominal values." (*ibidem*)

The interest rate then peaks during the crisis under the combined effect of four factors:

i because of the inactivity of capital blocked in one of the phases of its reproduction (M ... M′.) (one of the manifestations of the technological dimension, see further);
ii because confidence[16] in the continuity of the reproduction process, a fortiori on an extended basis, is shaken;
iii because the demand for industrial capital decreases (progressive disappearance of the motive of accumulation);
iv because the demand for credit motivated by the very high need for means of payment (and not for means of purchase or investment) (*ibid.*, III, XXX, p. 621) is increasing, with agents borrowing to pay for already made commitments, resulting in a break in the chain of payment obligations and thus in the credit system itself:

"The chain of payment obligations at specific dates is broken [...], and this is still further intensified by an accompanying breakdown of the credit system, which has developed alongside capital. All this therefore leads to violent and acute crises, sudden forcible devaluations, an actual stagnation and disruption in the reproduction process, and hence to an actual decline in reproduction." (*ibid.*, III, XV, p. 363)

The resulting phase of depression is then characterized, in the first place, by credit rationing (*ibid.*, III, XXVIII, pp. 580–581) amplifying the economic recession, thus the over-abundance of industrial capital:

> "Interest reaches its maximum again as soon as the new crisis breaks out, credit suddenly dries up, payments congeal, the reproduction process is paralysed and [...] there is an almost absolute lack of loan capital alongside a surplus of unoccupied industrial capital." (*ibid.*, III, XXX, p. 620)

This economic recession is coupled with a stock market crisis (*ibid.*, III, XXIX, pp. 598–599) which, combined with credit rationing, increases the interest rate and the mass of available monetary capital for which the context of devaluation or even "capital's lying idle or by its destruction" (*ibid.*, III, XV, p. 362) and bankruptcies constitute as many investment opportunities for financial capitalists, marking a potential hold of the financial dimension on the economic dimension:

> "in the bad phases of the industrial cycle, the rate of interest may rise so high that it temporarily swallows up profits entirely for some branches of business, particularly those unfavourably located. At the same time, the prices of government paper and other securities fall. This is the moment when money capitalists buy up this devalued paper on a massive scale, as it will soon go up again in the later phases, and even rise above its normal level. They will then sell it off, thereby appropriating a part of the public's money capital. Those securities that are not sold off yield a higher interest, since they were bought below their price. But all the profit which the money capitalists make, and which they turn back into capital, they transform first of all into money capital for loan." (*ibid.*, III, XXXI, pp. 634–635)

This reconstitution will allow the financing of the recovery[17] (*ibid.*, p. 619) and then the next phase of expansion, but the part retained by financial capitalists, notably banks and financial intermediaries ("money-dealers", *ibid.*, III, XXV, p. 528) within "joint-stock companies developed with the credit system" (hence the transformation of industrial capitalists into industrial managers,[18] *ibid.*, p. 510, 512), combined with their growing financial power, are likely to give rise to a banking and financial system, the ultimate degree of financialization, where the capitalist system would reach the extreme form of its alienation and fetishism of interest-bearing capital, where money breeds money in a self-creating logic of interest (*ibid.*, III, XXIV, pp. 515–516).

But, once again, contradiction is not an impossibility in capitalism since the recessionary phase of this cycle of the rate of profit and the rate of interest, through the devalorization or even the destruction of the over-abundant fixed capital, the rise of relative surplus population and thus the fall of wages (*i.e.* the labour dimension), the fall of prices and the "competitive struggle", and by allowing the experimentation of "new machinery, new and improved methods of labour and new forms of combination" (*ibid.*, III, XV, p. 363) (*i.e.* the technological dimension) allows the dynamics of the rate of profit to be reactivated and, hence, accumulation on a newly expanded basis of reproduction:

> "The stagnation in production that has intervened prepared the ground for a later expansion of production -within the capitalist limits. And so we go round the whole circle once again. One part of the capital that was devalued by the cessation of its function now regains its old value. And apart from that, with expanded conditions of production, a wider market and increased productivity, the same cycle of errors is pursued once more." (*ibid.*, III, XV, pp. 363–364)

However, the cyclicality of the rate of profit and the rate of interest illustrates the ambivalent nature of the credit system[19] as capitalism's response to the contradictory nature of capital development:

> "The credit system has a dual character immanent in it: on the one hand it develops the motive of capitalist production, enrichment by the exploitation of others' labour, into the purest and most colossal system of gambling and swindling, and restricts ever more the already small number of the exploiters of social wealth; on the other hand however it constitutes the form of transition towards a new mode of production. It is this dual character that gives the principal spokesmen for credit, from Law through to Isaac Péreire, their nicely mixed character of swindler and prophet." (*ibid.*, III, XXVII, pp. 572–573)

In other words, the bankers and other financial capitalists, like the industrial capitalists, earn profit, and not interest, from their activity. The development of this analysis shows that bankers and industrial capitalists share some common interests against workers in the distribution of the social product (*ibid.*, III, XIII, pp. 324–325). But we also noted that banks, because of their strategic position in the issuance and sale of new securities, play a peculiarly important role in the formation or the fusion of corporations. Banks appropriate to themselves a major share of profit, appoint their own representatives to sit on the directorates of corporations, and come to exercise a great influence in the sense of reducing competition and erecting monopolies. In this context, the financial dimension frame makes it possible to clarify that the relation between these two groups of capitalists also has an antagonistic character, which appears particularly in the analysis of the cyclical fluctuations of the interest rate. This conflictual relationship is exacerbated in the context of a very active technological dimension (with a high devaluation of capital and increased financing needs), together with competition among bankers themselves and the power of workers to resist reductions in their real wage (*i.e.* according to the configuration of the dimensions of labour and technology), can prevent the rate of profit from being fixed at a high level without excluding a fall in it.

Capital turnover cycles: the technological dimension

The technological dimension refers to the main characteristic of the capitalist mode of production, namely the "formal subsumption of labour under capital" (Marx, 1990, I, Appendix, pp. 1019–1023), and it is "the general form of every capitalist process of production [where] surplus-value can be created only [...] by increasing *absolute surplus-value*" (*ibid.*, p. 1019, 1021) but "a *specifically capitalist mode of production* [which does] not only transforms the situations of the various agents of production, it also *revolutionizes* their actual mode of labour and the real nature of the labour process as a whole" (*ibid.*, p. 1021, Marx emphasises). So with the "specific mode of capitalist production" (*ibid.*, pp. 1023–1025) as a mode of production *sui generis* (*ibid.*, p. 1035) this "formal subsumption" turns into "the real subsumption of labour under capital" with "the crucial importance of relative surplus-value" (*ibid.*, p. 1023) where science, technology and scientific knowledge, *via* "the use of *machinery*, and in general the transformation of production by the conscious *use* of the sciences, of mechanics, chemistry, etc. for specific ends, technology, etc." (*ibid.*, p. 1024) that allows a relative increase in the portion of capital as against the variable (see above), are subject to the development of the productive forces in the service of capitalism:

> "On a closer examination of the working machine proper we rediscover in it as a general rule, though often in highly modified forms, the very apparatus and tools used by the handicraftsman or the manufacturing worker; but there is the difference that instead of being the tools of a man they are the implements of a mechanism, mechanical implements [...] It is a part of the handicraftsman's implement [...] which is first seized on by the industrial revolution, leaving to the worker, in addition to his new labour of watching the machine with his eyes and correcting its mistakes with his hands, the merely mechanical role of acting as the motive power." (Marx, 1990, I, XV, p. 494, 496)

The technological dimension which, in the capitalist mode of production, can only be conceived in terms of the subjugation of the labour dimension, does not therefore refer to a narrative of technical and scientific discoveries applied to production, considered as autonomous in relation to social change, it shows the evolution of the technical conditions of extraction of (relative) surplus value turned towards the meticulous and systematic dispossession of workers' knowledge in the service of profit:

> "right down to the eighteenth century, the different trades were called "mysteries" (*mystères*),[20] into whose secrets none but those initiated by their profession and their practical experience could penetrate. Large-scale industry tore aside the veil that concealed from men their own social process of production and turned the various spontaneously divided

> branches of production into riddles, not only to outsiders but even to the initiated. Its principle, which is to view each process of production in and for itself, and to resolve it into its constituent elements without looking first at the ability of the human hand to perform the new processes, brought into existence the whole of the modern science of technology." (*ibid.*, I, XV, p. 616; see also, *ibid.*, p. 617, and I, Appendix, p. 1029)

In the capitalist system, the technological dimension marks the mutation of invention into innovation, that is to say, the moment of the concretization of its capitalist valorization, the prerogative of the modern bourgeoisie:

> "The bourgeoisie cannot exist without constantly revolutionizing the instruments of production, and thereby the relations of production, and with them the whole relations of society [...] Constant revolutionizing of production, uninterrupted disturbance of all social conditions, everlasting uncertainty and agitation distinguish the bourgeois epoch from all earlier ones [...] All that is solid melts into air, all that is holy is profaned, and man is at last compelled to face with sober senses, his real conditions of life, and his relations with his kind." (Marx & Engels, 2002, pp. 222–223)

And in this configuration, dissensions and conflicts are constitutive of social order, where the technical requirements of large-scale industry (parcelling out of repetitive tasks devolved to an easily substitutable labour force) constantly threatens the very existence of the worker "by taking away the instruments of labour, to snatch from his hands the means of subsistence, and, by suppressing his specialized function, to make him superfluous" (*ibid.*, I, XV, p. 618); Marx mobilizing here Shakespeare's *The Merchant of Venice* (Act IV, Scene I): "You take my life, When you do take the means whereby I live". In this framework, the Marxian explanation of economic cycles is centred on the "overall turnover of the capital advanced" (*i.e.* "turnover cycles") (Marx. 1992, II, IX, Part Two, pp. 231–424).

The reasoning is centred on the general formula for individual capital (knowing that "what is true for the individual capitalist, is true also for the capitalist class", *ibid.*, IV, p. 197); in other words, competition, promoted by the development of the credit system (illustration of financial dimension), reinforces the unity of the whole capitalist class and makes the individual capital a share of aggregate capital:

$$\mathbf{M} - \mathbf{C}\begin{cases} wf = V \\ mp = C \end{cases} - \mathbf{P}\begin{cases} V \\ k = C/V \\ C = \alpha Cf + Cc \end{cases} - \mathbf{C}'(= C + V + \sigma V) - \mathbf{M}'(= M + \Delta M = M + \rho(C + V)),\ with\ M' > M)$$

where (σ), (ρ) and (k) respectively are the rate of surplus value (or rate of exploitation), *i.e.* the capacity of the system to extract surplus-value, *i.e.* "surplus labour", *i.e.* ($\sigma = sv/V$) the rate of profit as the surplus value realized as remuneration of the total capital ($C + V$) advanced, *i.e.* ($\rho = sv/C + V$) and the organic composition of capital ($k = C/V$) which measures the capital intensity of the production process (P).

The rotation cycle or turnover of capital ($M \ldots M'$) as a periodic process,[21] is given by the sum of the production time[22] contained in (P) and the circulation time[23] contained in ($M - C$) and ($C' - M'$), *i.e.* "the overall time of circulation of a given capital": "It is the period of time that elapses from the moment that the capital value is advanced in a particular form until the return of the capital value in process in the same form. The specific purpose of capitalist production is always the valorization of the value advanced, whether this value is advanced in its independent form, *i.e.* the money form, or in commodities" (*ibid.*, II, VII, p. 233). The maximization of profit ($max\ \Delta M$) requires, then, two cumulative conditions, namely the continuity[24] and the temporal minimization of this rotation time, *i.e.* the sum of production time and circulation time,[25] and to take into account the specificity of the rotations of fixed (Cf) and circulating (or fluid) elements (Cc) of constant capital (C).[26]

(Cc) the value of a commodity, *i.e.* raw materials, energy, semi-processed goods, *etc.*, does not pose any particular problem since it transmits all of its value to the final goods produced during the constant capital turnover time (τ_C). This is because it is replaced as it is consumed, to the extent of the stocks, *i.e.* ($\tau_{Cc} = 1$). (Cf) the durable nature of capital, *i.e.* machinery, equipment, *etc.*, transfers only part of its value, *i.e.* wear and tear, (αCf) to the final commodities, another part $(1\text{-}\alpha)Cf$ remaining fixed in the means of production (mp) which continues to function despite wear and tear, *i.e.* ($\tau_{Cf} > 1$) until, all other things being equal, its total wear and tear ($\sum_{i=1}^{n} \alpha_i = 1,\ with\ \tau_{Cf} = n$). At this final moment, "the means of labour has lived out its time, and lost its value together with its use-value. It has ceased to be a bearer of value" (*ibid.*, II, VIII, p. 240):

> "As a means of labour functions and is used up, one part of its value passes over to the product, while another part remains fixed in the means of labour and hence in the production process. The value fixed in this way steadily declines, until the means of labour is worn out and has therefore distributed its value, in a longer or shorter period, over the volume of products that has emerged from a series of continually repeated labour processes. As long as a means of labour still remains effective, and does not yet have to be replaced by a new item of the same kind, some constant capital value remains fixed in it, while another part of the value originally fixed in it passes over to the product and thus circulates as a component of the commodity stock." (*ibid.*, II, VIII, pp. 237–238)

Depending on its wear rate,[27] each element of (Cf) has a particular rotation. But if the wear of (Cf) is regular, its replacement takes place in jerks, in discontinuous bursts, particularly when decisive technological revolutions have taken place, according to the rate of accumulation, the rate of exploitation (σ) (Marx, 1991, III, XV, pp. 373–374), the level of competition, the financing capacities of firms, the interest rate, and technical progress,[28] all of which are elements of the valorization of capital linked to the three interrelated dimensions. And in this framework, capital, constrained by its fixed component (Cf), central manifestation of the technological temporality, determines the extent of crises, "the effects of crises are more severe the more extensive the fixed capital, and most severe in those branches of production where the amount of fixed capital is greatest" (Hilferding, 1981, chap. 17). In order to evaluate the turnover time of (Cf) or (τ_{Cf}), Marx distinguishes between wear and tear or depreciation ("the portion of value that the fixed capital gradually gives up to the product as it is used, according to the average degree of its loss of use-value", Marx, 1992, II, VIII, p. 250) and "moral depreciation" (*ibidem*), *i.e.* obsolescence, which under the pressure of competition, crises and new innovations results in accelerated wear and tear and, consequently, in a premature renewal of the element of (Cf), which is suddenly outdated in terms of productivity, and therefore in terms of the value of the capital, *i.e.* ($\sum_{i=1}^{n} \alpha_i < 1$, $with\ \tau_{Cf} < n$):

> "The means of labour are for the most part constantly revolutionized by the progress of industry. Hence they are not replaced in their original form, but in the revolutionized form [...] competition forces the replacement of old means of labour by new ones before their natural demise, particularly when decisive revolutions have taken place [...] the constant revolutionizing of the means of production, which also increases steadily with the development of the capitalist mode of production also leads to changes in the mean of production; they constantly have to be replaced, because of their moral depreciation, long before they are physically exhausted." (*ibid.*, p. 250, 264)

The technological temporality, insofar as it allows the study of "capital confined by its fixed component" (*ibid.*, p. 264), thus shapes the material basis of periodic crises, and provides some insights into the duration of cycles.

The interrelation of the three dimensions

The interrelation of these three dimensions allows us to understand the mechanisms at work in the development of capitalism, understood as the capacity of the system to temporarily overcome its contradictions, which are expressed by two types of crisis (Sweezy, 1952, pp. 145–146), crises linked to the fall in the rate of profit (i) and crises of realization (ii). In the first case, crises refer to the conditions of extraction of surplus value, that is, to the *opposition* between the organic composition of capital (*i.e.* the expression of the technological dimension) on the one hand, and the rate of exploitation (*i.e.* the expression of the labour dimension) and the rate of interest (*i.e.* the expression of the financial dimension) on the other, in order to counteract the fall in the rate of profit, the exit from the crisis and the condition of recovery. In the second case, crises require, in order to be overcome, a double *compromise* (a proportional relation) between the rate of exploitation and the rate of profit on the one hand, and the rate of profit and the rate of interest on the other, in order to allow the realization of surplus value for a given level of technology.

i In the first scenario, the technological dimension is very active, characterized by a strong precipitous devalorization of (Cf) under the action of the high moral depreciation (*ibid.*, II, XIX, p. 264), it takes the form of a shortening of (τ_{Cf}) and an acceleration of the substitution of capital for labour, resulting in a rise in (k) and thus a fall in the rate of profit (ρ) (Marx, 1991, III, XIII, pp. 330–334), as the rise in (k) is only partially compensated by the increase in the "relative surplus working population" (*ibid.*, p. 328), the "permanent apparent surplus working population" (*ibid.*, p. 330), the "additional labour" (*ibid.*, p. 331) and/or in "the length and intensity of the working day" (*ibid.*, p. 329). These expressions of the labour dimension increase (σ), but only slow down the long-run tendency to the decrease of (ρ)[29]. In this case, financing needs, linked to the constantly premature renewal of (Cf) increase more than proportionally to the financing capacities constrained by the mass of profit (*i.e.* self-financing capacities), "the maximum limit of interest would seem to be the profit itself" or the "maximum limit of interest as the whole profit" (*ibid.*, III, XXII, p. 480), hence the need to have recourse to external financing, which is the first manifestation of the financial dimension. Furthermore, periods of economic crisis and recession offer, in this context, many opportunities for investment in industry for financial capitalists in search of devalued capital, "the most worthless and wretched kind of money-capitalists who flourish, thanks to their possession of cheaper buildings, machinery, etc." (*ibid.*, III, V, p. 199), second manifestation of the financial dimension, "the period during which moneyed interest enriches itself at the cost of industrial interest" (Marx, 1969, p. 496) that is, the opposition between rates of profit and interest, between the financial and technological dimensions.

Ultimately, when the technological dimension is very active, we must witness a shortening of the duration of cycles (or an increase in their frequency of occurrence), since $(\tau_{Cf} \rightarrow 1)$. This is coupled with a financialization of the economy as (ρ) diminishing "the absolute mass of profit appropriated by the social capital (*i.e.* by the totality of capitalists)" (Marx, 1991, III, XIII, p. 327) may no longer suffice for accumulation. Here, in the long run, we are in a "usual" Marxist reading of Capital (Henryk Grossmann (1929) for example) that of the decline of the capitalist mode of production, the "breakdown of the system" (Sweezy, 1952, pp. 190–213), characterized by "*memento mori*" crises (*ibid.*, p. 190), cumulative manifestations of the double opposition of the dimensions labour *vs.* technology and profit *vs.* interest, that rage and eventually lead to a collapse of the system itself, where industrial prosperity driven by the improvement, notably technical, of the conditions of exploitation of capital includes within it the forces that progressively worsen these same conditions, suggesting a worsening of the crises over time, and an acceleration of their recurrence:

> "The important thing in their [economists like Ricardo who take the capitalist mode of production as an absolute] horror at the falling rate of profit is the feeling that the capitalist mode of production comes up against a barrier to the development of the productive forces which has nothing to do with the production of wealth as such; but this characteristic barrier in fact testifies to the restrictiveness and the solely historical and transitory character of the capitalist mode of production; it bears witness that this is not an absolute mode of production for the production of wealth but actually comes into conflict at a certain stage with the latter's further development." (Marx, 1991, III, XV, p. 350)

However, Marx argues, on numerous occasions (see above), that for the most important branches of large-scale industry, an average value of (τ_{Cf}) equal to ten years could be derived from capitalist evolution:

> "To the same extent as the value and durability of the fixed capital applied develops with the development of the capitalist mode of production, so also does the life of industry and industrial capital in each particular investment develop, tending to several years, say an average of ten years [...] We can assume that, for the most important branches of large-scale industry, this life cycle is now on average a ten-year one. The precise figure is not important here. The result is that the cycle of related turnovers, extending over a number of years, within which the capital is confined by its fixed component, is one of the material foundations for the periodic cycle." (Marx, 1992, II, IX, p. 264)

ii Precisely, in the second scenario, the interrelation of the three dimensions enables us to show some of the conditions for the "invariance" of the duration of the cycles, and thus for their decennial recurrence. This requires a technological dimension that is not very active, *i.e.* a relative stabilization of the values of (τ_{Cf}) and (k) and therefore the rate of profit (ρ). In this case, the weakness of the technological dimension tends to exhaust the reserve army and lead to a condition in which available labour power is more or less fully utilized. Capitalists are forced to bid against one another for additional workers, wages rise, and surplus value is reduced. Whenever accumulation requires an extraordinary addition of paid labour, then wages rise, and, with all other circumstances remaining equal, the unpaid labour (surplus value) diminishes in proportion. The conditions of the recovery (*i.e.* the stabilization of (ρ)) require then a compromise (the proportional relation) between (k) et (σ), a neutralization of the labour and technological dimensions, which allows, by maintaining a wage level compatible with the requirements of profitability, the *realization* of the surplus value in profit (*ibid.*, II, XX, p. 486). The same is true of the "concentration of capital and the centralization of capital and the means of production in a few hands" (*ibid.*, III, XV, pp. 354–355, 375; see also *ibid.*, I, XXV, pp. 776–781), a combined manifestation of the financial and technological dimensions that results in a compromise between profit and interest rates, *i.e.* "surplus capital alongside surplus population" because "since beyond certain limits a large capital with a lower rate of profit accumulates more quickly than a small capital with a higher rate of profit" (*ibid.*, III, XV, p. 359) and the accumulation of large capital by the relative destruction of "the mass of small fragmented capitals" which allows the dissolution of the intermediate links between capital and labor and to correct the "fragmentation of the total social capital into many individual capitalists", amplified by the credit system (expression of the financial dimension, *i.e.* "the attraction of capital by capital"), "enormous social mechanism for the centralization of capitals" (*ibid.*, I, XXV, pp. 777–778).[30]

It is then the correspondence between the "mass of profit" thus released and the "financing needs of accumulation" (*ibid.*, III, XIII, p. 336) which becomes the primary condition for an "identical" perpetuation of the duration of the cycles. And if (ρ), second condition, is not "perfectly" stabilized (non-proportional variations in the opposite direction of (ρ) and (σ)), the result is a variability at the margin of the duration of the cycles, hence the "quasi" decennial cycle (*cf.* note 5). Finally, the distribution of the mass of profit between industrial *vs.* financial capitalists ("the ratio between interest and total profit", *ibid.*, III, XXII, p. 481) allows us to evaluate the comparative dynamics of the financial and technological dimensions, and thus the degree of financialization of the economy. In this case, the cycle would have been, once again, traversed "within the capitalist limits" (*Ibid.*, III, XV, p. 364), but with a lesser amplitude under the effect of the proportional relation between entre (k) et (σ) (*cf. supra*), suggesting, here, in the long run, the perpetuation of capitalism, without excluding the "pattern of a "stationary society"" (Schumpeter, 1966 p. 562, 651, 1131) evoked by Marx (*ibid.*, I, XXV, pp. 772–773), when "the increase of capital occurs while the technical composition of capital remains constant" (*ibid.*, p. 772), where the long-term stationarity of (σ), (ρ) and (k) would be symptomatic of the exhaustion of the operativity of the three dimensions or of a global compensation of their respective effects.

By grasping the crisis as a moment in a cycle, Marx makes it possible to grasp the dynamics of capitalism characterized by "the almost regular periodicity of crises on the world market" (Marx, 1969, p. 498), and thus, in the first place, to abstain from the "allegedly theoretical twaddle" (*ibid.*, p. 500), emanating from the "apologists" of capitalism,[31] relating to the impossibility of general crises of overproduction:

> "The constant recurrence of crisis has in fact reduced the rigmarole of Say and others to a phraseology which is now only used in times of prosperity but is cast aside in times of crises. In the crises of the world market, the contradictions and antagonisms of bourgeois production are strikingly revealed. Instead of investigating the nature of the conflicting elements which erupt in the catastrophe, the apologists content themselves with denying the catastrophe itself and insisting, in the face of their regular and periodic recurrence, that if production were carried on according to the textbooks, crises would never occur." (Marx, 1969, p. 500)

Marx shows that it is in crises that the contradictions and antagonisms of the capitalist mode of production burst forth, namely that production is motivated by the maximization of profit and not, in the first place, by the satisfaction of needs, and that this maximization is incompatible with that of collective well-being. The crisis as a "propitious moment" of the cycle, and thus its periodicity, is interpreted as the ability of the capitalist system to overcome its contradictions temporarily but periodically, crises not being merely possible, endowed with an "accidental occurrence and consequently whose occurrence is itself only "a matter of chance" (*ibid.*, p. 512), but becoming necessary, regular, and inherent to its regulation.

But the physiognomy of this regulation by the recurrence of crises, as a "moment" of the cycle, by its mechanistic process, is problematic, unless we consider the dynamic response of capitalism to its contradictions as an infallible "model" where crises become "providential moments". Therefore, while maintaining this demonstration of the necessity of crisis in capitalism, associated with the contingent character of economic laws and the observation of crises (and their recurrence) in history, the interest of the three interrelated dimensions scheme is to show the institutional, economic and ideological framework[32] within which capitalism, by periodically overcoming its contradictions through the interplay of these dimensions, *i.e.* through the interconnection of labour, technological and financial mechanisms, enjoys more flexibility, where the dynamics of "industrial reserve army", of profit and interest rates, and of fixed capital, are able to grant it a reprieve.

Notes

1 "The apologetic phrases used to deny crises are important in so far as they always prove the opposite of what they are meant to prove. In order to deny crises, they assert unity where there is conflict and contradiction. They are therefore important in so far as one can say they prove that there would be no crises if the

contradictions which they have erased in their imagination, did not exist in fact. But in reality crises exist because these contradictions exist. Every reason which they put forward against crisis is an exorcised contradiction, and, therefore, a real contradiction, which can cause crisis. The desire to convince oneself of the non-existence of contradictions, is at the same time the expression of a pious wish that the contradictions, which are really present, *should not* exist" (*ibid.*, p. 519; Marx emphasises).

2 For the ambiguity of Marx's attitude to Say's law, see Robinson (1966, pp. 86-87), Sweezy (1952, pp. 136-138).

3 "Both followers and enemies have experienced difficulty in attributing to Marx any clear-cut theory of cycles" (Schumpeter, 1966, p. 1131).

4 "The industrial cycle is such that the same circuit must periodically reproduce itself, once the first impulse has been given [...] the great general crisis representat [ing] a turning point. The acute form of the periodic process with its former ten-year cycle seems to have given way to a more chronic and drawn-out alternation, affecting the various industrial countries at different times between a relatively short and weak improvement in trade and a relatively long and indecisive depression [...] In the slack phase, production falls below the level it attained in the previous cycle and for which the technical basis is now laid. In the phase of prosperity - the middle period - it develops further on this basis. In the period of overproduction and swinding, the productive forces are stretched to their limit, even beyond the capitalist barriers to the production process." (Marx, 1991, III, XXX, pp. 620, 620n, 621).

5 This quasi-decennial periodicity, the basis of the "classical cycles" or "Juglar cycle" since Schumpeter (1939, I, p. 169), was outlined by Marx as early as 1848 in his "Discourse on Free Trade" and later clarified in Book I of Capital (*ibid.*, I, XXXV, p. 785, 786 n.) that "The path characteristically described by modern industry, which takes the form of a decennial cycle" or "Until now the duration of these cycles has been ten or eleven years, but there is no reason to consider this duration as constant" or again in Book III: "the great general crisis represented a turning-point. The acute form of the periodic process with its former ten-year cycle seems to have given way to a more chronic and draw-out alternation, affecting the various industrial countries at different times, between a relatively short and weak improvement in trade and a relatively long and indecisive depression. Perhaps what is involved is simply an extension of the cycle's duration." (*ibid.*, III, XXX, p. 620 n.). Meanwhile, Marx had, in a series of articles published in the "New York (Daily) Tribune", including "Pauperism and Free trade. The Approaching Commercial Crisis" of Nov. 1, 1852 and "The economic crisis in Europe" of Oct. 9, 1856, described a periodicity of cycles of 5/7 years, and listed the commercial crises of 1817, 1825, 1836, 1846–7 (Ledbetter and Wheen, eds., 2007). In Marxian thought, which associates the contingency of economic laws and the influence of history, this duration cannot be a precise temporal delimitation of each of the cycles and their turning point (Marx, 1992, II, XIX, p. 264), a thesis taken up by N. D. Kondratieff (1944, p. 32) for his "long cycles".

6 "This change in the technical composition of capital, this growth in the mass of the means of production, as compared with the mass of the labour-power that vivifies them, is reflected in its value-composition by the increase of the constant constituent of capital at the expense of its variable constituent." (*ibid.*, I, XXV, p. 773).

7 "Along with the tool, the skill of the worker in handling it passes over to the machine. The capabilities of the tool are emancipated from the restraints inseparable from human labour-power. This destroys the technical foundation on which the division of labour in manufacture was based. Hence, in place of the hierarchy of specialized workers that characterizes manufacture, there appears, in

the automatic factory, a tendency to equalize and reduce to an identical level every kind of work that has to be done by the minders of the machines [...] All work at a machine requires the worker to be taught from childhood upwards, in order that he may learn to adapt his own movements to the uniform and unceasing motion of an automaton." (*ibid.*, I, XV, pp. 545–546).

8 "Factory work exhausts the nervous system to the uttermost; at the same time, it does away with the many-sided play of the muscles, and confiscates every atom of freedom, both in bodily and in intellectual activity." (*ibid.*, p. 548).

9 "In so far as machinery dispenses with muscular power it becomes a means for employing workers of slight muscular strengh [...] The labour of women and children was therefore the first result of the capitalist application of machinery! [...] Compulsory work for the capitalist usurped the place, not only of the children's play, but also of independent labour at home, within customary limits, for the family itself [...] Machinery, by throwing every member of that family onto the labour-market, spreads the value of the man's labour-power over his whole family. It thus depreciates it." (*ibid.*, I, XV, pp. 517–518).

10 "It is assumed throughout, that the commodity is sold at its value" (Marx, 1969, p. 492).

11 "Acceleration, through credit, of the individual phases of circulation or commodities metamorphosis, then an acceleration of the metamorphosis of capital and hence an acceleration of the reproduction process in general [...] The credit system hence accelerates the material development of the productive forces and the creation of the world market, which it is the historical task of the capitalist mode of production to bring to a certain level of development, as material foundations for the new form of production. At the same time, credit accelerates the violent outbreaks of this contradiction, crises, and with these the elements of dissolution of the old mode of production." (*ibid.*, p. 567, 572).

12 "By and large, therefore, the movement of loan capital, as expressed in the rate of interest, runs in the opposite direction to that of industrial capital [...] At the beginning of the industrial cycle, however, a low rate of interest coincides with a contraction of industrial capital, and at the end of the cycle a high rate of interest coincides with an over-abundance of industrial capital." (*ibid.*, III, XXX, p. 620).

13 It should be noted that Marx twice quotes Smith's analysis of the role of capital and bank deposits in money lending, in the face of the risk of "runs" (*ibid.*, pp. 601–603). See part I, below.

14 In this line, Marx, in June-July 1856, published no less than three articles entitled "The French Credit Mobilier" in the "New York Tribune" (Ledbetter & Wheen eds., 2007, pp. 171–188), relating to the financial speculations and credit policies of the Frères Pereire's "Crédit Mobilier", symptomatic of the banking behaviour at the root of the global financial panic of 1857.

15 "Moral hazard" occurs when the provision of insurance against a given risk encourages behaviour that makes it more likely that the risk will materialize.

16 Confidence is crucial as regards financial temporality (*cf. ibid.*, III, XXX, p. 614, 620; III, XXXI, p. 631, for ex.).

17 "If the reproduction process has reached the flourishing stage that precedes that over-exertion, commercial credit undergoes a very great expansion, this is turn actually forming the "healthy" basis for a ready flow of returns and an expansion of production. In this situation, the rate of interest is still now, even if it has risen above its minimum. This is actually the *only* point in time at which it may be said that a low rate of interest, and hence a relative abundance of loanable capital, coincides with an actual expansion of industrial capital." (*ibid.*, III, XXX, p. 619, Marx emphasises).

18 "Capitalist production has itself brought it about that the work of supervision is readily available, quite independent of the ownership of capital [...] After every crisis one can see many ex-manufacturers [...] who are now supervising their own former factories as managers for the new owners, often their creditors, in return for a modest wage [...] the functioning capitalist confronts the mere owner of capital, the money capitalist, and with the development of credit this money capital itself assumes a social character, being concentrated in banks and loaned out by these, no longer by its direct proprietors; and since on the other hand the mere manager, who does not possess capital under any title, neither by loan nor in any other way, takes care of all real functions that fall to the functioning capitalist as such, there remains only the functionary, and the capitalist vanishes from the production process as someone superfluous." (*ibid.*, III, XXIII, pp. 511–512).

19 which makes the social character of capital predominant with respect to its private character.

20 "In the famous *Livre des métiers* of Etienne Boileau, we find it prescribed that a journeyman, on being admitted among the masters, has to swear "to love his brethren with brotherly love, to support them in their respective trades, not willfully to betray the secrets of the trade."" (*ibid.*, I, XV, p. 616).

21 "The circuit of capital, when this is taken not as an isolated act but as a periodic process, is called its turnover." (*Ibid.*, II, VII, p. 235).

22 "The duration of [capital] stay in the production sphere forms its production time [...] the production time is always the time that the capital takes to produce use-values and valorize itself, hence to function as productive capital" (*ibid.*, II, V, p. 200, 203).

23 "Circulation time and production time are mutually exclusive. During its circulation time, capital does not function as productive capital, and therefore produces neither commodities nor surplus-value [...] The expansion and contraction of the circulation time hence acts as a negative limit on the contraction or expansion of the production time, or of the scale on which a capital of a given magnitude can function. The more that the circulation metamorphoses of capital are only ideal, i.e. the closer the circulation time comes to zero, the more the capital functions, and the greateris its productivity and self-valorization." (*ibid.*, II, V, p. 203).

24 "the total process is in fact the unity of the three circuits [($M - C$), (P), ($C' - M'$)], which are the different forms in which the continuity of the process is expressed. The total circuit presents itself for each functional form of capital as its own specific circuit, and indeed each of these circuits conditions the continuity of the overall process; the circular course of one functional form determines that of the others. It is a necessary condition for the overall production process, in other words for the social capital, that this is at the same time a process of reproduction, and hence the circuit of each of its moment [...] As a whole, then, the capital is simultaneously present, and spatially coexistent, in its various phases. But each part is constantly passing from one phase or functional form into another, and thus functions in all of them in turn. The forms are therefore fluid forms, and their simultaneity is mediated by their succession." (*ibid.*, II, IV, pp. 183–184).

25 "the movements of capital through the production sphere and the two phases of the circulation sphere are accomplished successively in time. The duration of its stay in the production sphere forms its production time, that in the circulation sphere its circulation time. The total amount of time it takes to describe its circuit is therefore equal to the sum of its production time and its circulation time [...] It is clear that the nearer the production time and working time approach to equality, the greater the productivity and valorization of a given productive capital in a given space of time. The tendency of capitalist production is therefore to shorten as much as possible the excess of production time over working time [...] During

its circulation time, capital does not function as productive capital, and therefore produces neither commodities nor surplus-value [...] The more that the circulation metamorphoses of capital are only ideal, i.e. the closer the circulation time comes to zero" (*ibid.*, II, V, pp. 200, 202–203).

26 "The formal characteristics of fixed and fluid capital arise only from the different turnovers of the capital value or *productive capital* that functions in the production process. This difference in turnover arises for its part from the different ways in which the various components of the productive capital transfer their value of the product, though not from their different share in the production of the product's value or from their characteristic behaviour in the valorization process." (*ibid.*, II, VIII, p. 246).

27 "The longer the means of labour lasts and the more slowly it wears out, the longer the constant capital value remains fixed in this use-form. But whatever its degree of durability, the proportion in which it gives up value is always in inverse ratio to the overall duration of its function." (*ibid.*, II, VIII, p. 238).

28 "The necessity of technical progress for the maintenance of the capitalist system is deduced in Marxian economics by showing that only in a progressive economy can capitalist profit and interest exist". (Lange 1935, p. 198).

29 On this controversial link, *cf.* Robinson (1966, p. viii-ix ; and Chapter V) for the labour-saving technical progress and the "fundamental Marxian theorem" initiated by Okishio and systematized by Morishima (1973, p. 53): "the exploitation of labourers by capitalists is necessary and sufficient for the existence of a price-wage set yielding positive profits or, in other words, for the possibility of conserving the capitalist economy."

30 "The growth of the social capital is accomplished through the growth of many individual capitals." (*ibid.*, I, XXV, p. 776).

31 "The apologetic phrases used to deny crises are important in so far as they always prove the opposite of what they are meant to prove. In order to deny crises, they assert unity where there is conflict and contradiction. They are therefore important in so far as one can say they prove that there would be no crises if the contradictions which they have erased in their imagination, did not exist in fact. But in reality crises exist because these contradictions exist." (Marx, 1969, p. 519).

32 which is not unrelated to O. Lange's "institutional framework": "The superiority of Marxian economics on the problem of the evolution of Capitalism is due to the exact specification of the institutional datum which distinguishes Capitalism from "einfache Warenproduktion". It was thus that Marx was able to discover the peculiarities of the capitalist system and to establish a theory of economic evolution." (Lange, 1935, p. 196).

Bibliography

Goodwin, Richard M. (1967). A growth cycle. In Charles H. Feinstein (Ed.), *Socialism, capitalism and economic growth. Essays presented to Maurice Dobb* (pp. 54–58). Cambridge: Cambridge University Press.

Grossmann, Henrik (1992). *The law of accumulation and breakdown of the capitalist system. Being also a theory of crises* (1929). London: Pluto Press.

Hansen, Alvin Harvey, & Clemence, Richard Vernon (1953). *Readings in Business Cycles and National Income*, New York, W.W. Norton & Cy. Inc.

Hilferding, Rudolf (1981). *Finance capital. A study of the latest phase of capitalist development*, (1910), From Translations by Morris Watnick & Sam Gordon. London: Abingdon, New York, Routledge.

Kondratieff, Nikolaï Dmitrievitch (1944). The long waves in economic life. *The review of economic statistics*, *XVII*(6), November 1935, 105–115; also in *Readings in business cycle theory*, Philadelphia, Toronto, The Blakiston Company, pp. 20–42.

Lange, Oskar Ryszard (1935). Marxian economic and modern economic theory. *The Review of Economic Studies*, *2*(3), June, 189–201.

Ledbetter, James, & Wheen, Francis (Eds.) (2007). *Dispatches for the New York Tribune. Selected journalism of Karl Marx*. London, New York: Penguin Books, Coll. "Penguin Classics".

Leontief, Wassily (1938). The significance of Marxian Economics for present-day economic theory. *The American Economic Review*, *28*(1), supplement March, 1–9.

Marx, Karl (1969). *Theories of surplus value*, Part II (1862–3). London: Lawrence & Wishart; Moscow, Progress Publishers, 1968.

Marx, Karl (1990). *Capital. A critique of political economy*, Volume I (1867), Translated by Ben Fowkes. London: Penguin Books in association with New Left Review, Penguin Classics.

Marx, Karl (1991). *Capital. A critique of political economy*, Volume III (1864–75). Translated by David Fernbach. London: Penguin Books in association with New Left Review, Penguin Classics.

Marx, Karl (1992). *Capital. A critique of political economy*, Volume II (1869–79), Translated by David Fernbach. London: Penguin Books in association with New Left Review, Penguin Classics.

Marx, Karl, & Engels, Friedrich (2002). *The Communist Manifesto*, (1848), With an Introduction and Notes by Gareth Stedman Jones, London, Penguin Books, coll. "Penguin Classics".

Minsky, Hyman P. (1975). *John Maynard Keynes*. New York: Columbia University Press.

Morishima, Michio (1973). *Marx's Economics, A Dual Theory of Value and Growth*. Cambridge, London, New York, Melbourne: Cambridge University Press.

Natakani, Takeshi, & Hagiwara, Taiji (1997). Product innovation and the rate of profit. *Kobe University Economic Review*, *43*, 39–51.

Robinson, Joan Violet (1966). *An essay on Marxian economics*, Second edition, London and Basingstoke, The MacMillan Press Ltd.

Schumpeter, Joseph Alois (1939). *Business cycles. A theoretical, historical, and statistical analysis of the capitalist process*. New York and London, MacGraw-Hill Book Company, Inc., 2 volumes.

Schumpeter, Joseph Alois (1966). *History of economic analysis* (1954). New York: Oxford University Press, sixth printing.

Sweezy, Paul Marlor (1952). *The theory of capitalist development. Principles of Marxian political economy* (1942), With a Foreword by Maurice Dobb, London, Dennis Dobson Limited, 12 Park Place, St James's.

Part III

John Maynard Keynes (Cambridge 1883, Firle 1946) and "the General Theory of employment, interest, and money" (1936)

Introduction

In 1930, when John Maynard Keynes pondered the question of "Economic possibilities for our grandchildren" in his *Essays in Persuasion* (1931), he began by pointing out the unfoundedness of the severe economic pessimism (*i.e.* "a bad attack of economic pessimism", *ibid.*, p. 358) resulting from the "Great Depression":

> "We are suffering, not from the rheumatics of old age, but from the growing-pains of over-rapid changes, from the painfulness of readjustment between one economic period and another. The increase of technical efficiency has been taking place faster than we can deal with the problem of labour absorption; the improvement in the standard of life has been a little too quick; the banking and monetary system of the world has been preventing the rate of interest from falling as fast as equilibrium requires [...] The prevailing world depression, the enormous anomaly of unemployment in a world full of wants, the disastrous mistakes we have made, blind us to what is going on under the surface – to the true interpretation of the trend of things." (1930 in 1931, pp. 358–359)

Elaborating on the reasons why we were, at the time, in "a temporary phase of mal-adjustment" (*ibid.*, p. 364), "a nightmare which will pass away with the morning" ("The Great Slump of 1930" in 1931, p. 135), a "magneto trouble" (*ibid.*, p. 140), Keynes emphasized that, in the long term, "mankind is solving its economic problem", *i.e.* that "the standard of life in progressive countries one hundred years hence will be between four and eight times as high as it isto-day" ("Economic possibilities ...", *ibid.*, pp. 364–365), while simultaneously noting, with extreme lucidity that:

> "We are being afflicted with a new disease of which some readers may not yet have heard the name, but of which they will hear a great deal in the years to come – namely, *technological unemployment*. This means unemployment due to our discovery of means of economising the use of labour outrunning the pace at which we can find new uses for labour." (*ibid.*, p. 364, Keynes emphasises)

DOI: 10.4324/9781032649054-13

Indeed, although the crisis of 1929 was part of a "classic cycle" following the reorganization crisis of 1920 (Gilles, 2009, p. 145 ff.), it was "A Year to Remember", "a year of notable economic events", "the property of the economists" according to Galbraith (1955, p. 11, 12), "one of the greatest economic catastrophes of modern history" for Keynes ("The great ...", *op. cit.*, p. 135), insofar as it marked a break in the dynamics of capitalism due to i) the absence of spontaneous recovery (the depression lasted a decade [1929–39]) (*ibid.*, pp. 145–146), ii) the collapse of production and prices, and massive unemployment, which gave it a hitherto unprecedented scale (*ibid.*, pp. 136–137). Explaining and solving these problems, which empirically refute the belief that market economies are automatically capable of generating full employment, is a twofold theoretical and practical challenge that the "Keynesian Revolution" was to meet. The first is directly by Keynes, who demonstrates, in The General Theory of Employment, Interest and Money (1936) (henceforth GT[1]), that not only is there no mechanism in a competitive economy that guarantees full employment, but that the "normal destiny" of this economy is to be trapped in a chronic state of "underemployment"[2]:

> "it is an outstanding characteristic of the economic system in which we live that, whilst it is subject to severe fluctuations in respect of output and employment, it is not violently unstable. Indeed it seems capable of remaining in a chronic condition of sub-normal activity for a considerable period without any marked tendency either towards recovery or towards complete collapse. Moreover, the evidence indicates that full, or even approximately full, employment is of rare and short-lived occurrence [...] an intermediate situation which is neither desperate nor satisfactory is our normal lot." (GT, 18, pp. 249–250)

Keynes's teaching then becomes a warning not to rely on the automatic adjustment mechanism of competition, in order to assign real objectives to economic policy, such as full employment. And this "lesson" engages the responsibility of "the accepted classical theory of economics" for its inability to "solve the economic problems of the concrete world" (GT, 24, p. 378), first and foremost "the outstanding faults of the economic society in which we live", namely i) that "its failure to provide for full employment" and ii) that "its arbitrary and inequitable distribution of wealth and incomes" (*ibid.*, p. 372); inability that has less to do with "logical flaws in its analysis" than with the fact that "its tacit assumptions are seldom or never satisfied" (*ibid.*, p. 378). Alongside utilitarianism (the calculating spirit as a force of capitalism) and individualism, which now embody the calculations of Utility[3], these assumptions include the belief in the self-regulation of markets, where in an economy characterized by an ideal distribution of productive resources, the maximum collective well-being results from the rational pursuit of self-interest by each individual, and thus that the famous "invisible hand" of Smith's "obvious and simple system of natural liberty" (*cf. supra*, Part I, chapter 2) operates. In this matter, Keynes writes:

> "It is *not* true that individuals possess a prescriptive "natural liberty" in their economic activities [...] The world is *not* so governed from above that private and social interest always coincide. It is *not* so managed here below that in practice they coincide. It is *not* a correct deduction from the Principles of Economics that enlightened self-interest always operates in the public interest. Nor is it true that self-interest generally *is* enlightened; more often individuals acting separately to promote their own ends are too ignorant or too weak to attain even these. Experience does *not* show that individuals, when they make up a social unit, are always less clear-sighted than when they act separately." (Keynes, "The End of Laissez-faire", 1926, pp. 39–40, Keynes emphasises)

In other words, in the face of the illusory effectiveness of the "invisible hand" in the "best of all possible worlds" of laissez-faire[4], concrete solutions must come from the exercise of individual freedom, framed and supported by the visible hand of politics. Hence the need to know "what the State ought to take upon itself to direct by the public wisdom, and what it ought to leave, with as little interference as possible, to individual exertion" (Burke quoted by Keynes, *ibid.*, p. 40).

This is how to meet the second practical challenge, through the action of "the modern State", having "whose criterion of action is solely the public good" (*ibid.*, p. 41), in cooperation with "individual initiative" (GT, 24, p. 378):

> "The most important Agenda of the State relate not to those activities which private individuals are already fulfilling, but to those functions which fall outside the sphere of the individual, to those decisions which are made by *no one* if the State does not make them. The important thing for Government is not to do things which individuals are doing already, and to do them a little better or a little worse; but to do these things which at present are not done at all." ("The End of Laissez-faire", *op. cit.*, p. 46; Keynes emphasises)

It is within this framework that economic policy (fiscal and monetary) can remedy depression and unemployment, marking the end of the "laissez-faire doctrine" in favour of a "New Deal" (GT, 22, p. 331) in the face of the "Great Depression", a veritable plea for "capital works, if these works are any use at all" ("Economy", *in* 1931, p. 161) financed *via* "Government deficits" by "a policy of government borrowing" (*ibid.*, p. 161), denying the effectiveness of nominal wage cuts in combating unemployment. The diagnosis and remedies proposed here by Keynes stand in opposition to the two main "postulates of the classical economics" (GT, Chapter 2), "supposedly simple and obvious" (*ibid.*, 2, p. 5), *i.e.* i) "The wage is equal to the marginal product of labour" and ii) "The utility of the wage when a given volume of labour is employed is equal to the marginal disutility of that amount of employment" (*ibidem*), by virtue of which the system converges, naturally, towards full employment since i) specifies "the demand schedule for employment" and ii) "the supply schedule", "the amount of employment" being fixed at "point where the utility of the marginal product balances the disutility of the marginal employment" (*ibid.*, p. 6). This "classical system" is brought to macroeconomic closure by the adoption of Say's Law, according to which any increase in production automatically generates an equivalent increase in income and expenditure, so as to maintain the economy at full employment:

> "From the time of Say and Ricardo, the classical economists taught that supply creates its own demand; – meaning by this in some significant, but not clearly defined, sense that the whole of the costs of production must necessarily be spent in the aggregate, directly or indirectly, on purchasing the product [...] Thus Say's Law, that the aggregate demand price of output as a whole is equal to its aggregate supply price for all volumes of output, is equivalent to the proposition that there is no obstacle to full employment. If, however, this is not the true law relating the aggregate demand and supply functions, there is a vitally important chapter of economic theory which remains to be written and without which all discussions concerning the volume of aggregate employment are futile." (Keynes, GT, 2, p. 18; 3, p. 26)

It was precisely the real consequences, in terms of unemployment and misery, of the crisis of 1929 and the resulting "Great Depression" that gave Keynes the opportunity to write this vital chapter in economic theory, the "raison d'être" of the General Theory, *i.e.* to challenge classical assumptions and supersede classical theory: "It may well be that the classical theory represents the way in which we should like our Economy to behave. But to assume that it actually does so is to assume our difficulties away." (GT, 3, p. 34). But the response to the urgency and human distress of the 1930s cannot be the exclusive domain of Theory, but must be combined with pragmatism in the philosophical sense of the term, a doctrine which takes as the criterion of truth of an idea or a theory its possibility of acting on reality, *i.e.* reconnect with "the practical influence of economic theory" (GT, Preface, p. vi). It is therefore necessary, for Keynes, to abstract from "the ideal commonwealth men", *i.e.* to affirm that "the task of transmuting human nature must not be confused with the task of managing it." (GT, 24, p. 374). Thus, aware of the impossibility of transforming "human nature", strongly imbued with "the money-making passion"[5], the modern state, for Keynes, must exercise "the management of this nature", dictated by "wisdom and prudence", so that capitalism is practised "subject to rules and limitations" (*ibidem*), with a "certain central controls in matters which are now left in the main to individual initiative", such as the propensity to consume and the incentive to invest *via* tax policy and interest rate setting, for example, while at the same time "wide fields of activity which are unaffected" so that "public authority will co-operate with private initiative." (*ibid.*, pp. 377–378).

Here we are at the very foundation of Keynes' heterodoxy, that of "pragmatic reformism", the genesis of which predates the Great Depression, taking the form of what is today called "mixed economy", which Keynes calls "semi-socialism" ("The End of Laissez-faire", *op. cit.*, p. 45), and consisting of finding "improvements in the technique of modern Capitalism by the agency of collective action" (*ibid.*, p. 50). This reformism is situated between, on the one hand, the "many people, who are really objecting to Capitalism as a way of life [who] argue as though they were objecting to it on the ground of its inefficiency in attaining its own objects" (*ibid.*, p. 52) and, on the other hand, the "devotees of Capitalism [...] often unduly conservative, and reject reforms in its technique, which might really strengthen and preserve it, for fear that they may prove to be first steps away from Capitalism itself." (*ibid.*). In other words, between two pessimisms, "the pessimism of the revolutionaries who think that things are so bad that nothing can save us but violent change" and "the pessimism of the reactionaries who consider the balance of our economic and social life so precarious that we must risk no experiments." ("Economic Possibilities for our Grandchildren", *op. cit.*, pp. 359–360).

The other aspect of Keynes' heterodoxy is epistemological and theoretical. Here, Keynesian heterodoxy is inscribed as the desire to "persua[de] economists to re-examine critically certain of their basic assumptions", to "emanci[pate ourselves] from preconceived ideas" (GT, Preface, p. v, vi), and "that in writing this book, we felt we were abandoning this orthodoxy, reacting strongly against it, breaking chains and conquering freedom." (GT, Preface to the French edition, Cambridge, February 20 1939)[6]. This abandonment of orthodoxy takes the form of two recusals: i) that of "Say's Law" and the fallacy according to which "demand is created by supply", and by virtue of which "the economic system is constantly working at full capacity", hence the impossibility of conceiving, a fortiori dealing with, the problems of unemployment and the business cycle (*ibidem*), and ii) that of "Quantitative Theory", which has "misled us" about the level and setting of prices (*ibidem*), in order to replace it with a qualitative theory of money and the interest rate, where the demand for and supply of money refer to "the demand for cash and [the] means of satisfying it" (*ibidem*), which governs the interest rate and, together with other factors (confidence, for example), the incentive to invest, then the level of income, production and employment and, ultimately, the general price level.

This is the scope of GT's program: to break with faith in the ability of competitive forces to lead the economy into a stable situation of full employment without state intervention, and to propose a general theory, with classical theory as a "special case" (GT, Preface p. vii)[7], making it possible to specify, for any period, the main determinants of the level of employment. This explains why Keynes dedicates his book above all to "fellow economists" (*ibid.*, p. v)[8], while wishing "that it will be intelligible to others" (*ibidem*), even likening it, in the Preface to the French edition, to a message *ad urbem et orbem* ("to the City and the World") addressed "directness to outside opinion" (*ibid.*, p. 5). In this context, the title "General Theory" refers to the dual macroeconomic dimension of Keynesian analysis, i) with the need to study the economic system "considered globally":

> "I have called my theory a *general* theory. I mean by this that I am chiefly concerned with the behaviour of the economic system as a whole,—with aggregate incomes, aggregate profits, aggregate output, aggregate employment, aggregate investment, aggregate saving rather than with the incomes, profits, output, employment, investment and saving of particular industries, firms or individuals. And I argue that important mistakes have been made through extending to the system as a whole conclusions which have been correctly arrived at in respect of a part of it taken in isolation." (GT, Preface to the French edition, Cambridge, 1939, p. 6)

ii) to demonstrate the inseparable and interactive nature of individual behaviour and macroeconomic configurations in this "system as a whole", where "the demand arising out of the consumption and investment of one individual is the source of the incomes of other individuals, so that incomes, in general, are not independent, quite the contrary, of the disposition of individuals to spend and invest" (*ibid.*, pp. 6–7). Where the macroeconomic configuration becomes the resultant of "on the current decisions to produce which depend in turn on current decisions to invest and on present expectations of current and prospective consumption [i.e.] the individual psychological inclinations as to how to dispose of given incomes" (*ibid.*, p. 7), which themselves depend on the situation of the "whole system" (*ibidem*).

It is from this angle of "Modern Macroeconomics" that Schumpeter (1966, p. 1170) considers The General Theory, the book that enjoyed "the greatest literary success of our epoch", written by a "forceful and dauntless leader of public opinion" who accomplished, with this book, "a similar feat of leadership"; a work hailed for "the intellectual performance spiced by the – real or putative – relevance to burning questions of the time" (*ibid.*, p. 1181). For Schumpeter, GT therefore offers an "analytic apparatus" (*ibid.*, pp. 41–42, 1174), consisting of an appropriate interpretation of the "outstanding characteristics of the economic system in which we live that" (GT, 18, p. 255), even if "these facts of experience do not follow of logical necessity" (*ibidem*), hence the need for a "highly abstract argument" and also "much controversy" (GT, Preface, p. v). This leads Blaug (1985, p. 780, 798) to say that GT is "an ambiguous and undigested book, full of digressions and undeveloped themes, running in all directions", "an untidy book [...] that contains not one, not two, but three or four 'models' of the workings of a modern economy.". In other words, to paraphrase Dostaler (2007), GT is a work that falls into no particular category, since it is neither a book for the general public, like The Economic Consequences of the Peace (1920) for example, nor a scholarly treatise, like the Treatise on Money or the Treatise on Probability, nor a textbook, even if this book is, in the field of economics, "the most famous and influential of the twentieth century"; assessments that Samuelson (1946, pp. 187, 190) summarizes as:

> "The General Theory caught most economists under the age of 35 with the unexpected virulence of a disease first attacking and decimating an isolated tribe of South Sea islanders. Economists beyond 50 turned out to be quite immune to the ailment. With time, most economists in-between began to run the fever, often without knowing or admitting their condition [...] the General Theory is a badly written book, poorly organized; any layman who, beguiled by the author's previous reputation, bought the book was cheated of his 5 shillings. It is not well suited for classroom use. It is arrogant, bad-tempered, polemical, and not overly-generous in its acknowledgments. It abounds in mares' nests and confusions [...]. In it the keynesian system stands out indistinctly, as if the author were hardly aware of its existence or cognizant of its properties [...]. Flashes of insight and intuition intersperse tedious algebra. An awkward definition suddenly gives way to an unforgettable cadenza. When it finally is mastered, we find its analysis to be obvious and at the same time new. In short, it is a work of genius."

Ultimately, the GT is like a "patchwork of ideas, concepts and theories" that includes a doctrine, apparently constructed in the world of pure abstractions, but which is not, however, unrelated to the practice and concerns of the time, and which remain relevant today. Hence Galbraith's recommendation (1952, p. 72, 75) that GT "could not normally be read, even by the intelligent layman, unless he was schooled in the language and, even more, in the abstractions of economics" so that his "major conclusion", could be understood, that "depression and unemployment are in no sense abnormal", that "the economy can find its equilibrium at any level of performance" thus destroying "the old faith in a full-employment equilibrium". It is this "schooling" that motivates the developments that follow.

Notes

1 References to General Theory, for example (GT, 3, p. 30), will henceforth read as follows: in General Theory, Chapter 3, page 30.

2 The concept of an "underemployment equilibrium" is not explicitly Keynes', but rather a conjecture in the form of an implicit challenge to standard economics: to demonstrate the possibility of a general equilibrium with persistent involuntary unemployment (*i.e.* "stable equilibrium with N at a level below full employment", GT, 3, p. 30) in an economy of perfect competition with flexible prices and wages. It

was Hicks (1937; 1939) who first took up this challenge by developing the idea of a temporary equilibrium, an equilibrium distinct from full employment equilibrium, but at the cost of a "translation" of GT compatible with the formalization of Walrasian general equilibrium, from which the (IS-LM) model was derived. In this vein, disequilibrium theorists also move away from the Keynesian system, excluding system imbalances (contained in the GT) and conceiving only operating imbalances. Involuntary unemployment is thus considered an imbalance, i.e. the major imbalance in the system that is not only important for economic analysis, but also, or even above all, for economic policy, becoming a question of society: is the latter capable of regulating the level of employment more or less spontaneously through the market or, if unable to do so, can this regulation be ensured by economic policy?

3 A conjunction that solves many philosophical difficulties thanks to "The idea of a divine harmony between private advantage and the public good": "Suppose that by the working of natural laws individuals pursuing their own interests which enlightenment in conditions of freedom always tend to promote the general interest at the same time!" (Keynes, "The end of laissez-faire", 1926, pp. 10–11).

4 "Peace on earth to men of good means. A rich man could, after all, enter into the Kingdom of Heaven – if only he saved. A new harmony sounded from the celestial spheres. "It is curious to observe how, through the wise and beneficient arrangement of Providence, men thus do the greatest service to the Public, when they are thinking of nothing but their own gain"; so sang the angels." (Keynes, "Social Consequences of Changes in the Value of Money", 1923, in 1931, p. 85), and to add, in GT (3, p. 33; Keynes emphasises): "The celebrated *optimism* of traditional economic theory, which has led to economists being looked upon as Candides, who, having left this world for the cultivation of their gardens, teach that all is for the best in the best of all possible worlds provided we will let well alone, is also to be traced, I think, to their having neglected to take account of the drag on prosperity which can be exercised by an insufficiency of effective demand."

5 Or again in "The End of Laissez-faire" (*op. cit.*, p. 50): "the essential characteristic of Capitalism, namely the dependence upon an intense appeal to the money-making and money-loving instincts of individuals as the main motive force of the economic machine."

6 "Mais nous-même, en écrivant ce livre [GT], nous avons senti que nous abandonnions cette orthodoxie, que nous réagissions fortement contre elle, que nous brisions des chaînes et conquerrions une liberté." ["But I myself in writing it [GT], and in other recent work which has led up to it, have felt myself to be breaking away from this orthodoxy, to be in strong reaction against it, to be escaping from something, to be gaining an emancipation"], (Keynes, 1969, p. 5).

7 "I shall argue that the postulates of the classical theory are applicable to a special case only and not the general case, the situation which it assumes being a limiting point of the possible positions of equilibrium." (GT, 1, p. 3).

8 "The matters at issue are of an importance which cannot be exaggerated. But, if my explanations are right, it is my fellow economists, not the general public, whom I must first convince. At this stage of the argument the general public, though welcome at the debate, are only eavesdroppers at an attempt by an economist to bring to an issue the deep divergences of opinion between fellow economists which have for the time being almost destroyed the practical influence of economic theory, and will, until they are resolved, continue to do so." (GT, Preface, p. vi).

7 The General Theory as the foundation of modern macroeconomics

From the demonstration of underemployment to economic policy proposals for a return to full employment

From criticism of "postulates of the Classical economics" to Keynesian pragmatism

Keynesian pragmatism, as defined above, manifests itself in GT as a theoretical "entre-deux", the willingness to oppose classical postulates while accepting the language of standard economic theory[1] in order to expose his theoretical developments, including the most heterodox, with the aim of convincing his fellow economists and then the general public. The potential ambiguity of this position was largely removed by the urgency and need to provide answers, even if theoretical, to the context of the Great Depression, where "people [were] unusually expectant of a more fundamental diagnosis" (GT, 24, p. 383), and by the desire to translate analysis into operational proposals:

> "By the mid-thirties, the layman — whether worker, business¬ man, farmer or unemployed — had undoubtedly reached his own conclusions concerning American capitalism. Asked were its norm an equilibrium of stable prices and full employment, the conclusion of the competitive model, he would have recommended his interrogator to the care of a good doctor. But, as ideas to be influential need the support of experience, so experience needs interpretation by ideas. Only then does it become the basis for generalization — for a theory. The Great Depression might, conceivably, have remained the great accident if ideas had not again intervened [...] The ideas which interpreted the depression, and which warned that depression or inflation might be as much a part of the free-enterprise destiny as stable full employment, were those of John Maynard Keynes." (Galbraith, 1952, pp. 70–71)

This passage from John Kenneth Galbraith illustrates "the Social Philosophy towards which the General Theory might lead", (GT, Chapter 24) where Keynes shows the need to be (what he will be), both a committed theorist and practitioner of economics, the two being inextricably linked, in order to specify "the practical measures in which they might be gradually clothed" (*ibid.*, p. 383), and to respond to the challenges of the world, by establishing a diagnosis based on observation and analysis of the facts, the

DOI: 10.4324/9781032649054-14

one according to which "if effective demand is deficient, not only is the public scandal of wasted resources intolerable, but the individual enterpriser who seeks to bring these resources into action is operating with the odds loaded against him" (*ibid.*, pp. 380–381), whereas "if effective demand is adequate, average skill and average good fortune will be enough." (*ibid.*, p. 381). And "Classical theory" is incapable of conceiving, let alone dealing with this "waste", "involuntary unemployment", because of the "postulates" of "the classical theory of employment", supposedly so "simple and obvious" (*ibid.*, 2, p. 5) that it is never questioned, despite the facts, admitting only "frictional unemployment", resulting from "various inexactneness of adjustment which stand in the way of continuous full employment" due to "a temporary want of balance between the relative quantities of specialised resources as a result of miscalculation or intermittent demand" (*ibid.*, p. 6), and "voluntary unemployment" due to "the refusal or inability of a unit of labour, as a result of legislation or social practices or of combination for collective bargaining or of slow response to change or of mere human obstinacy, to accept a reward corresponding to the value of the product attributable to its marginal productivity" (*ibidem*). As a result, this theory applies only to a "special case" (and not to the "general case" of "the economic society in which we actually live", that of the "facts of experience", GT, 1, p. 3), "full employment", *i.e.* "the maximum quantity of employment which is compatible with a given real wage" (GT, 2, p. 12) achievable by activating, in a competitive framework, "Say's law" according to which "Supply creates its own Demand" (*ibid.*, 3, p. 25), which states that "the aggregate demand price is equal to the aggregate supply price for all levels of output and employment" (*ibid.*, 2, p. 22). In this framework of guaranteed outlets, the maximizing calculation of the labour demander (*i.e.* the entrepreneur) is limited to equalizing marginal labour productivity at the real wage rate (w/p) and, hence, increasing employment if the labour suppliers (*i.e.* employees) agree to a reduction in (w/p), hence the possibility for them to influence the level of employment which, in a situation of price and wage flexibility, can only be "full employment" (*i.e.* validation of the second postulate of "classical theory", *ibid.*, 2, pp. 5–6). Consequently, in this doctrinaire universe of "classical postulates", which is "only applicable to the case of full employment", involuntary unemployment cannot be conceived, and therefore cannot exist (TG, 2, p. 16). As we can see, this inability of "classical theory" to enable "scientific prediction" stems from the fact that these postulates, these "implicit hypotheses", which naturally lead to optimum employment of productive resources, have never been verified against "the facts of common observation" (TG, 3, pp. 32–33):

> "For professional economists, after Malthus, were apparently unmoved by the lack of correspondence between the results of their theory and the facts of observation; -a discrepancy which the ordinary man has not failed to observe, with the result of his growing unwillingness to accord to economists that measure of respect which he gives to other groups of

> scientists whose theoretical results are confirmed by observation when they are applied to the facts [...] It may well be that the classical theory represents the way in which we should like our economy to behave. But to assume that it actually does so is to assume our difficulties away." (GT, 3, pp. 33–34)

GT is therefore conceived as a manifesto expressing Keynes's desire to persuade economists "to re-examine critically some of their basic assumptions" (GT, Preface, p. v), *i.e.* to revise their representation of the world, so that economic theory regains "the practical influence" (*ibid.*, p. vi), become operational again, thereby constituting an epistemological break with classical theory, in the name of its weak applicability, whose "main objective is to deal with difficult theoretical questions, and only secondarily with the application of this theory to practice" (*ibid.*, p. v).

It was in this context that Keynes dared to take up the challenge of the facts of the 1929 crisis and the Great Depression, which, for him, constituted both a field of operation for curative economic policies and a scathing denial of the supposedly infallible virtues of competition upheld by the "Classics", who, for their part, found themselves totally bereft with their traditional conception of a stabilized equilibrium at the level of full employment of resources and the ideology of "laissez-faire" (see above). It is this undermining of the *ideals* of "full employment equilibrium" and "laissez-faire" that is well illustrated by Henri Guitton's (1979, p. 59) formulation of "l'ambition du savoir parfait [the ambition of perfect knowledge]", according to which "quand on se rapproche de la réalité, on s'éloigne de l'équilibre. Et quand on démontre l'équilibre, on n'est plus dans la réalité [when you get closer to reality, you get further away from equilibrium. And when we demonstrate equilibrium, we are no longer in reality]", and the need to propose a theoretical alternative, which explains why the thirties were, simultaneously, the darkest years in economic history ("black decade") and "years of high theory" (Shackle, 1967).

The scale and severity of the Great Depression also influenced the theoretical construction of GT, which was based on a perspective of lasting or even endemic, *i.e.* structural, underemployment:

> "an insufficiency of effective demand may, and often will, bring the increase of employment to a standstill *before* a level of full employment has been reached. The insufficiency of effective demand will inhibit the process of production in spite of the fact that the marginal product of labour still exceeds in value the marginal disutility of employment." (GT, 3, pp. 30–31)

Hence the explanation of the "paradox of poverty in the midst of plenty" when "the richer the community, the wider will tend to be the gap between its actual and its potential production; and therefore the more obvious and outrageous the defects of the economic system", GT, 3, pp. 30–31), while

GT only marginally addresses the "business cycle", studied in, the last Chapter 24, through "Concluding Notes on the Social Philosophy towards which the General Theory might lead" (GT, 24, pp. 372–384) or incidentally in Chapter 18 ("The General Theory of Employment Re-stated"), where fluctuations are dampened by the interplay of "conditions of stability" (GT, 18, pp. 250–251) linked to the marginal propensity to consume *via* the multiplier, and to variations in "the prospective yield of capital" and/or the rate of interest, and/or money-wages and/or rate of investment (*ibid.*, pp. 250–251) (see below).

Faced with the extraordinary challenges posed by the Great Depression, the general fall in prices, the collapse of share prices, a contraction in industrial production and world trade, high unemployment and major currency crises (Gilles, 2009, pp. 168–169), all typical problems calling for solutions, GT must propose a model, indeed a method of political action (with the economist as "advisor to the Prince"[2]), where the economist's knowledge is based on knowledge of the actors and their behaviours (*i.e.* motives to act), first and foremost the entrepreneur's decision to invest. For a period (t, $\forall t$), these behaviours interact with "dependent variables", such as "the existing skill and quality of available labour", "the existing quality and quantity of available equipment", "the existing technique", "the degree of competition", "the tastes and habits of the consumer", "the disutility of different intensities of labour and of the activities of supervision and organisation", *etc.* (GT, 18, p. 245) which determine "the volume of employment and the national income (or national dividend) measured in wage-units" (*ibidem*), and "independent variables" as "the propensity to consume", "the schedule of the marginal efficiency of capital" and "the rate of interest" (r), driven by "three fundamental psychological factors": "the psychological propensity to consume"[3], "the psychological expectation of future yield from capital-assets"[4] and "the psychological attitude to liquidity"[5] (GT, 18, pp. 246–247). And axiomatizing this set of behaviours, variables, motives, beliefs, circumstances and situations by activating the "Principle of Effective Demand" (GT, Chapter 3), the GT's "Keynesian model", yields the "amount of national income" corresponding to the "volume of employment", *i.e.* "the national income dépend[ent] on the volume of employment, *i.e.* on the quantity of effort currently devoted to production, in the sense that there is a unique correlation between the two" (GT, 18, p. 246):

> "Our present object is to discover what determines at any time the national income of a given economic system and (which is almost the same thing) the amount of its employment; which means in a study so complex as economics, in which we cannot hope to make completely accurate generalisations, the factors whose changes *mainly* determine our *quaesitum*. Our final task might be to select those variables which can be deliberately controlled or managed by central authority in the kind of system in which we actually live." (GT, 18, p. 247, Keynes emphasises)

Keynes' model

In opposition to the School of automatic adjustment, the School of full employment equilibrium and the classical model enclosed in "Say's law", the "Keynes' model" contained in the GT is based on four main lemmas (*L*) whose interaction leads to two demonstrations (*D*):

L1. An economy of decisions and behaviours in an uncertain and risky future[6] specified by the model's "independent variables" linked to psychological factors (or laws) that condition certain behaviours in terms of liquidity, investment and consumption (*cf. supra*), framed by institutional variables (the exogeneity of the money supply, supposedly controlled by the monetary authority, GT, 15, p. 205) and conventional variables, where "convention" (see further) is a non-price mode of coordination (or socialization) that ensures a certain continuity and stability in the system.

> "In practice we have tacitly agreed, as a rule, to fall back on what is, in truth, a *convention*. The essence of this convention [...] lies in assuming that the existing state of affairs will continue indefinitely, except in so far as we have specific reasons to expect a change." (GT, 12 p. 152, Keynes emphasises)

Keynes's major contribution here is to show that macroeconomic dynamics rest on microeconomic foundations, *i.e.* the adaptation and decision-making of agents in a changing, even uncertain environment. The unpredictability of an unstable world, combined with the limits of human understanding, means that when we leave the comfortable confines of certainty to enter a world where a cause lacks its accustomed effect, and where our inductions no longer follow the habit that determines us to transpose the past into the future (Hume, 1739, Book I, Part III, "of knowledge and probability," pp. 69–179), we see uncertainty as central to the study of individual decisions and behaviour.

This observation of the instability of a complex world is shared by Keynes (1921) when he expresses his skepticism about Nature's principle of uniformity, characterized by the immutability of natural laws (*ibid.*, 276)[7]. Within this framework, according to Hume[8] (*ibidem*), when we observe different effects resulting from apparently similar causes, these different effects must be taken into account whenever we need to determine the probability of an event. In other words, probabilistic reasoning enables individuals to build up "the *corpus* of knowledge" (Keynes, 1921, I, p. 7), to establish hypotheses to guide their decisions and actions "in the ordinary course of thought and argument" (*ibid.*, p. 5). Hence the need to take into account the destabilizing effects of uncertainty and risk, and the volatility of expectations (agents' visions of the future) and behaviour, which now mobilize two factors: the evaluation of a probability and the degree of confidence in the evaluation methods and criteria adopted, *i.e.* a two-level probability used by Keynes and Knight to identify uncertainty:

> "a judgment of probability is actually made in such cases. The business man himself not merely forms the best estimate he can of the outcome of his actions, but he is likely also to estimate the probability that his estimate is correct. The "degree" of certainty or of confidence felt in the conclusion after it is reached cannot be ignored, for it is of the greatest practical significance. The action which follows upon an opinion depends as much upon the amount of confidence in that opinion as it does upon the favorableness of the opinion itself. The ultimate logic, or psychology, of these deliberations is obscure, a part of the scientifically unfathomable mystery of life and mind. We must simply fall back upon a "capacity" in the intelligent animal to form more or less correct judgments about things, an intuitive sense of values. We are so built that what seems to us reasonable is likely to be confirmed by experience, or we could not live in the world at all. Fidelity to the actual psychology of the situation requires, we must insist, recognition of these two separate exercises of judgment, the formation of an estimate and the estimation of its value." (Knight, 1921, pp. 226–227)

Where the interest rate (*r*) ("a highly psychological phenomenon", TG, 15, p. 202), not "the absolute level of (*r*)" but "the degree of its divergence from what is considered a fairly *safe* level of (*r*), having regard to those calculations of probability which are being relied on" (*ibid.*, p. 201), is a measure of our doubt about the valuation methods used, in the sense that the higher the degree of confidence, the lower the level of (*r*) and this divergence. In this context, (*r*) is akin to the cost of this "safety" and money as the supreme convention, the one to which agents relate when insecurity is high, in a situation of generalized distrust and pessimism, a form of protection in the face of uncertainty.

Two main points can be highlighted here, ensuring an analytical link between the *Treatise on Probability* and GT.

Firstly, the usefulness of reasoning in an inter-temporal framework, where decisions involve events in different periods, with behaviours likely to be guided by different time horizons. For Keynes, for example, the propensity to consume depends, among other things, on the "Changes in expectations of the relation between the present and the future level of income" (GT, 8, p. 95), hence:

> "The psychological time preferences of an individual require two distinct sets of decisions to carry them out completely. The first is concerned with that aspect of time-preference which I have called the *propensity to consume*, which [...] determines for each individual how much of his income he will consume and how much he will reserve in *some* form of command over future consumption. But this decision having been made, there is a further decision which awaits him, namely, in *what form* he will hold the command over future consumption which he has reserved, whether out of his current income or from previous savings. Does he

want to hold it in the form of immediate, liquid command (i.e. in money or its equivalent)? Or is he prepared to part with immediate command for a specified or indefinite period" (GT, 13, p. 166, Keynes emphasizes)

In other words, what is the degree of his "liquidity-preference"[9]? (*ibidem*). As we can see, consumption depends positively on income throughout the life cycle, but the effect of the interest rate is indeterminate. Similarly, some of the "objective factors" (GT, 8, p. 91) that influence the propensity to consume, such as "Changes in the rate of time-discounting, *i.e.* in the ratio of exchange between present goods and future goods" (*ibid.*, p. 93, *i.e.* approximately, the interest rate) and/or "Changes in expectations of the relation between the present and the future level of income" (*ibid.*, p. 95) and/or "Changes in fiscal policy" (*ibid.*, p. 94) are typically part of an intertemporal framework, even if uncertainty and the quality of information disrupt these choices and may lead to a lack of coordination between agents.

Secondly, and related to the above, economic action takes place in the context of a plurality of actions carried out by a plurality of actors, and these combined pluralities prevent us from knowing with certainty the consequences of our actions. In other words, the complexity of the world in which individuals must make decisions and take action results both from the incompleteness and imperfection of the information that diminishes its intelligibility, and from the plurality of actions carried out by a plurality of actors, preventing us from knowing with certainty the consequences of our actions, given that the distinctions between "true" and "false" and/or between "certain" and "probable" depend on our knowledge, which in turn depends on "circumstances" (Keynes, 1921, I, p. 3), probabilities being the product of an "intellectual construction" ("argument", *ibidem*). More specifically, after quoting Leibniz as an exergue of *A Treatise on Probability* ("J'ai dit plus d'une fois qu'il faudrait une nouvelle espèce de logique, qui traiteroit des degrés de Probabilité", ["I've said more than once that we need a new kind of logic, one that deals with degrees of Probability"]), Keynes understands "probability" to mean any knowledge obtained indirectly by intellectual construction ("argument"):

"Part of our knowledge we obtain direct; and part by argument. The Theory of Probability is concerned with that part which we obtain by argument, and it treats of the different degrees in which the results so obtained are conclusive or inconclusive" (Keynes, 1921, I, p. 3)

Keynes thus assumes that rationality stems from a validation of the relationship between elements known with certainty (or even those that can be made so through knowledge) and the consequences of these elements, which are in turn probable; in other words, it is the ability of individuals to perceive, in their immediate real environment, the elements of proof (*i.e.* "evidence"[10]), the logical relationships linking the present situation to probable future evolutions, and to measure the degree of effectiveness of these evolutions, probabilities as "a guide of life" (Keynes, 1921, XXVI, p. 323)[11]. Rationality here is therefore not a maximizing calculation (of expected utility), but the ability (empirical expertise) of the individual i) to perceive and process the relevant information and elements present, ii) to deduce the results of possible interrelations between these elements and information:

> "We are merely reminding ourselves that human decisions affecting the future, whether personal or political or economic, cannot depend on strict mathematical expectation, since the basis for making such calculations does not exist; and that it is our innate urge to activity which makes the wheels go round, our rational selves choosing between the alternatives as best we are able, calculating where we can, but often falling back for our motive on whim or sentiment or chance." (GT, 12, pp. 162–163)

As we can see, Keynes considers that knowledge of the past and present does not exhaust uncertainty about the future. In order to grasp the possible logical relationships between the present and the as-yet-unknown future, Keynes believes that, in addition to sound empirical knowledge, intuition is required. For Keynes, following Moore, intuition enables the agent to escape from his own subjectivity, to sublimate it, to reach the level of objective knowledge. Within this framework, the treatment of uncertainty becomes central to the study of individuals' decisions and behaviour, and probabilistic reasoning enables them to build up "a *corpus* of knowledge" (Keynes, 1921, p. 4), to establish hypotheses to guide their decisions and actions. Intuition at the service of empirical expertise is thus at the heart of Keynes' decision-making and individual behaviour, forming a "humanized rationality" in opposition to the "standard rationality" based on a universally idealized, "calculatory" approach to the future (the purview of the Rationality of Reality, determinism and objective probabilities[12]), founded on the conception of the Laplace's school (1921, IV, p. 44 ff), a system driven by the principle of generalized intelligibility, an entirely predictable mechanical World[13], which excludes "feelings" in favour of a rationality dictated by mathematics (*ibid.*, IV, p. 55 ff), in particular, the "Principle of Indifference" (*ibid.*, IV, p. 53 ff; VII, p. 82 ff):

> "No other formula in the alchemy of logic has exerted more astonishing powers. For it has established the existence of God from the premise of total ignorance; and it has measured with numerical precision the probability that the sun will rise to-morrowtomorrow" (Keynes, 1921, VII, p. 82).

Faced with this indifference, humanized rationality, rooted in reality, opposes the pragmatic "Weight of Arguments" (Keynes, 1921, Chapter VI, pp. 71–78), a weighted reasoning that allows each individual to make his or her own "balance, not between the favourable and the unfavourable evidence, but between the absolute amounts of relevant knowledge and of relevant ignorance respectively." (*ibid.*, VI, p. 71, Keynes emphasises), a context which, *via* a "simple" footnote in the General Theory (GT, 12, p. 148), refers to the "state of confidence" on which the state of long-term expectation is based:

> "It would be foolish, in forming our expectations, to attach great weight to matters which are very uncertain (fn.: By "very uncertain" I do not mean the same thing as "very improbable".)". (GT, 12, p. 148)

Very prosaically, what Keynes means is that certain and/or relatively complete information weighs more heavily in our reasoning than uncertain and/or less credible and/or incomplete information:

> "It would be foolish, in forming our expectations, to attach great weight to matters which are very uncertain. It is reasonable, therefore, to be guided to a considerable degree by the facts about which we feel somewhat confident, even though they may be less decisively relevant to the issue than other facts about which our knowledge is vague and scanty." (GT, 12, p. 148)

The fact remains that the individual is a *social being*, hence the need to take into account, and even coordinate, his or her behaviour with that of others in order to understand how capitalism works in society. So, what happens when an individual in society, in a critical situation where uncertainty is irreducible (*i.e.* where the future is non-probabilizable), has no criterion for discriminating between different proposals or different types of possible behaviour within which he must choose (temporary withdrawal may be another solution)? In this context of uncertainty irreducible to the calculation of probabilities, agents must proceed differently and resort to "the inductive method", since "An inductive argument affirms, not that a certain matter of fact *is* so, but that *relative to certain evidence* there is a probability in its favour" (Keynes, 1921, XVIII, p. 221, Keynes emphasises), supported by "the analogy", whether "positive" or "negative", in the sense of similarities and differences respectively (*ibid.*, XIX, p. 223).

In the absence of conclusive knowledge and in the context of similarity research, Keynes (1937, p. 214) argues that mimetic (or gregarious) behaviour becomes opportune because it makes it possible to benefit from the information, supposedly less incomplete, conveyed by "others", *i.e.* the "rest of the world", in other words, the market, according to a rationality of the type: "in uncertainty, where I have no idea about the phenomenon I'm trying to evaluate, copying the other can only improve my performance since either the other shares my ignorance and my position remains unchanged, or he knows something and, by imitating him, I improve my situation." Keynes' argument is spelt out in his major article "The General Theory of Employment" (1937, p. 214, Keynes emphasizes):

> "Knowing that our own individual judgment is worthless, we endeavor to fall back on the judgment of the rest of the world which is perhaps better informed. That is, we endeavor to conform with the behavior of the majority or the average. The psychology of a society of individuals each of whom is endeavoring to copy the others leads to what we may strictly term a *conventional* judgment."

This heterodox form of rationality proposed by Keynes is opposed to that of the optimizing *homo oeconomicus* of the Classics and their successors (*ibid.*, p. 212), based on "methodological individualism", which evolves in a stable universe defined by certain economic laws, therefore known to all (symmetrical and complete information), where anticipations are easily calculable and where uncertainty is reduced to an expression, itself calculable (*ibid.*, p. 213).

In a process of generalized imitation, where markets operate according to a dynamic in which everyone copies everyone else, price becomes the result of "the mass psychology of the market" (GT, 12, p. 155), where the cost of singularity (*i.e.* emboldening oneself to do differently) becomes exorbitant, with "mass psychology", even when it emanates from "a large number of ignorant individuals", becoming "a conventional valuation" (*ibid.*, p. 154), with the consequent imperative need to follow it according to the "logic" of "you can't be right against everyone":

> "Worldly wisdom teaches that it is better for reputation to fail conventionally than to succeed unconventionally." (GT, 12, p. 158).

In addition, a process of self-fulfilling expectations can operate, in and through which a price will self-confirm even if it differs from its fundamental equilibrium level - in other words, a form of non-fundamental uncertainty (based on agents' beliefs) influencing equilibrium grandeurs. Consequently, each average market opinion corresponds to a different equilibrium, and successive shifts from one equilibrium to another *via* expectations, what contemporary theory calls conjectural (or multiple) equilibria, or even "sunspot" equilibria, which invalidate the standard view that market dynamics, particularly financial ones, converge towards a single, stable stationary equilibrium.

L2. An economy of effective demand. Let us start by noting the ambiguity of Keynes' term "effective demand", since he does not mean demand effectively realized or present on the market, but demand *anticipated* by entrepreneurs:

> "let D be the proceeds which entrepreneurs expect to receive from the employment of N men, the relationship between D and N being written D = *f*

(N), which can be called the *Aggregate Demand Function*. Now if for a given value of N the expected proceeds are greater than the aggregate supply price [Z], *i.e.* if D is greater than Z, there will be an incentive to entrepreneurs to increase employment beyond N and if necessary, to raise costs by competing with one another for the factors of production, up to the value of N for which Z has become equal to D [...] The value of D at the point of the aggregate demand function, where it is intersected by the aggregate supply function, will be called *the effective demand*." (GT, 3, p. 25, Keynes emphasizes)

Consequently, it is the aggregate effective demand (D), *i.e.* "the aggregate income (or proceeds) which the entrepreneurs expect to receive [...] from the amount of current employment which they decide to give" (GT, 6, p. 55), which determines the level of production implemented, *i.e.* the aggregate supply (Z), hence the meaning of the title of Chapter 5 of GT: "Expectation as determining output and employment". Entrepreneurs' short- and long-term forecasts (production costs *via* "user cost" [GT, Appendix on user cost, pp. 66–73][14] and sale-proceeds), as determining output and employment (GT, Chapter 5, pp. 46–51), are subject to the same problems as those noted above (*cf. L1*), and if these forecasts are subject to error, the possibility of fluctuations in employment and inventories.

With these reservations, (D) corresponds to the maximum profit forecast by entrepreneurs, and therefore ensures the optimum for producers, but not necessarily for employees. The quantity of labour that entrepreneurs decide to employ (N) is therefore the result of ($D = f(N) = D_1 + D_2$), with (D_1) the amount of aggregate consumption expected, *i.e.* "the amount which the community is expected to spend on consumption",GT, 3, p. 29), which depends on "The fundamental psychological law" (or "psychological law", Keynes, 1937, p. 220) (*cf. supra*), and (D_2) the amount of expected new investment, *i.e.* "the amount which the community is expected to devote to new investment" (GT, 3, p. 29), linked to "the psychological expectation of future yield from capital".

The general theory of employment, then, is as follows: the level of employment (N) is set in order to achieve the production planned by firms, in other words, it is determined on the basis of the expected outlets that make up effective demand:

"We have shown that when effective demand is deficient there is under-employment of labour sense that there are men unemployed who would be willing to work at less than the existing real wage." (GT, 20, p. 289)

L3. An economy of involuntary unemployment. It follows from (*L2*) that the primary cause of unemployment is not a dysfunction (rigidity) of the real wage adjustment mechanism in a hypothetical labour market, *i.e.* "the equality of the real wage to the marginal disutility [...] corresponds to the absence of 'involuntary' unemployment" (GT, 2, p. 15), second classical postulate. Keynes' antiphrase can be explained as follows: while admitting the first "fundamental postulate" of classical employment theory (*ibid*., p. 5), according to which "the wage is equal to the marginal product of labour", Keynes rejects the second, according to which "the utility of the wage when a given volume of labour is employed is equal to the marginal disutility of that amount of employment" (*ibidem*). In other words, Keynes accepts the "Classical" labour demand function but rejects the supply curve, hence the impossibility of conceiving of a "labour market", since the initiative for employment belongs to entrepreneurs. In this framework, involuntary unemployment is defined as follows:

> "Men are involuntary unemployed if, in the event of a small rise in the price of wage-goods relatively to the money-wage, both the aggregate supply of labour willing to work for the current money-wage and the aggregate demand for it at that wage would be greater than the existing volume of employment." (GT, 2, p. 15)

As we can see, involuntary unemployment emerges, here, with a fall in the real wage (resulting not from a fall in the nominal wage, favoured by the "Classics", but from a rise in the prices of consumer goods, *i.e.* $[\downarrow(w/p)\,with(w \rightarrow /p\uparrow)]$), which generates a higher level of employment (*via* the increase in labour demand) through the absorption of a hitherto unemployed labour supply. The origin of this fall is important because, for Keynes, individuals do not necessarily adopt the same behaviour (*i.e.* behavioural heterogeneity) when faced with situations that, in turn, generate the same effect, in this case, the fall in their purchasing power ($\Delta(w/p) < 0$):

> "although a reduction in the existing money-wage would lead to a withdrawal of labour, it does not follow that a fall in the value of the existing money-wage in terms of wage-goods would do so, if it were due to a rise in the price of the latter. In other words, it may be the case that within a certain range the demand of labour is for a minimum money-wage and not for a minimum real wage. The classical school have tacitly assumed that this would involve no significant change in their theory. But this is not so. For if the supply of labour is not a function of real wages as its sole variable, their argument breaks down entirely and leaves the question of what the actual employment will be quite indeterminate [...] Whilst workers will usually resist a reduction of money-wages, it is not their practice to withdraw their labour whenever there is a rise in the price of wage-goods." (GT, 2, pp. 8–9)

These different interpretations of the same phenomenon can be explained by the imperfection of information (or a "money illusion" as to how it is processed[15]) that affects the optimization calculation performed by each agent, which consists of equalizing his marginal rate of substitution "consumption *vs.* leisure" with the real wage rate given as a condition for his participation in the labour market. Another explanation lies in what may be termed equity sensitivity, *i.e.* "social justice" (TG, 19, p. 268), *i.e.* a nominal wage cut (*w*) may be perceived as an individual or categorical measure, or even disciplinary (*i.e.* a sanction) by the agent concerned, whereas a decrease in (*w*/*p*) through inflation concerns "the purchasing-power of money which affects all workers alike" (TG, 2, p. 14), thus appearing as more "equitable" (or less discriminatory):

> "since there is, as a rule, no means of securing a simultaneous and equal reduction of money-wages in all industries, it is in the interest of all workers to resist a reduction in their own particular case. In fact, a movement by employers to revise money-wage bargains downward will be much more strongly resisted than a gradual and automatic lowering of real wages as a result of rising prices." (GT, 19, p. 264).

Finally, the "consent" of the workforce to lower wages (real or nominal) depends on the levels and dynamics of employment (*N*) (GT, 2, p. 10) and the way they are perceived by agents. The behaviours resulting from these different situations are different: when (*w*) decreases, the agent does not hastily conclude that it is the same in other companies. He may be encouraged to resign and look elsewhere for a better-paid job. When (*p*) increases, employees believe that the drop in (*w*/*p*) affects all activities. In the absence of opportunity, they keep their jobs. Hence the downward rigidity of (*w*) and the relative disconnection of the "existing level of money-wage" with "the marginal disutility of labour" (GT, 2, p. 8), *i.e.* the opposite of the presuppositions of the "classical economists", from which it follows that "within a certain range the demand of labour is for a minimum money-wage and not for a minimum real wage" (*ibidem*). But Classic theory "maintains, in short, that the wage bargains between the entrepreneurs and the workers determine the real wage" (GT, 2, p. 11). If this is not verified in practice, so if these negotiations do indeed determine (*w*) and not (*w*/*p*), "then there is no longer any reason to expect a tendency towards equality between the real wage and the marginal disutility of labour." (*ibidem*). *In fine*, Keynes remarks mischievously:

> "Thus it is fortunate that the workers, though unconsciously, are instinctively more reasonable economists than the classical school [...] Every trade union will put up some resistance to a cut in money-wage, however small. But since no trade union would dream of striking on every occasion of a rise in the cost of living, they do not raise the obstacle to any increase in aggregate employment which is attributed to them by the classical school." (GT, 2, pp. 14–15)

As we can see, unemployment is explained not by the operating characteristics of a hypothetical competitive "labour market" but fundamentally by those of the goods and money markets, which condition monetary purchasing power, *i.e.* the value of (*w*/*p*):

> "Thus the volume of employment is not determined by the marginal disutility of labour measured in terms of real wages, except in so far the supply of labour available at a given real wage sets a *maximum* level to employment. The propensity to consume and the rate of new investment determine between them the volume of employment, and the volume of employment is uniquely related to a given level of real wages – not the other way round." (GT, 3, p. 30)

Consequently, it is the propensity to consume and the amount of new investment, as determinants of effective demand (*cf. L2*), that set (*N*) (and not the "price" of labour, which would be the wage), and it is the insufficiency of this aggregate effective demand (*D*) (GT, 20, p. 289) which is the cause of involuntary unemployment, establishing an equivalence between involuntary unemployment and deficient effective demand, with insufficient anticipation of the revenues expected from the sale of production leading to job creation below "full employment":

> "the volume of employment (and consequently of output and real income) is fixed by the entrepreneur under the motive of seeking to maximise his present and prospective profits [...] whilst the volume of employment which will maximise his profit depends on the aggregate demand function given by his expectations of the sum of the proceeds resulting from consumption and investment respectively on various hypotheses [...] the object of the employment function being to relate the amount of the effective demand, measured in terms of the wage-unit, directed to a given firm or industry or to industry as a whole with the amount of employment, the supply price of the output of which will compare to that amount of effective demand." (GT, 7, p. 77; 20, p. 280)

L4. An economy of money and interest within an economy of production, as opposed to the "classical" dichotomous conception of an economy of exchange, in which money has the same importance as goods in the formation and enjoyment of wealth. Thus, money wages represent a *prevision* of money liquidity, enabling the acquisition of an as yet undetermined quantity of goods. In other words, they represent an *advance*, and therefore uncertain, purchasing power, which must be applied to the monetary value of goods yet to be produced. Similarly, the recruitment of an employee is characterized by the *advance* of this money wage by the entrepreneur, who *hopes* that it will be at least equal to the marginal productivity of this employee, who, for his part, is unaware of the precise purchasing power vested in this wage, and therefore of the level of compensation for the disutility associated with this work.

Here again, as in (*L1*), (*L2*) and (*L3*), future events inform present decisions to consume or produce, which depend, moreover, on the intensity of the desire to hold and accumulate wealth. Consequently, each agent has two decisions to make in order to realize his time preferences: the first concerns his propensity to consume (cf. above), the second refers to the unconsumed part of his income (*i.e.* his "some form of command over future consumption", GT, 13, p. 166), which he can keep in liquid form ("the form of immediate, liquid command") or place (*i.e.* "prepared to part with immediate command for a secified or indefinite period") for future return, depending on the "degree of his liquidity-preference" (*ibidem*). On the entrepreneur's side, it is also necessary to take time into account, due to i) production lead times, ii) the dependence of current production decisions on the choice between immediate or deferred use of available resources.

In both cases, money, "*par excellence* 'liquid'" (GT, 17, p. 234), constitutes "a link between the present and the future" (GT, 21, p. 293); by its perennial existence, it makes up for our legitimate anxiety about the future by giving us, through its attribute of liquidity, *i.e.* its total availability, its universal character and its capacity to be accumulated "without limits" (*i.e.* money with nil yield and negligible cost of carrying, but with a substantial liquidity-premium, GT, 17, p. 226), a hold on the totality of goods and securities, a security aimed at allaying our legitimate anxieties[16] linked to the fact that we have "only the vaguest idea of any but the most direct consequences of our acts", "the fact that we know very little about the future" (Keynes, 1937, p. 213, 215), our knowledge of the future being, contrary to classical postulates, "fluctuating, vague and uncertain" (*ibidem*), since factors such as fear, hope, disillusionment, *etc.* condition human conduct (*ibid.*, p. 215). The counterpart of this "insurance" is a "liquidity premium" (GT, 17, pp. 226–227), a kind of opportunity cost paid by its holders (*ibid.*, p. 227).

Considering the special status of money, the monetary interest rate (r) becomes central as a reward for the renunciation of liquidity, (r) becomes a psychological monetary element, setting the "price" of liquidity, the premium necessary to compensate for the cost of its separation. Faced with this separation, the uniqueness of the market rate of interest (r), for a given period, resembles a convenience, a simplification of the "complex of rates of interest for various terms" (GT, 11, p. 143), where the plurality of rates, the expression of agents' expectations, can be explained by the duration for which liquidity is renounced:

> "For the sake of simplicity of statement I have slurred the point that we are dealing with complexes of rates of interest and discount corresponding to the different lengths of time which will elapse before the various prospective returns from the asset are realised. But it is not difficult to re-state the argument so as to cover this point [knowing that] expectations, which are held concerning the complex of rates of interest for various terms which will rule in the future, will be partially reflected in the complex of rates of interest which rule to-day." (GT, 11, p. 137 n., 143)

(r) is therefore a "price", that of liquidity for a given money supply ($\bar{M}$), the one required for the agent to consent to the marginal disutility of reducing his liquid holdings:

> "the rate of interest at any time, being the reward for parting with liquidity, is a measure of the unwillingness of those who possess money to part with their liquid control over it. The rate of interest is not the "price" which brings into equilibrium the demand for resources to invest with the readiness to abstain from present consumption. It is the "price" which equilibrates the desire to hold wealth in the form of cash with the available quantity of cash; which implies that if the rate of interest were lower, *i.e.* if the reward for parting with cash were diminished, the aggregate amount of cash which the public would wish to hold would exceed the available supply, and that if the rate of interest were raised, there would be a surplus of cash which no one would be willing to hold." (GT, 13, p. 167)

The setting of the interest rate in relation to the "psychological preferences" of agents is the subject of a specific "General Theory" (GT, Chapter 13, pp. 165–174), in which Keynes first opposes the classical tradition of the "natural rate of interest", asserting that "the rate of interest cannot be a return to saving or waiting as such" (GT, 13, pp. 166–167), which would balance "the demand for investment and the willingness to save" (GT, 14, p. 175), by mobilizing a simple argument: "For if a man hoards his savings in cash, he earns no interest, though he saves just as much as before" (GT, 13, p. 167), while this hoarding can (and should) be understood as "a first approximation to the concept of *Liquidity-preference*", a factor in determining the level of (*r*) at which "the aggregate desire to hoard" becomes compatible with "the available cash" (*ibid.*, p. 174), hence the idea of an interest rate as "the reward of not-hoarding" and not as "the reward of not-spending" (*ibid.*). Secondly, like rates of return on loans and investments, (*r*) cannot be a simple reward of waiting as such, but "the reward of running the risk":

> "There is, in truth, no sharp line between [the rates of return on loans or investments] and so-called "pure" rate of interest, all of them being the reward for running the risk of uncertainty of one kind or another. Only in the event of money being used solely for transactions and never as a store of value [*i.e.* "Partial money" in the sense of Hicks, see Box, Part II, chap.4], would a different theory become appropriate." (GT, 14, p. 182)

Within this framework, alongside "rational" transaction and precautionary motives, there are "instinctive grounds" (Keynes, 1937, p. 216) for holding cash as a store of value, found at the deepest level of our motivations, which act as "a barometer of the degree of our distrust of our own calculations and conventions concerning the future" (*ibidem*). Money "takes charge" at times when the most precariously scaffolded conventions have weakened (*ibidem*). Ultimately, the possession of money soothes our anxiety, and the premium (*r*) that we require to separate ourselves from the money fairly accurately reflects our level of disquiet.

The interaction of these four lemmas {*L*1 ... *L*4}, *i.e.* an economy of 1) decisions in an uncertain and risky future, 2) effective demand, 3) involuntary unemployment, 4) money and interest, leads Keynes to two demonstrations {*D*1, *D*2}:

D1. A stable and durable state of underemployment. The flexibility of the money-wage rate (w) does not necessarily ensure a return to full employment, as a decrease in (w) by "the reduction in money-wage [is] reducing the purchasing power of some workers" (TG, 19, p. 258) can lead to a drop in effective demand. Consequently, a fall in (w) increases employment only if it i) lowers the interest rate, ii) increases the marginal efficiency of capital, becoming "a stimulus to output" (*ibid.*, p. 257). (i) means that a fall in (w) leads to a fall in prices (*ibid.*, p. 258, 262) and in money income, reducing the need for liquid cash (*i.e.* the preference for liquidity)[17] thus lowering the interest rate (r) (*ibid.*, p. 263). (ii) means that a rise in the marginal productivity of capital relative to (r) stimulates investment (*ibid.*, p. 267) (fuelled by an "optimistic tone in the minds of entrepreneurs" due to the fall in (r) (*cf.* i) and the fall in (w), *ibid.*, p. 264), with agents anticipating that (w) has fallen relative to its future level ("a reduction relatively to money-wages in the future", *ibid*, p. 263), without inscribing this reduction in the long term (*i.e.* "the expectation, or even to the serious possibility, of a further wage-reduction in prospect", *ibidem*) because in the latter case, ($\Delta w < 0$) can lead to the "postponement" of consumption and investment, and thus a reduction in the marginal efficiency of capital (*ibid.*). As a result:

> "There is, therefore, no ground for the belief that a flexible wage policy is capable of maintaining a state of continuous full employment; - any more than for the belief than an open-market monetary policy is capable, unaided, of achieving this result. The economic system cannot be made self-adjusting along these lines." (GT, 19, p. 267)

The rarity and ephemeral nature (*i.e.* "short-lived occurrence") of "full or even approximately full employment", and therefore the ability of this system to evolve durably, with relative stability (apart from social and political risks, see above), in "a chronic condition of sub-normal activity for a considerable period" (GT, 18, p. 249) is explained not by the flexibility of nominal wages[18], than by "conditions of stability" such as: i) when the marginal propensity to consume, which conditions the induced effects in terms of the level of production, converges the value of the multiplier "is greater than unity but not very large" (*ibid.* p. 250), which corresponds to a "psychological characteristic of human nature" insofar "as real income increases, both the pressure of present needs diminishes and the margin over the established standard of life is increased; and as real income diminishes the opposite is true"[19]; ii) when the prospective yield on capital or the level of the interest rate varies moderately, which stabilizes "the rate of investment" (*ibid.*, p. 250) and thus, by increasing the predictability of the future, also stabilizes the volatility of behavior in business communities: "this condition sets a limit to the instability resulting from rapid changes in the prospective yield of capital-assets due to sharp fluctuations in business pschology or to epoch-making inventions" (*ibid.*, p. 252) ; iii) because investment flows linked to the wear and tear of capital and its necessary replacement, or to obsolescence as premature wear and tear (by technology) of capital, ensure stabilization (and downward rigidity) of "the marginal efficiency of capital" and thus smooth the scale of "alternate recession and recovery" (*ibid.*, p. 253).

As we can see, Keynes' reasoning does not explicitly refer to the problem of specifying an "underemployment *equilibrium*", but rather to describing, with the help of a General Theory, the "outstanding characteristic of the economic system in which we live that" of not being "violently unstable" (*ibid.*, p. 249):

> "Indeed [our economic system] seems capable of remaining in a chronic condition of sub-normal activity for a considerable period without any marked tendency either towards recovery or towards complete collapse. Moreover, the evidence indicates that full, or even approximately full, employment is of rare and short-lived occurrence. Fluctuations may start briskly but seem to wear themselves out before they have proceeded to great extremes, and a intermediate situation which is neither desperate nor satisfactory is our normal lot." (GT, 18, pp. 249–250)

But, Keynes continues:

> "we must not conclude that the mean position thus determined by "natural" tendencies, namely, by those tendencies which are likely to persist, failing measures expressly designed to correct them, is, therefore, established by laws of necessity. The unimpeded rule of the above conditions is a fact of observation concerning the world as it is or has been, and not a necessary principle which cannot be changed." (GT, 18, p. 254)

D2. The effectiveness of government and economic policies in converging towards full employment. As the level of employment results from the level of effective demand, any economic policy oriented towards (*D*) is likely to compensate for its deficiencies and reduce its fluctuations, making it possible, respectively, to approximate the level of demand for full employment and to reduce the uncertainty of forecasts, a condition for the coordination of individuals' expectations, and, more generally, for the definition of an environment allowing "curbed" or "guided" "the free play of economic forces" in order to realize all "the full potentialities of production" (GT, 24, p. 379):

> "The central controls necessary to ensure full employment will, of course, involve a large extension of the traditional functions of government [...] But there will still remain a wide field for the exercise of private initiative

and responsibility. Within this field the traditional advantages of individualism will still hold good [...] the enlargement of the functions of government, involved in the task of adjusting to one another the propensity to consume and the inducement to invest [...] both as the only practicable means of avoiding the destruction of existing economic forms in their entirety and as the condition of the successful functioning of individual initiative." (TG, 24, pp. 379–380)

As we can see, public interventionism is primarily at the service of employment, and while this mission is *essential*, since the problem of unemployment is a global economic phenomenon and not the effect of the incapacity of certain individuals, it remains *limited*: i) in time, since it is a question of correcting a situation of underemployment resulting from a low "degree of consilience between private and public advantage" (*ibid.*, p. 379) until "central controls" succeed in establishing "an aggregate volume of output corresponding to full employment as nearly as is practicable" (*ibidem*); ii) in its ambitions, as regards the activities concerned and the instruments implemented:

"For whilst it indicates the vital importance of establishing certain central controls in matters which are now left in the main to individual initiative, there are wide fields of activity which are unaffected. The State will have to exercise a guiding influence on the propensity to consume partly through its scheme of taxation, partly by fixing the rate of interest [Furthermore] a somewhat comprehensive socialisation of investment will prove the only means of securing an approximation to full employment; though this need not exclude all manner of compromises and of devices by which public authority will co-operate with private initiative." (GT, 24, pp. 377–378).

Thus, the "socialisation of investment" (GT, 24, p. 378) is akin to the state *correcting* the failure of the competitive market to coordinate heterogeneous agents (rather than substituting them), which leads to unemployment. It is therefore not a question of "socialising economic life" (*ibid.*, p. 379), *a fortiori* of constituting a "homogeneous or totalitarian state" that could solve the problem of unemployment but "at the expense of efficiency and of freedom" (*ibid.*, p. 381), but of correcting the unemployment inevitably associated "with present-day capitalistic individualism" (*ibidem*).

The remedy for the "greatest economic evils of our time", such as the "great inequalities of wealth" and/or "the unemployment of Labour" and/or "the disappointment of reasonable business expectations" and/or "the impairment of efficiency and production", then necessarily lies "outside the operations of individuals", as they are the fruits "of risk, uncertainty, and ignorance" that "particular individuals, fortunate in situation or in abilities" use for their own strict purposes (Keynes, 1926, p. 47), hence the need for "deliberate control of the currency and of credit by a central institution" (*ibid.*, p. 48), for the full publication, by legal constraint if necessary, of the facts that it is useful to know in business markets, in order to reduce informational asymmetries and incompleteness and provide society with "better knowledge than we have now for taking the next step" (*ibidem*), or for the State to take greater responsibility for "directly organizing investment" (GT, 12, p. 164), in order to bring private initiative and entrepreneurship back into line with "the general social advantage" (*ibidem*). But once these corrections have been made, the market economy, with an individualism freed of "its defects and its abuses", as "the best safeguard of personal liberty [that] greatly widens the field for the exercise of personal choice" (TG, 24, p. 380), will have to be restored to its legitimacy and operability. Public action, as a "co-ordinated act of intelligent judgment" (Keynes, 1926, p. 48), then becomes the very condition for the durability of the reformed exercise of individual liberties, which would no longer be entirely abandoned "to the chances of private judgment and private profits" (*ibid.*, p. 49), by guaranteeing a stable and secure institutional framework, favouring predictability and therefore projection into the future, and, in so doing, allowing these initiatives, decisions and individual behaviours to flourish.

Notes

1 An example from the classic literature may illustrate our point: when Keynes refers to "effective demand" (GT, Chapter 3), he repeatedly refers to Malthus (GT, 3, p. 32; 23, pp. 362–364, 369, 371) without once mentioning the "radical" Sismondi. The same is true when, in his "Essays in Biography", he pays tribute to Malthus, "The First of the Cambridge Economists" (Keynes, 1951, pp. 81–124).

2 In this respect, it is interesting to reproduce the first paragraph of "An open letter to President Roosevelt", written by Keynes on December 31, 1933, whose content also illustrates the "entre-deux" described above: "You have made yourself the Trustee for those in every country who seek to mend the evils of our condition by reasoned experiment within the framework of the existing social system. If you fail, rational change will be gravely prejudiced throughout the world, leaving orthodoxy and revolution to fight it out. But if you succeed, new and bolder methods will be tried everywhere, and we may date the first chapter of a new economic era from your accession to office. This is a sufficient reason why I should venture to lay my reflections before you, though under the disadvantages of distance and partial knowledge."

3 "The fundamental psychological law, upon which we are entitled with great confidence both *a priori* from our knowledge of human nature and from the detailed facts of experience, is that men are disposed, as a ruleand on the average, to increase their consumption as their income increases, but not by as much as the increase in their income." (GT, 8, p. 96).

4 "the marginal efficiency [...] depends on the *prospective* yield of capital, and not merely on its current yield" (GT, 11, p. 141) hence the first risk, "the entrepreneur's or borrower's risk and arises out of doubts in his own mind as to the probability of his actually earning the prospective yield for which he hopes" (*ibid.*, 11, p. 144), accompanied, in the case of loans, by the "lender's risk" caused by "the possible insufficiency of the margin of security, i.e. involuntary default due to the disappointment of expectation", second risk that affects the calculation of the "minimum prospective yield which will induce the investment" (*ibidem*). All these forecasts, these visions of the future, which determine the expected yield on capital,

are, finally, conditioned by "The State of Long-Term Expectation" (GT, chapter 12), which depends on "not solely on the most forecast we can make [but] also depends on the *confidence* with which we make this forecast – on how highly we rate the likelihood of our best forecast turning out quite wrong." (GT, 12, p. 148)

5 "in any given state of expectation, there is in the minds of the public a certain potentiality towards holding cash beyond what is required by the transactions-motive or the precautionary-motive, which will realise itself in actual cash-holdings in a degree which depends on the terms on which the monetary authority is willing to create cash." (GT, 15, p. 205)

6 The representation of uncertainty and risk in economic life is based on the now classic distinction made by Knight (1921, VIII, p. 233) : "The practical difference between the two categories, risk and uncertainty, is that in the former the distribution of the outcome in a group of instances is known (either through calculation *a priori* or from statistics of past experience), while in the case of uncertainty this is not true, the reason being in general that it is impossible to form a group of instances, because the situation dealt with is in a high degree unique." In a situation of risk, agents can therefore associate a probability distribution of outcomes with each of their strategies, whereas in a situation of uncertainty, the decision-maker is unable to establish such distributions. This dichotomy makes it possible to apply the criterion of maximizing expected utility to a situation of risk, and the criterion of statistical decision theory to a situation of uncertainty.

7 "The Law of the Uniformity of Nature appears to me to amount to an assertion that an analogy which is perfect, except that mere differences of position in time and space are treated as irrelevant" (*ibid.*, XIX, p. 226) and, further on: "The Principe of the Uniformity of Nature [...] supplies the answer, if it is correct, to the criticism that the instances, on which generalisations are based, are all alike in being past, and that any generalisation, which is applicable to the future, must be based, for this reason, upon imperfect analogy." (*ibid.*, XXII, p. 256).

8 It is interesting to note, in the context of this book, that Keynes (with Piero Sraffa) was the editor of the "Abstract of a Treatise of Human Nature" (Hume, 1938) where in the introduction he questions the identity of a certain "Mr Smith" (wondering whether this is "Adam" or not, *ibid.*, p. xiii and ff), contained in a letter, dated March 4, 1740, written by David Hume and addressed to Francis Hutcheson: "My bookseller has sent to Mr Smith a Copy of my Book [*i.e.* the *Abstract*], which I hope he has receiv'd, as well as your Letter. I have not yet heard what he has done with the Abstract. Perhaps you have. I have got it printed in London; but not in the Works of the Learned; there having been an article with regard to my Book, somewhat abusive, printed in that Work, before I sent up the Abstract." (*ibid.*, p. xiii)

9 "an individual's liquidity-preference is given by a schedule of the amounts of his resources, valued in terms of money or of wage units, which he will wish to retain in the form of money in different sets of circumstances." (GT, 13, p. 166). Under uncertainty, investors, for example, may choose to suspend their decision and delay their commitment until they have more (or better) information. Here, the level of holding of cash, an asset with no intrinsic return at zero risk, *i.e.* the "liquidity premium", will depend not on investors' beliefs about the possible outcomes of investment choices as such, but on investors' distrust of their calculations and conventions concerning the future or the conventions adopted to dispense with these calculations (see below).

10 "the probability of the same statement varies with the evidence presented, which is, as it were, its origin of reference." (*ibid.*, I, p. 7).

11 "The importance of probability can only be derived from the judgment that it is *rational* to be guided by it in action; and a practical dependence on it can only be

justified by a judgment that in action we *ought* to act to take some account of it. It is for this reason that probability is to us the "guide of life"", (*ibid.*, XXVI, p. 323; Keynes emphasises)

12 For Keynes, Subjective probabilities are "a sort of Probability which depends upon knowledge and ignorance, and is relative, in some manner, to the mind of the subject" (*ibid.*, XXIV, p. 281) which differ from Objective probabilities "which is not thus dependent, or less completely so, though precisely what this conception stands for is not plain" (*ibidem*). *i.e.* "the antithesis between knowledge and ignorance, between events, that is to say, which we have some reason to expect, and events which we have no reason to expect, which gives rise to the theory of subjective probability and subjective chance; and, connected with this, the distinction between "random" selection and "biased" selection. There are next objective probability and objective chance, which are as yet obscure, but which are commonly held to arise out of the antithesis between "cause" and "chance," between events, that is to say, which are causally connected and events which are not causally connected." (*ibidem*). Here Keynes relies partly on David Hume's taxonomy (1739, Book II, Part III, Section IX, p. 444): "Probability is of two kinds, either when the object is really in itself uncertain, and to be determined by chance; or when, though the object be already certain, yet 'tis uncertain to our judgment, which finds a number of proofs on each side of the question. Both these kinds of probabilities cause fear and hope; which can only proceed from that property, in which they agree, viz. the uncertainty and fluctuation they bestow on the imagination by that contrariety of views, which is common to both."

13 In his "Théorie analytique des Probabilités", Laplace (1812) states in his introduction (*ibid.*, p. 3) that: "Si l'on considère les méthodes analytiques auxquelles la théorie des probabilités a déjà donné naissance, et celles qu'elle peut faire naître encore; la justesse des principes qui lui servent de base, la logique rigoureuse et délicate qu'exige leur emploi dans la solution des problèmes; les établissements d'utilité publique qui s'appuient sur elles: si l'on observe ensuite que dans les choses même qui ne peuvent être soumises au calcul, cette théorie donne les aperçus les plus sûrs qui puissent nous guider dans nos jugemens, et qu'elle apprend à se garantir des illusions qui souvent nous égarent; on verra qu'il n'est point de science plus digne de nos méditations, et dont les résultats soient plus utiles." [If we consider the analytical methods to which the theory of probabilities has already given rise, and those which it may yet give rise to; the soundness of the principles on which it is based, the rigorous and delicate logic required for their use in the solution of problems; the establishments of public utility which rely on them: if we then observe that, even in things that cannot be subjected to calculation, this theory provides the surest insights that can guide us in our judgments, and that it teaches us to guard against the illusions that often lead us astray; we will see that there is no science more worthy of our meditations, and whose results are more useful].

14 "User cost constitutes one of the links between the present and the future." (GT, p. 69) since the entrepreneur is faced with a choice between "using up his equipment now and preserving it to be used later on" (*ibid.*, p. 70). As a result, "it is the expected sacrifice of future benefit involved in present use which determines the amount of the user cost, and it is the marginal amount of this sacrifice which, together with the marginal factor cost and the expectation of the marginal proceeds, determines his scale of production." (*ibidem*)

15 This "money illusion" operates on the employee side, by underestimating the loss of purchasing power linked to a more than proportional rise in (p) compared to the (possible) rise in (w), *i.e.* a fall of (w/p), but can also operate on the entrepreneurial side: "For a time at least, rising prices may delude entrepreneurs into increasing

employment beyond the level which maximises their individual profits measured in terms of the product." (GT, 20, p. 290)

16 "The possession of actual money lulls our disquietude; and the premium which we require to make us part with money is the measure of our disquietude." (Keynes, 1937, p. 216)

17 if and only if the reduction in (w) does not cause social tensions and political instability because "if the reduction in wages disturbs political confidence by causing popular discontent, the increase in liquidity-preference due to this cause may more than offset the release of cash from the active circulation [in other words] labour troubles may offset this favourable factor" (GT, 19, pp. 263–264)

18 "When there is a change in employment, money-wages tend to change in the same direction as, but not in great disproportion to, the change in employment; *i.e.* moderate changes in employment are not associated with very great changes in money-wages. This is a condition of the stability of prices rather than of employment." (GT, 18, p. 251)

19 So that: "it is natural – at any rate on the average of the community – that current consumption should be expanded when employment increases, but by less than the full increment of real income; and that it should be diminished when employment diminishes, but by less than the full decrement of real income." (GT, 18, p. 251)

Bibliography

Blaug, Mark (1985). *Economic theory in retrospect (1962)*. Cambridge: Cambridge University Press, fourth edition.

Dostaler, Gilles (2007). *Keynes and his battles*, Cheltenham (UK), Northampton, MA, (USA): Edward Elgar Publishing Limited. An augmented and revised edition of *Keynes et ses combats*, Paris, Albin Michel, 2005.

Galbraith, John Kenneth (1952). *American capitalism. The concept of countervailing power*. Cambridge, MA: Houghton Mifflin Company Boston, The Riverside Press Cambridge.

Galbraith, John Kenneth (1955). *The great crash 1929. A striking study of the greatest speculative boom in history and of the catastrophe which followed it*. London: Hamish Hamilton Ltd.

Gilles, Philippe (2009). *Histoire des crises et des cycles économiques. Des crises industrielles du 19ème siècle aux crises actuelles*. Paris: A. Colin, coll. "U", 2ème édition.

Guitton, Henri (1979). *De l'imperfection en économie*. Paris: Calmann-Lévy, coll. "Perspectives de l'économique".

Hicks, John Richard (1937). Mr. Keynes and the "Classics"; a suggested interpretation. *Econometrica*, *5*(2), April, 147–159.

Hicks, John Richard (1939). *Value and capital: An inquiry into some fundamental principles of economic theory*. Oxford: Clarendon Press.

Hume, David (1739). *A treatise on human nature: Being an attempt to introduce the experimental method of reasoning into moral subjects*. London: Printed for John Noon, at the White-Hart, near Mercer's-Chapel in Cheapside..

Hume, David (1938). *An abstract of a treatise of human nature (1740)*. Cambridge: At the University Press. A Pamphlet hitherto unknow by David Hume, Reprinted with an Introduction by J. M . Keynes and P. Sraffa.

Keynes, John Maynard (1921). *A treatise on probability*. London: MacMillan and Co, Limited, St. Martin's Street.

Keynes, John Maynard (1926). *The end of Laissez-Faire*. London: Hogarth Press.
Keynes, John Maynard (1931). *Essays in Persuasion*. London: MacMillan and Co, Limited, St. Martin's Street.
Keynes, John Maynard (1936). *The general theory of employment interest and money*. London: MacMillan and Co, Limited, St. Martin's Street.
Keynes, John Maynard (1937). The general theory of employment. *The Quarterly Journal of Economics*, *51*(2), February, 209–223.
Keynes, John Maynard (1951). *Essays in biography (1933)*, New Edition with Three Additional Essays edited by. In Geoffrey Keynes (Eds.). London: Rupert Hart-Davis, 36 Soho Square.
Keynes, John Maynard (1969). *Théorie générale de l'emploi, de l'intérêt et de la monnaie* (1936). Paris: Payot, "Bibliothèque scientifique Payot".
Knight, Frank Hyneman (1921). *Risk, uncertainty and profit*. Boston and New York: Houghton Mifflin Company, The Riverside Press Cambridge.
Laplace, Pierre-Simon de (1812). *Théorie analytique des Probabilités*, Paris: Mme Veuve Courcier, Imprimeur-Libraire pour les Mathématiques, Quai des Augustins, n°57.
Samuelson, Paul Anthony (1946). Lord Keynes and the general theory. *Econometrica*, *14*(3), July, 187–200.
Schumpeter, Joseph Alois (1966). *History of economic analysis (1954)*. New York: Oxford Universty Press, sixth edition.
Shackle, George Lennox Sharman (1967). *The years of high theory. Invention & tradition in economic thought 1926–1939*. Cambridge (Ill.): Cambridge University Press.

8 Enterprise, speculation, convention, and human nature or economic instability as a consequence of the state of long-term expectation

Investment decisions and the "state of the long-term expectation"

As defined above, the "Keynes model" contained in GT, according to which capitalism produces unemployment even in a competitive environment (with flexible prices and wages), functions as "the theory of a system in which changing views about the future are capable of influencing the present situation [capable of analysing] the problems of the real world in which our previous expectations are liable to disappointment and expectations concerning the future affect what we doto-day" (GT, 21, pp. 293–294). This "theory of shifting equilibrium" must necessarily be conceived within the framework of a monetary economy, since money constitutes "a link between the present and the future" (*ibid.*, p. 293):

> "Money in its significant attributes is, above all, a subtle device for linking the present to the future; and we cannot even begin to discuss the effect of changing expectations on current activities except in monetary terms. We cannot get rid of money even by abolishing gold and silver and legal tender instruments. So long as there exists any durable asset, it is capable of possessing monetary attributes and, therefore, of giving rise to the characteristic problems of a monetary economy." (GT, 21, p. 294)

In addition to money, the link between the present and the future is provided by certain assets characterized by three attributes (GT, 17, pp. 225–226): i) "some assets produce a yield or output [...] by assisting some process of production or supplying services to a consumer"; ii) "Most assets, except money, suffer some wastage or involve some cost through the mother passage of time [...] irrespective of their being used to produce a yield"; iii) "the power of disposal over an asset during a period may offer a potential convenience or security, which is not equal for assets of different kinds, though the assets themselves are of equal initial value". The amount concerning by iii) is called by Keynes "liquidity-premium".

Among these assets, "the investment or capital-asset" best illustrates these intertemporal effects *via* "the schedule of the marginal efficiency of capital":

DOI: 10.4324/9781032649054-15

> "The schedule of the marginal efficiency of capital is of fundamental importance because it is mainly through this factor (much more than through the rate of interest) that the expectation of the future influences the present [...] The fact that the assumptions of the static state often underlie present-day economic theory, imports into it a large element of unreality. But the introduction of the concepts of user cost [cf. supra] and of the marginal efficiency of capital [...] will have the effect, I think, of bringing it back to reality [...] It is by reason of the existence of durable equipment that the economic future is linked to the present. It is, therefore, consonant with, and agreeable to, our broad principles of thought, that the expectation of the future should affect the present through the demand price for durable equipment." (GT, 11, pp. 145–146)

More precisely, the link between the current period and future periods depends on agents' decisions to build up, use and pass on their capital stocks (money for everyone and investment assets for entrepreneurs), based on their expectations of the amount and type of capital likely to be used (or transmitted) in subsequent periods, and on the expected return. At the same time, money, as a store of value, makes it possible to abstract oneself momentarily from the market by constituting an option value conducive to better predictability of future prices, and the liquidity of financial markets makes individual investment choices reversible. Thus, these decisions will depend, on the one hand, on the "prospective yield of the investment" as a function of "the supply price of the capital-asset" or its "replacement cost", *i.e.* "the marginal efficiency of capital" (GT, 11, p. 135) by which "the expectation of the future influences the present" (*ibid.*, p. 145), and on the other hand, on the interest rate (*r*) set on the money market (*ibid.*, p. 137).

The expected return on capital will be calculated on the basis of two types of factors: on the one hand, "existing facts", known "more or less for certain" such as the present stock of capital assets and "the strength of the existing consumers' demand for goods"; on the other hand, the forecast made "with more or less confidence" of "future events" (GT, 12, p. 147), such as quantitative (stock) and qualitative (incorporated technical progress) changes in "capital assets", the "tastes of the consumer", "the strength of effective demand from time to time during the life of the investment under consideration" and the evolution of (*w*) during the period of effectiveness of the investment under consideration (*ibidem*). The assessment of these future events will then depend on a "state of psychological expectation" which, for Keynes, refers to "the state of long-term expectation" (*ibid.*, pp. 147–148) which will depend on "the most probable forecast we can make" but also on "the state of confidence" in which it is made, *i.e.* "on how highly we rate the likelihood of our best forecast turning out quite wrong" (*ibid.*, p. 148), a combination of practical market observation and "business psychology" (*ibid.*, p. 165) that will condition not only the evaluation of the marginal efficiency of capital and thus the investment decision, but also, in part, the levels and variations of (*r*). Thus, the decision to invest today depends on forecasting tomorrow's competition with capital assets and labour costs, whose qualities (new inventions and techniques) and levels (wage unit), respectively, are "unknowns":

> "The output from equipment produced to-day will have to compete, in the course of its life, with the output from equipment produced subsequently, perhaps at a lower labour cost, perhaps by an improved technique, which is content with a lower price for its output and will be increased in quantity until the price of its output has fallen to the lower figure with which it is content. Moreover, the entrepreneur's profit (in terms of money) from equipment, old or new, will be reduced, if all output comes to be produced more cheaply. In so far as such developments are foreseen as probable, or even as possible, the marginal efficiency of capital produced to-day is appropriately diminished." (GT, 11, p. 141)

As we can see, the assessment of the evolution of (w) conditions that of the marginal efficiency of capital, and therefore the investment decision. So, if forecasts concerning (Δw) are inelastic to present variations in (w) then the marginal efficiency of capital increases until it equals (r). In this case, the "Keynes effect" operates, investment and employment rise, and unemployment falls as long as (r) is not too low. Conversely, if entrepreneurs anticipate ($\Delta w < 0$) for the future, then the marginal efficiency of capital decreases and investment may be deferred. In this case, the "Keynes effect" does not operate, resulting in higher involuntary unemployment:

> "If the reduction of money-wages is expected to be a *reduction relatively to money-wages in the future*, the change will be favourable to investment, because [...] it will increase the marginal efficiency of capital; whilst for the same reason it may be favourable to consumption. If, on the other hand, the reduction leads to the expectation, or even to the serious possibility, of a further wage-reduction in prospect, it will have precisely the opposite effect. For it will diminish the marginal efficiency of capital and will lead to the postponement both of investment and of consumption." (GT, 19, p. 263, Keynes emphasizes)

In the "old fashioned type" (GT, 12, p. 150), the one before organized financial markets, where "enterprises were mainly owned by those who undertook them or by their friends and associates" (*ibidem*), *i.e.* before the split between ownership and management of capital, the investment decision depended on the will of "individuals of sanguine temperament and constructive impulses who embarked on business as a way of life, not really relying on a precise calculation of prospective profit" (*ibidem*), who trust their market knowledge and intuition, guided by the "temptation to take a chance" rather than "cold calculation" (*ibidem*). In this context, investment decisions were largely "irrevocable", and in the absence of stock exchanges (*i.e.* financial market that calls to order or sanctions, and the multiplicity of new opportunities to be seized), "there is no object in frequently attempting to revalue an investment to which we are committed" (*ibid.*, p. 151). Hence the stability of the operative convention, as a "tacitly agreed" (*ibid.*, p. 152) mode of non-price coordination between agents (cf. box), *i.e.* the relationship between the marginal efficiency of capital and the interest rate, and thus the stability of the system, since through this relationship "the expectation of the future influences the present" (GT, 11, p. 143), where (*r*) is a highly "conventional phenomenon": "its actual value is largely governed by the prevailing view as to what its value is expected to be. *Any* level of interest which is accepted with sufficient conviction as *likely* to be durable *will* be durable; subject, of course, in a changing society to fluctuations for all kinds of reasons round the expected normal." (GT, 15, p. 203). As a result:

> "the inducement to invest depends partly on the investment demand-schedule and partly on the rate of interest. [Therefore] The schedule of the marginal efficiency of capital may be said to govern the terms on which loanable funds are demanded for the purpose of new investment; whilst the rate of interest governs the terms on which funds are being currently supplied." (GT, 11, p. 137; 13, p. 165)

Conventions

A "convention", in Keynes' sense, can be defined as a set of shared rules or collective knowledge which, when added to the knowledge and cognitive capacities of individuals taken in isolation, enable them to broaden their skills and analytical capacities, particularly their perceptions of the "future", and thus influence their present decisions, by facilitating the coordination of their anticipations and behaviours.

This definition can be likened to that of Poincaré (1905) applied to scientific reasoning, where convention guides us by helping us to discern the most convenient path:

"If we insert at the beginning of every problem an explicit convention, well and good! We then have nothing to do but to apply the rules of arithmetic and algebra, and we complete our calculation, when our result cannot be called in question. But if we wish to make the slightest application of this result, we must prove that our convention is legitimate, and we shall find ourselves in the presence of the very difficulty we thought we had avoided. It may be said that common-sense is enough to show us the convention that should be adopted" (*ibid.*, p. 206)

Or Einstein (1949, p. 10), who likens "convention" to "a far-reaching agreement concerning the elements and rules of the game".

This definition can also be understood in relation to the analogy contained in the General Introduction (*cf. supra*) concerning the "Early

Music Interpretation Movement", when Gardiner (2014, Chapter 3, p. 15) notes, with regard to the Motets:

"the convention of assigning the voice of God to a single voice (or to twin voices)" adding that the composer's role at the time was "to explain the self-evident and, through music, to release the turbulent emotions that rack people's lives even (or especially) when they try to suppress or deny them" (*ibid.*, p. 16, 19).

All these definitions refer, *in fine*, to Vico (1710, Chapter VII, § IV, p. 116) when he writes that the faculty of knowledge ("*facultas ingenium*") "is the ingenium, by which man is able to see resemblances and to produce them. Indeed, we see that in children, in whom nature is more upright and less corrupted by beliefs and prejudices, the first faculty to emerge is that of perceiving resemblances."

"Organised investment markets" and the need for conventions

These investment decisions are seriously complicated by the spread of organised financial markets (notably stock exchanges, GT, 12, pp. 150–151), as they dissociate economic property and power, "the ownership and management of capital" (*ibid.*, p. 150), and involve stock market prices in the estimation of the marginal efficiency of capital, instead of (*r*), which "sometimes facilitates investment but sometimes adds greatly to the instability of the system" (*ibidem*). So:

> "the daily revaluations of the Stock Exchange, though they are primarily made to facilitate transfers of old investments between one individual and another, inevitably exert a decisive influence on the rate of current investment. For there is no sense in building up a new enterprise at a cost greater than that at which a similar existing enterprise can be purchased; whilst there is an inducement to spend on a new project what may seem an extravagant sum, if it can be floated off on the Stock Exchange at an immediate profit [So] when a company's shares are quoted very high so that it can raise more capital by issuing more shares on favourable terms, this has the same effect as if it could borrow at a low rate of interest [i.e.] a high quotation for existing equities involves an increase in the marginal efficiency of the corresponding type of capital and therefore has the same effect [...] as a fall in the rate of interest. Thus certain classes of investment are governed by the average expectation of those who deal on the Stock Exchange as revealed in the price of shares, rather than by the genuine expectations of the professional entrepreneur." (GT, 12, p. 151)

These stock market prices respond to a new conventional logic (*i.e.* a new mode of off-price coordination in an uncertain future) according to which "the existing market valuation, however arrived at, is uniquely *correct*" (*ibid.*, p. 152) with regard to current knowledge of the facts likely to influence future returns, and that this valuation "will only change in proportion to changes in this knowledge" (*ibidem*); the stability between two given states of knowledge, between two conventional bases of valuation, can be accorded with the principle of sufficient reason[1].

This conventional logic behind the pricing of securities is fundamentally different from the classic market valuation that sets the price of goods, since it requires a collective assessment (*i.e.* by financial market agents) of the financial convention, *i.e.* an implicit agreement on the forecasts for the value of a security. The latter depends on the way in which the other agents will value it, since each individual's valuation depends on that of the others:

> "Knowing that our own individual judgment is worthless, we endeavor to fall back on the judgment of the rest of the world which is perhaps better informed. That is, we endeavor to conform with the behavior of the majority or the average. The psychology of a society of individuals each of whom is endeavoring to copy the others leads to what we may strictly term a *conventional* judgment." (Keynes, 1937, p. 214, Keynes emphasises)

As a result, this "practical theory of the future", based on i) the principle that "the present is a much more serviceable guide to the future" (Keynes, 1937, p. 214); ii) the idea that "the existing state of opinion as expressed in prices and the character of existing output is based on a correct summing up of future prospects"; iii) in a societal context where "each of individuals is endeavouring to copy the others" (*ibidem*), is subject to "sudden and violent changes", increasing our inability to conceive of a veritable "knowledge of the future" (*ibid.*, p. 213):

> "The practice of calmness and immobility, of certainty and security, suddenly breaks down. New fears and hopes will, without warning, take charge of human conduct. The forces of disillusion may suddenly impose a new conventional basis of valuation. All these pretty, polite techniques, made for a well-panelled Board Room and a nicely regulated market, are liable to collapse. At all times the vague panic fears and equally vague and unreasoned hopes are not really lulled, and lie but a little way below the surface." (Keynes, 1937, p. 215).

One of the factors contributing to the instability and complexity of organized financial markets is the fact that two types of forecasting activities operate within them, each characterized by different time horizons, "the genuine expectations of the professional entrepreneur" and "the average expectation of those who deal on the Stock Exchange as revealed in the price of shares" (GT, 12, p. 151). In other words, the activity of "*enterprise*", which "forecasting the prospective yield of assets over their whole life" (*ibid.*, p. 158), and the activity of "*speculation*", which "forecasting the psychology of the market" (*ibidem*). This means that financial markets must coordinate both the short-term forecasts needed for portfolio investment and the long-term forecasts needed for investment in new production assets. This presupposes agreement, or at least implicit (peaceful) coexistence, on "visions of the future", which is very difficult to achieve, especially if speculation prevails over enterprise: "As the organization of investment markets improves, the risk of the predominance of speculation does increase" (*ibidem*):

> "The spectacle of modern investment markets has sometimes moved me towards the conclusion that to make the purchase of an investment permanent and indissoluble like marriage, except by reason of death or other grave cause might be a useful remedy for our contemporary evils. For this would force the investor to direct his mind to the long-term prospects and to those only. But a little consideration of this expedient brings us up against a dilemma, and shows us how the liquidity of investment markets often facilitates, though it sometimes impedes, the course of new investment." (GT, 12, p. 160)[2]

From then on, what becomes "the basis of conventional valuation" (GT, 12, p. 155; 1937, p. 215), on which the formation of agents' forecasts, decisions and behaviour is based, will depend on the ratio between enterprise activity and speculative activity, which is itself a function of the degree of market liquidity, in the sense that the more liquid the asset (*i.e.* capable of being traded "without" cost, delay and risk of capital loss), more speculation takes place, driven by the "fetish of liquidity" (*ibid.*, p. 155). In the latter situation, the characteristic of organized financial markets, agents bet "not so much to its prospective yield, as to a favourable change in the conventional basis of evaluation" (*ibid.*, p. 159), where the future price of an asset depends not (or little) on its fundamental value, but on the beliefs of operators, self-validated on/by the market, leading to upward or downward dynamics in asset prices, the motives and results of the expectations that coordinate agents' behaviour. We therefore understand that:

> "Speculators may do no harm as bubbles on a steady stream of enterprise. But the position is serious when enterprise becomes the bubble on a whirlpool of speculation. When the capital development of a country becomes a by-product of the activities of a casino, the job is likely to be ill-done. The measure of success attained by Wall Street, regarded as an institution of which the proper social purpose is to direct new investment into the most profitable channels in terms of future yield, cannot be claimed as one of the outstanding triumphs of *laissez-faire* capitalism – which is not surprising, if I am right in thinking that the best brains of Wall Street have been in fact directed towards a different object." (GT, 12, p. 159)

And these conditions, dominated by speculation, become precisely "the spectacle of modern investment markets" (*ibid.*, p. 160), made up of instability and "precariousness", where average opinion becomes the legitimate evaluation, the referent, condemning *ipso facto* "genuine long-term expectations" (*ibid.*, p. 156), "so difficult to-day as to be scarcely practicable" (*ibid.*, p. 157)[3] in favour of behaviour centred on "near-term market fluctuations" (*ibidem*).

This precariousness is also accentuated by i) "the gradual increase in the proportion of the equity in the community's aggregate capital investment which is owned by persons who do not manage and have no special knowledge of the circumstances, either actual or prospective, of the business in question, the element of real knowledge in the valuation of investments by those who own them or contemplate purchasing them has seriously declined" (*ibid.*, p. 153). The result of this situation is an increase in informational incompleteness and asymmetry for owners and potential buyers, linked to the disconnect between fundamental value and market price, between the reality of economic activities and the related quotations; ii) "Day-to-day fluctuations in the profits of existing investments", which, although ephemeral and meaningless, exert a short-termist influence on the markets, such as "*now-nowism*", "altogether excessive, and even absurd" (*ibid.*, pp. 153–154); iii) a "conventional evaluation which is established as the outcome of the mass psychology of a large number of ignorant individuals" (*ibid.*, p. 154) resulting in "violent changes" following "sudden fluctuation of opinion" (*i.e.* the tipping of expectations) caused by factors of little importance in terms of "prospective yield" (*ibidem*); iv) the "competition between expert professionals", which far from "correct[ing] the vagaries of the ignorant individual", leads most of them to guess "changes in the conventional basis of valuation a short time ahead of the general public" rather than making long-term forecasts of the "probable yield of an investment over its whole life" (*ibid.*, p. 154).

These combined factors contribute to the existence of organised financial markets driven not by the considered financing of investments calculated on their "true values" (*i.e.* "fundamental values") but on values that the market, under the influence of "mass psychology", will fix for an instant (t), conditioning the behaviour of financial operators to anticipate "impending changes, in the news or in the atmosphere, of the kind by which experience shows that the mass psychology of the market is most influenced" (*ibid.*, p. 155); judicious investments consisting, from now on, no longer "to defeat the dark forces of time and ignorance which envelop our future" (GT, 12, p. 155), but "to beat the gun", "to outwit the crowd" or "to pass the bad, or depreciating, half-crown to the other fellow" or even to find "gulls amongst the public to feed the maws of the professional" (*ibidem*).

This type of market functioning, where players' ignorance of the future forces them to guess and then adopt the market's average opinion, can then be likened, metaphorically, to a game of "Musical Chairs", "a pastime in which he is victor who says *Snap* neither too soon nor too late [...] secures a chair for himself when the music stops" (*ibid.*, p. 156), or a "beauty contest game" such as those organised by newspapers. In the latter case, for example, "the competitors have to pick out the six prettiest faces from a hundred photographs, the prize being awarded to the competitor whose choice most nearly corresponds to the average preferences of the competitors as a whole". (*ibid.*, p. 156). As we can see, winning the competition is not a matter of selecting the six faces you think are the prettiest, but those you think are the most likely to win the votes of the other competitors, those you think the others will find the prettiest. Solving this problem is no simple matter, insofar as this strategy becomes "Common Knowledge", "all of [competitors] are looking at the problem from the same point of view" (*ibidem*), according to an *ad infinitum* logic of the type "I think the other thinks that I think the other thinks …" where "we devote our intelligences to anticipating what average opinion expects the average opinion to be." (*ibid.*), a situation of specularity where no considered decision can be taken. To close this situation where each anticipation is reflected in the others, *i.e.* a self-referential dynamic (Orléan, 1988), and make a decision, agents must refer to a convention, *i.e.* a "Common Thought", a representation of the world commonly accepted, "tacitly agreed", GT, 12, p. 152), (here, the criteria of a beautiful face and, more generally, the specification of what is Beautiful [*i.e.* the "canons of beauty"], shared by the community for an instant (t)), necessary for "a considerable measure of continuity and stability in our affairs, *so long as we can rely on the maintenance of the convention*" (*ibid.*, p. 152, Keynes emphasizes). In this case, the convention provides a "reasonably "safe"" (GT, 12, p. 153), by which the agent can embolden himself to make a decision "with the idea that the only risk he runs is that of a genuine change in the news *over the near future*, as to the likelihood of which he can attempt to form his own judgment, and which is unlikely to be very large" (*ibid.*, pp. 152–153, Keynes emphasizes). As a result, everyone's decision is based not so much on what they think others think, but on what they believe to be the "conventional basis of valuation" (*cf. supra*) capable of "managing", for the period of validity of this conventional basis, some of the coordination and cognitive constraints which, until then, prevented the agent from "taking action", from leaving the safe haven of hoarding, of his preference for liquidity. And if they do not, everyone "estimat[ing] the prospects differently" (GT, 13, p. 169), it is because their assessment "differs from the predominant opinion as expressed in market quotations [and thus] may have a good reason for keeping liquid resources" (*ibid.*). This is why the stability of financial markets depends fundamentally on the diversity of opinions expressed on them:

> "Just as we found that the marginal efficiency of capital is fixed, not by the "best" opinion, but by the market valuation as determined by mass psychology, so also expectations as to the future of the rate of interest as fixed by mass psychology have their reactions on liquidity-preference; - but with this addition that the individual, who believes that future rates of

> interest will be above the rates assumed by the market, has a reason for keeping actual liquid cash [...] It is interesting that the stability of the system and its sensitiveness to changes in the quantity of money should be so dependent on the existence of a *variety* of opinion about wat is uncertain. Best of all we should know the future. But if not, then, if we are to control the activity of the economic system by changing the quantity of money, it is important that opinions should differ." (GT, 13, p. 170, 172, Keynes emphasizes)

Hence, the widely shared belief of agents in a representation, which becomes the "conventional basis of evaluation" (*cf. supra*), specifies one (or several in the case of "sunspots") referent(s) among the possible conjectures, in relation to which their forecasts and behaviours will be polarized, or at least coordinated: if I believe that "everyone" (or at least the dominant opinion) is based on this convention, and I have good reason to believe that others think the same is true for me, then it is in my interest to conform to it, and vice versa[4]. And this coordination will be self-perpetuating or even reinforced by the dynamics of "self-fulfilling prophecies", a process well described by Keynes, notably for the setting of the long-term interest rate, "a highly psychological phenomenon" (GT, 15, p. 202), which can easily be extended to financial assets in general:

> "It might be more accurate, perhaps, to say that the rate of interest is a highly conventional, rather than a highly psychological, phenomenon. For its actual value is largely governed by the prevailing view as to what its value is expected to be. *Any* level of interest which is accepted with sufficient conviction as *likely* to be durable *will* be durable" (GT, 15, p. 203, Keynes emphasizes)

On the one hand, we understand that "there is no clear evidence from experience that the investment policy which is socially advantageous coincides with that which is most profitable" knowing that "It needs *more* intelligence to defeat the forces of time and our ignorance of the future than to beat the gun." (GT, 12, p. 157); especially since "life is not long enough; - human nature desires quick results, there is a peculiar zest in making money quickly, and remoter gains are discounted by the average man at a very high rate." (*ibidem*).

On the other hand, the instability of the financial market is linked to the interdependence of beliefs and behaviours between agents, each one questioning what the others are thinking and going to do, as soon as they no longer count on the maintenance of the convention as a rule of conduct: "it is not surprising that a convention, in an absolute view of things so arbitrary, should have its weak points. It is its precariousness which creates no small part of our contemporary problem of securing sufficient investment." (*ibid.*, p. 153). In the latter case, if I think that some people are no longer going to respect the convention, or if I think that others think that some people (possibly myself) are no longer going to respect it, then I have an incentive to do the same. Ultimately, it is "the state of confidence" (*ibid.*, p. 158) that agents demonstrate in the convention (*i.e.* the strength of the convention) that specifies the degree of stability of financial markets, the whole remaining subordinate to "a political and social atmosphere which is congenial to the average business man" (*ibid.*, p. 162).

Here, the motives for securities transactions are similar to those for holding money and setting (*r*) (see above):

> "Because, partly on reasonable and partly on instinctive grounds, our desire to hold Money as a store of wealth is a barometer of the degree of our distrust of our own calculations and conventions concerning the future. Even tho this feeling about Money is itself conventional or instinctive, it operates, so to speak, at a deeper level of our motivation. It takes charge at the moments when the higher, more precarious conventions have weakened. The possession of actual money lulls our disquietude; and the premium which we require to make us part with money is the measure of the degree of our disquietude." (Keynes, 1937, p. 216)

In the end, whatever the case, the common denominator is always "human nature" (GT, 12, p. 161), "deep in our subconsciousness" that sometimes wants to satisfy "strong instincts" (Keynes, "auri sacra fames", 1930 dans 1931, p. 182), such as holding gold ("*auri sacra fames*" since Virgil and his Aeneid (Book III, v. 57)[5]) as a "refuge value", "a garment of respectability" (*ibid.*, p. 183), and which, when this human nature translates into economic instability, is made up of impatience that demands "quick results and making money quickly" (GT, 12, p. 157), "animal spirits" characterized by "a spontaneous urge to action" (*ibid.* p. 161), very difficult to domesticate:

> "a large proportion of our positive activities depend on spontaneous optimism rather than on a mathematical expectation, whether moral or hedonistic or economic. Most, probably, of our decisions to do something positive, the full consequences of which will be drawn out over many days to come, can only be taken as a result of animal spirits - of a spontaneous urge to action rather than inaction, and not as the outcome of a weighted average of quantitative benefits multiplied by quantitative probabilities." (GT, 12, p. 161)

As we can see, in the face of this radical uncertainty, the need for individuals to act refers back to a "practical theory of the future" (1937, p. 214) based on "our own individual judgment" (*ibidem*), and if this is *a priori* "worthless", as on financial markets with speculative activity[6], then the reference becomes "the judgment of the rest of the world which is perhaps better informed" (*ibidem*). Here, the risk of economic instability stems from the possible abandonment (or even condemnation) of investment prospects, and more generally of entrepreneurial activity, which is particularly demanding compared to speculative activity, since it requires that "the reasonable calculation is supplemented and supported by animal spirits" (GT, 12, p. 162):

> "Thus if the animal spirits are dimmed and the spontaneous optimism falters, leaving us to depend on nothing but a mathematical expectation, enterprise will fade and die; - though fears of loss may have a basis no more reasonable than hopes of profit had before." (GT, 12, p. 162)

But, despite the fact that "we have only the vaguest idea of any but the most direct consequences of our acts" (1937, p. 213), and that "our knowledge of the future is fluctuating, vague and uncertain" (*ibid.*), since "we simply do not know" (*ibid.*, p. 214), Keynes' message remains optimistic for the long term, since "certain important factors which somewhat mitigate in practice the effects of our ignorance of the future" (TG, 12, p. 163), and guide us in our forecasts and behaviour. This is the case for an "important class of long-term investment", namely "public utilities" for which "a substantial proportion of the prospective yield is practically guaranteed by monopoly privileges coupled with the right to charge such rates as will provide a certain stipulated margin" (*ibidem*) or for "investments entered upon by, or at the risk of, public authorities" (*ibidem*):

> "public authorities [...] are frankly influenced in making the investment by a general presumption of there being prospective social advantages from the investment, whatever its commercial yield may prove to be within a wide range, and without seeking to be satisfied that the mathematical expectation of the yield is at least equal to the current rate of interest, - though the rate which the public authority has to pay may still play a decisive part in determining the scale of investment operations which it can afford." (GT, 12, pp. 163–164)

Nor is Keynes' message to warn that "human decisions affecting the future, whether personal or political or economic" would be subject to "waves of irrational psychology" (GT, 12, p. 162), the state of long-term expectation often being quite stable despite crises and depressions. Rather, it is a matter of alerting us (economists, in particular), warning us against a supposedly omniscient and omnipotent "mathematical expectation", because "it is our innate urge to activity which makes the wheels go round, our rational selves choosing between the alternatives as best we are able, calculating where we can, but often falling back for our motive on whim or sentiment or chance." (*ibid.*, p. 163).

This is perhaps the main theoretical message of the General Theory, this warning against certain "symbolic pseudo-mathematical methods of formalising a system of economic analysis" (GT, 21, p. 297) which provide a symbolic, disembodied figuration of a system of economic analysis, but which lose "their cogency and authority if this hypothesis is disallowed" (*ibid.*), which are pure speculations, "as imprecise as the initial assumptions" allowing their authors "to lose sight of the complexities and interdependencies of the real world in a maze of pretentious and unhelpful symbols" (*ibid.*, p. 298):

> "The object of our analysis is, not to provide a machine, or method of blind manipulation, which will furnish an infaillible answer, but to provide ourselves with an organised and orderly method of thinking out particular problems; and, after we have reached a provisional conclusion by isolating the complicating factors one by one, we then have to go back on ourselves and allow, as well as we can, for the probable interactions of the factors amongst themselves. This is the nature of economic thinking." (GT, 21, p. 297)

a praxeology that Smith and Marx would not have disowned, and which is still relevant today.

Notes

1 In the analogical line of the previous box on "conventions", this conventional logic associated with the "principle of sufficient reason" can be defined as follows (Poincaré, 1905, XI, p. 234): "To undertake the calculation of any probability, and even for that calculation to have any meaning at all, we must admit, as a point of departure, an hypothesis or convention which has always something arbitrary about it. In the choice of this convention, we can be guided only by the principle of sufficient reason. Unfortunately, this principle is very vague and very elastic, and in the cursory examination we have just made we have seen it assume different forms. The form under which we meet it most often is the belief in continuity, a belief which it would be difficult to justify by apodeictic reasoning, but without which all science would be impossible."

2 "For the fact that each individual investor flatters himself that his commitment is "liquid" (though this cannot be true for all investors collectively) calms his nerves and makes him much more willing to run a risk. If individual purchases of investments were rendered illiquid, this might seriously impede new investment, so long as *alternative ways* in which to hold his savings are available to the individual. This is the dilemma. So long as it is open to the individual to employ his wealth in hoarding or lending *money*, the alternative of purchasing actual capital assets cannot be rendered sufficiently attractive [...] except by organising markets wherein these assets can be easily realised for money." (*ibid.*, pp. 160–161, Keynes emphasises).

3 "Finally it is the long-term investor, he who most promotes the public interest, who will in practice come in for most criticism, wherever investment funds are managed by committees or boards or banks. For it is in the essence of his behaviour that he should be eccentric, unconventional and rash in the eyes of average opinion. If he is successful, that will only confirm the general belief in his rashness; and if in the short run he is unsuccessful, which is very likely, he will not receive much mercy. Worldly wisdom teaches that it is better for the reputation to fail conventionally than to succeed unconventionally." (GT, 12, pp. 157–158).

4 "If I think that some will not respect the convention, or if I think that others think that some (including myself) will not respect it, then it is appropriate not to respect it."
5 "Accursed hunger for gold, to what do you not drive human hearts!"
6 "Why should anyone outside a lunatic asylum wish to use money as a store of wealth?" (Keynes, 1937, p. 216).

Bibliography

Einstein, Albert (1949). Notes for an autobiography. *The Saturday Review of Literature*, November 26, 1949.

Gardiner, John Eliot (2014). *Music in the castle of heaven. A portrait of Johann Sebastian Bach*. London: Penguin Books Ltd.

Keynes, John Maynard (1921). *A treatise on probability*. London: MacMillan and Co, Limited, St. Martin's Street.

Keynes, John Maynard (1931). *Essays in Persuasion*. London: MacMillan and Co, Limited, St. Martin's Street.

Keynes, John Maynard (1936). *The general theory of employment interest and money*. London: MacMillan and Co, Limited, St. Martin's Street.

Keynes, John Maynard (1937). The general theory of employment. *The Quarterly Journal of Economics*, *51*(2), February, 209–223.

Orléan, André (1988). "L'auto-référence dans la théorie keynésienne de la spéculation". *Cahiers d'économie politique*, *14*(1), 229–242.

Poincaré, Henri (1905). *Science and hypothesis*. London and Newcastle-on-Tyne: The Walter Scott Publishing Co, Ltd.

Vico, Johann Baptistae (1710). *De Antiquissima Italorum Sapienta ex Linguae Latinae Originibus eruenda*. Napoli: Napoli, Ex Typographia Felicis Mosca.

General conclusion

In the preface to the 1st edition of "Economic Theory in Retrospect", Mark Blaug points out that: "There is a mutual interaction between past and present economic thinking for, whether we set it down in so many words or not, the history of economic thought is being rewritten every generation" (Blaug, 1985, p. vii). To understand this *continuum* of rewritings, this cumulative dynamic of knowledge, ideas and techniques of observation and data processing that make up the History of Economic Thought, to which this book contributes, we need to consider three complementary aspects:

i This *continuum*, in the field of the Humanities and Social Sciences, and therefore in Economics, admits, in diversity, the coexistence at a given moment (*t*), of several paradigms, which contradicts Kuhn's analysis, centered on the "hard" Sciences, where incommensurability designates the fact that paradigms are irreconcilable, synonymous with radical ruptures (*i.e.* "scientific revolutions") between successive paradigms:

> "What differentiated these various schools was not one or another failure of method—they were all "scientific"—but what we shall come to call their incommensurable ways of seeing the world and of practicing science in it." (Kuhn, 1970, p. 4)

In this excerpt, the term "incommensurable" is used to refer to the relationship between Schools of thought with incompatible worldviews and divergent scientific practices, which impose "gestalt switches" according to a "destructive-constructive paradigm changes" logic (Kuhn, 1970, VII, p. 66). In this context, the way we perceive and understand reality is radically altered, incommensurability here referring to a relationship between different worlds:

> "Therefore, at times of revolution, when the normal-scientifc tradition changes, the scientist's perception of his environment must be re-educated—in some familiar situations he must learn to see a new gestalt. After he has done so the world of his research will seem, here and there, incommensurable with the one he had inhabited before [...] though the world does not change

DOI: 10.4324/9781032649054-16

with a change of paradigm, the scientist afterward works in a different world." (*ibid.*, X, p. 112, 121)

In Economics, as more generally in the Humanities and Social Sciences, to paraphrase Kuhn, the economic world is changing, leading to the emergence of new, competing paradigms that encourage controversy, the development of knowledge and a better understanding of the world.

ii Like hiking trails, the identification of this *continuum* of rewritings requires that it be marked out with the help of what Schumpeter (1966, p. 51) called "Classical Situations", which appear at key moments in the development of economic analysis or when Karl Pribram (1986, p. 137) likens The Wealth of Nations to "a signpost at the crossroads of economic reasoning". Faced with the "lacking direction and meaning" (Schumpeter, 1966, p. 4), these beacons take the form of innovations or consolidations and syntheses of scientific advances made up to that point or compared to them, and are embodied in an author and a work, the "paradigmatic books" (*cf.* General introduction) whose influence will extend over several decades. In this book, we have identified and analyzed three main "paradigmatic books", three "great books" in Blaug's sense (1985, p. vii), constituting three still-operating paradigms: by means of Wealth of Nations, the Smithian paradigm, based on the infallibility of the "system of natural liberty", and therefore conservative in its principles; by means of Capital, the Marxian paradigm, based on the contingent and historically-dated nature of a "specifically capitalist mode of production", and therefore revolutionary in its principles; by means of the General Theory, the Keynesian paradigm, based on the perfectibility of "the economic society in which we live" and therefore reformist in its principles.

iii This *continuum* is part of a long period, one that enables us to move beyond "a history that is almost changeless, the history of man in relation to his surroundings" (Braudel, 1982, p. 3) to join a "social history" that "look[s] successively at economies and states, societies and civilizations, and finally attempt[s] to show [...] how all the forces from the depths came into play" (*ibidem*), and only the "great books" can pass this hurdle, the one that enables us "to distinguish equally surely the lasting from the ephemeral [...] the continuity from discontinuity of our social destiny" (*ibid.*, p. 17). Where the work of epigones feeds schools of thought that ensure the continuity and updating of founding principles, such as the classical and neo-classical schools in the tradition of Wealth of Nations; Marxian and neo-Marxist schools in the tradition of Capital; and neo- and post-Keynesian schools in the tradition of General Theory.

Here, the correspondence and literature of epigones bear witness to the perpetuation of the original ideas contained in the "great books", and their updating without departing from their fundamental principles, which remain relevant today. "Honour where honour is due", this paradigmatic *continuum* begins with Adam Smith at the centre of the History of Economic Thought, for example by Galbraith (1987), who entitles Chapter 2 of his "History of Economics": "After Adam", and develops "The new world of Adam Smith" in Chapter 4, while Blaug (1985) begins his work with a first chapter devoted to "Pre-Adamite Economics" and Pribram (1986, p. 126) situates economics as an "independent discipline" with Adam Smith and the Wealth of Nations.

This was also the case for Jean-Baptiste Say, when he wrote to Thomas Robert Malthus in 1820:

> "Loin d'ébranler les célèbres Recherches sur la richesse des nations, je les appuie dans ce qu'elles ont d'essentiels [...] Je révère Adam Smith : il est mon maître. Lorsque je fis les premiers pas dans l'économie politique, et lorsque, chancelant encore, poussé d'un côté par les docteurs de la balance du commerce, et de l'autre par les docteurs du produit net, je bronchais à chaque pas, il me montra la bonne route. Appuyé sur sa Richesse des nations, qui nous découvre en même temps la richesse de son génie, j'appris à marcher seul [...] Je ne suis soumis qu'aux décrets de l'éternelle raison, et ne crains pas de le dire : Adam Smith n'a pas embrassé l'ensemble du phénomène de la production et de la consommation des richesses ; mais il a tant fait, que nous devons être pénétrés pour lui de reconnaissance. Grace à lui, la plus vague, la plus obscure des sciences, deviendra bientôt la plus précise, et celle de toutes qui laissera le moins de faits inexpliqués" (Say, 1820, pp. 41–43)[1]

Sometimes with the risk, highlighted by Sen (1986), of seeing the ideas contained in The Wealth of Nations diverted from their original meaning through extreme, even caricatural simplification, as the price to be paid for notoriety:

> "Shakespeare did not say it, but it is true that some men are born small, some achieve smallness, and some have smallness thrust upon them. Adam Smith, the father of modern economics, has had to cope with a good deal of such thrusting. That conclusion is inescapable, reading some of the recent pronouncements of conservative extremism [...] with persistent attempts to implicate Adam Smith in justifying the straight and the narrow. The invoking of Adam Smith and "the invisible hand" is a widespread phenomenon, varying from explicit attribution to implicit use of Smith's authority [...] The Wealth of Nations is, however, a complex book [...] The latter-day "Smithians" may have a simple enough message to enhance our wisdom on economic affairs, but Adam Smith was scarcely capable of such heroic simplicity. The tradition of using Adam Smith for defending simple (and frequently obtuse) political decisions goes back a long time." (*ibid.*, p. 28)

The *continuum* described above feeds on controversies and debates of ideas, and from this point of view, Marx's work, and in particular Capital, has been and continues to be a great contributor and purveyor of inspiration, as W. Leontief points out:

> "In the very first pages of the first volume of Capital, Marx raised against the "vulgar" (I guess he would call them today "orthodox" or "neo-classical") economists the accusation of "fetishism." Instead of looking for the ultimate deep-lying price determinants, they operate, according to Marx, with superficial, imaginary concepts of supply and demand, money costs, etc., all of which refer to purely fictitious relations. Although these subjective concepts acquire in the mind of acting economic individuals the quality of independent, tyrannically dominating forces, actually they are nothing but the products of deliberate actions of the same individuals. This typically Hegelian observation is strickingly correct. Is, however, the theoretical conclusion which Marx seems to draw from it actually justified? If it were, his criticism would indict modern price theory even in a greater degree than any of the theories of his contemporaries, John Stuart Mill, Senior, or Malthus." (Leontief, 1938, p. 1)

In the first chapter of "The Accumulation of Capital" (2003, p. 3), Rosa Luxemburg highlights one of the major aspects of the Marxian paradigm: the reproduction of social capital:

> "Karl Marx made a contribution of lasting service to the theory of economics when he drew attention to the problem of the reproduction of the entire social capital. It is significant that in the history of economics we find only two attempts at an exact exposition of this problem: one by Quesney [*sic*], the father of the Physiocrats, at its very inception; and in its final stage, this attempt by Marx. In the interim, the problem was ever with bourgeois economics. Yet bourgeois economists have never been fully aware of this problem in its pure aspects, detached from related and intersecting minor problems; they have never been able to formulate it precisely, let alone solve it. Seeing that the problem is of paramount importance, their attempts may all the same help us to some understanding of the trend of scientific economics." (Luxemburg, 2003, p. 3)

The trend of scientific economics that can be completed by the *continuum* between Marx and Keynes, for which it is interesting to note the testimony of Joan Robinson contained in the Preface to the second edition of her "Essay on Marx Economics":

> "I began to read *Capital*, just as one reads any book, to see what was in it; I found a great deal that neither its followers nor its opponents had prepared me to expect. Piero Sraffa teased me, saying that I treated Marx as a little-known forerunner of Kalecki. There is a certain sense in which this is not a

joke. There are many pointers in *Capital* to a theory of effective demand. Marx's disciples could have worked it out before Keynes and Kalecki learned it from the brutal teaching of the great slump; but they did not do so. The professed Marxists in England greeted the *General Theory* with the slogans of sound finance. The "Keynesian" element in Marx *was* little-known. The academics did not even pretend to understand Marx. It seemed to me that, apart from prejudice, a barrier was created for them by his nineteenth-century metaphysical habits of thought, which are alien to a generation brought up to inquire into the meaning of meaning. I therefore tried to translate Marx's concepts into language that an academic could understand. This puzzled and angered the professed Marxists, to whom the metaphysic is precious for its own sake." (Robinson, 1966, p. vi, vii)

A *continuum* that comes to a temporary halt here, provisionally, at the General Theory, whose importance for John Kenneth Galbraith lies not only in the innovative ideas it contains but also in the personality of its author:

"The General Theory owed much of its acceptance to the Great Depression and to the failure of classical economics to contend with that pervasively unsettling event. But it also owed much to Keynes's assurance in economic argument and analysis, the confident originality of his expression and mood. The confidence should especially be stressed. No economist is ever more highly regarded than he regards himself or followed with more certainty than that which he himself manifests. And Keynes's influence also owed much to his personal background, reputation and prestige. Had The General Theory come from someone who lacked these qualifications, it might well have sunk without trace." (Galbraith, 1987, pp. 227–228)

Or Paul Samuelson's (1946) tribute to the recently deceased Keynes, marking the 10th anniversary of the General Theory:

"In this case, gradually and against heavy resistance, the realization grew that the new analysis of effective demand associated with the General Theory was not to prove such a passing fad, that here indeed was part of "the wave of the future." This impression was confirmed by the rapidity with which English economists, other than those at Cambridge, took up the new Gospel: e.g. Harrod, Meade, and others at Oxford; and still more surprisingly, the young blades at the London School like Kaldor, Lerner, and Hicks, who threw off their Hayekian garments and joined in the swim [...] Instead of burning out like a fad [...] the General Theory is still gaining adherents and appears to be in business to stay. Many economists who are most vehement in criticism of the specific Keynesian policies-which must always be carefully distinguished from the scientific analysis associated with his name-will never again be the same after passing through his hand." (Samuelson, 1946, p. 188)

Finally, it is perhaps Galbraith in his "History of Economics" who can conclude for us the "bien-fondé" of the earlier developments that make up this book:

> "However, none of this earlier effort ranked in importance with the publication of The General Theory of Employment Interest and Money in 1936, which was an event in the history of economics comparable in significance with the publication of Wealth of Nations in 1776 and the first edition of Capital in 1867. It was, as Keynes intended it to be, a lethal blow at the classical conclusions as to demand, production and employment and the resulting policy." (Galbraith, 1987, p. 227)

Note

1 ["Far from undermining the famous "Recherches sur la richesse des nations," I support them in their essentials [...] I revere Adam Smith: he is my master. When I took my first steps into political economy, and when, still faltering, pushed on one side by the doctors of the balance of trade, and on the other by the doctors of the net product, I stumbled at every step, he showed me the right way. Leaning on his Wealth of Nations, which reveals to us at the same time the wealth of his genius, I learned to walk alone [...] I am subject only to the decrees of eternal reason, and I am not afraid to say it: Adam Smith has not embraced the whole phenomenon of the production and consumption of wealth; but he has done so much, that we must be grateful to him. Thanks to him, the vaguest, most obscure of sciences will soon become the most precise, and the one of all that will leave the fewest facts unexplained."]

General bibliography

Blaug, Mark (1985). *Economic theory in retrospect (1962)*. Cambridge: Cambridge University Press, fourth edition.

Braudel, Fernand (1982). *On history*. Translated by Sarah Matthews. Chicago: The University of Chicago Press.

Bray, John Francis (1839). *Labour's wrongs and labour's remedy; or the age of might and the age of right*. Leeds, UK: Published by David Green, Briggate.

Diemer, Arnaud & Guillemin, Hervé (2012). "Adam Smith et la physique de Newton". *Œconomia*, *2*(3), Septembre, 327–363.

Dostaler, Gilles (2007). *Keynes and his battles*. Cheltenham (UK), Northampton, MA, (USA): Edward Elgar Publishing Limited. An augmented and revised edition of *Keynes et ses combats*, Paris, Albin Michel, 2005.

Einstein, Albert (1949). Notes for an autobiography. *The Saturday Review of Literature*, November 26, 1949.

Galbraith, John Kenneth (1952). *American capitalism. The concept of countervailing power*. Cambridge, MA: Houghton Mifflin Company Boston and the Riverside Press Cambridge.

Galbraith, John Kenneth (1955). *The Great Crash 1929. A striking study of the greatest speculative boom in history and of the catastrophe which followed it*. London: Hamish Hamilton Ltd.

Galbraith, John Kenneth (1987). *A history of economics. The past as the present*. London: Hamish Hamilton Ltd.

Gardiner, John Eliot (2014). *Music in the castle of heaven. A portrait of Johann Sebastian Bach*. London: Penguin Books Ltd.

Gilles, Philippe (2009). *Histoire des crises et des cycles économiques. Des crises industrielles du 19ème siècle aux crises actuelles*. Paris: A. Colin, coll. "U", 2ème édition.

Goodwin, Richard M (1967). A growth cycle. In Charles H. Feinstein (Ed.), *Socialism, capitalism and economic growth. Essays presented to Maurice Dobb* (pp. 54–58). Cambridge: Cambridge University Press.

Grossmann, Henrik (1992). *The law of accumulation and breakdown of the capitalist system. Being also a theory of crises (1929)*. London: Pluto Press.

Guitton, Henri (1979). *De l'imperfection en économie*. Paris: Calmann-Lévy, coll. "Perspectives de l'économique".

Hansen, Alvin Harvey & Clemence, Richard Vernon (1953). *Readings in business cycles and national income*. New York: W.W. Norton & Cy. Inc.

Harrod, Roy Forbes (1951). *The life of John Maynard Keynes*. London: MacMillan & Co. Ltd.

Hicks, John Richard (1935). A suggestion for simplifying the theory of money. *Economica*, *2*(5), February, 1–19.

Hicks, John Richard (1937). Mr. Keynes and the "classics"; a suggested interpretation. *Econometrica*, *5*(2), April, 147–159.

Hicks, John Richard (1939). *Value and capital: An inquiry into some fundamental principles of economic theory*. Oxford: Clarendon Press.

Hilferding, Rudolf (1981). *Finance capital. A study of the latest phase of capitalist development, (1910)*. Translated by Morris Watnick & Sam Gordon. London, Abingdon, New York: Routledge.

Hippocrates from Cos (1983). *Hippocratic writings*. Edited by G.E.R. Lloyd and translated by J. Chadwick & W.N. Mann. London: Penguin Books Ltd, "Penguin Classics".

Hirschman, Albert Otto (2013). *The passions and the interests. Political arguments for capitalism before its triumph* (1977). Princeton and Oxford: Princeton University Press, "Princeton Classics".

Hume, David (1739). *A treatise on human nature: Being an attempt to introduce the experimental method of reasoning into moral subjects*, London, Printed for John Noon, at the White-Hart, near Mercer's-Chapel in Cheapside.

Hume, David (1938). An Abstract of a Treatise of Human Nature (1740). A Pamphlet hitherto unknow by David Hume, Reprinted with an Introduction by J. M . Keynes and P. Sraffa, Cambridge, At the University Press.

Kahneman, Daniel & Tversky, Amos (1979). Prospect theory: An analysis of decisions under risk. *Econometrica*, *47*(2), March, 263–291.

Keynes, John Maynard (1921). *A treatise on probability*. London: MacMillan and Co, Limited, St. Martin's Street.

Keynes, John Maynard (1926). *The end of Laissez-Faire*. London: Published by Leonard & Virginia Woolf at the Hogarth Press, 52 Tavistock Square.

Keynes, John Maynard (1931). *Essays in Persuasion*. London: MacMillan and Co, Limited, St. Martin's Street.

Keynes, John Maynard (1936). *The general theory of employment interest and money*. London: MacMillan and Co, Limited, St. Martin's Street.

Keynes, John Maynard (1937). The general theory of employment. *The Quarterly Journal of Economics*, *51*(2), February, 209–223.

Keynes, John Maynard (1951). *Essays in biography (1933)*, New Edition with Three Additional Essays edited by Geoffrey Keynes , London: Rupert Hart-Davis, 36 Soho Square.

Keynes, John Maynard (1969). *Théorie générale de l'emploi, de l'intérêt et de la monnaie (1936)*. Paris: Payot, "Bibliothèque scientifique Payot".

Keynes, John Maynard (2013). A monetary theory of production (1933). In D. Moggridge (Ed.), *The collected writings of John Maynard Keynes vol. XIII "The general theory and after: Part I, preparation"* (pp. 408–411). Cambridge: Cambridge University Press for the Royal Economic Society.

Knight, Frank Hyneman (1921). *Risk, uncertainty and profit*. Boston and New York: Houghton Mifflin Company and the Riverside Press Cambridge.

Kondratieff, Nikolaï Dmitrievitch (1944). The long waves in economic life. *The Review of Economic Statistics*, *XVII*(6), November 1935, 105–115; also in *Readings in business cycle theory*, Philadelphia, Toronto, The Blakiston company, p. 20–42.

Kuhn, Thomas Samuel (1970). *The structure of scientific revolutions (1962)*. Enlarged, Chicago: The University of Chicago Press, International Encyclopedia of Unified Science, second edition.

Lange, Oskar Ryszard (1935). Marxian economic and modern economic theory. *The Review of Economic Studies*, *2*(3), June, 189–201.

Laplace, Pierre-Simon de (1812). *Théorie analytique des Probabilités*. Paris: Mme Veuve Courcier, Imprimeur-Libraire pour les Mathématiques, Quai des Augustins, n°57.

Ledbetter, James & Wheen, Francis (Eds.) (2007). *Dispatches for The New York tribune. Selected journalism of Karl Marx*. London and New York: Penguin Books, Coll. "Penguin Classics".

Leibniz, Gottfried Wilhelm (1951). *Essays on the goodness of God, the freedom of man and the origin of evil (1710)*. London: Routledge & Kegan Paul Ltd.

Leontief, Wassily (1938). The significance of Marxian economics for present-day economic theory. *The American Economic Review*, *28*(1), supplement March, 1–9.

Luxemburg, Rosa (2003). *The accumulation of capital, (1913)*. Translated by Agnes Schwarzschild. London and New York: Routledge "Classics".

Marx, Karl (1892). *The poverty of philosophy. Answer to the "philosophy of poverty" by M. Proudhon (1874)*. Moscow. Foreign Languages Publishing House.

Marx, Karl (1965). *Œuvres Economie*, Tome I, Paris, Edition établie et annotée par Maximilien Rubel, Editions Gallimard, NRF, coll. "Bibliothèque de la Pléiade".

Marx, Karl (1969). *Theories of surplus value, part II (1862–3)*. London and Moscow: Lawrence & Wishart and Progress Publishers.

Marx, Karl (1977). *Economic and philosophic manuscripts of 1844*. Moscow: Progress Publishers, fifth revised edition.

Marx, Karl (1990). *Capital. A critique of political economy*, volume I (1867). Translated by Ben Fowkes. London: Penguin Books in association with New Left Review, Penguin Classics.

Marx, Karl (1991). *Capital. A critique of political economy*, volume III (1864–75). Translated by David Fernbach. London: Penguin Books in association with New Left Review, Penguin Classics.

Marx, Karl (1992). *Capital. A critique of political economy*, volume II (1869–79). Translated by David Fernbach. London: Penguin Books in association with New Left Review, Penguin Classics.

Marx, Karl & Engels, Friedrich (2002). *The communist manifesto, (1848)*, with an Introduction and Notes by Gareth Stedman Jones. London: Penguin Books, coll. "Penguin Classics."

Mathiot, Jean (1990). *Adam Smith. Philosophie et Economie. De la sympathie à l'échange*. Paris: PUF, coll. "Philosophies" n° 24.

Minsky, Hyman P (1975). *John Maynard Keynes*. New York: Columbia University Press.

Morishima, Michio (1973). *Marx's economics: A dual theory of value and growth*. Cambridge, London, New York, Melbourne: Cambridge University Press.

Natakani, Takeshi & Hagiwara, Taiji (1997). Product innovation and the rate of profit. *Kobe University Economic Review*, *43*, 39–51.

Orléan, André (1988). L'auto-référence dans la théorie keynésienne de la spéculation. *Cahiers d'économie politique*, *14*(1), 229–242.

Poincaré, Henri (1905). *Science and hypothesis*. London and Newcastle-on-Tyne: The Walter Scott Publishing Co, Ltd.

Polanyi, Karl (2001). *The great transformation. The political and economic origins of our time (1944)*. Boston, MA: Beacon Press.

Pribram, Karl (1986). *Les fondements de la pensée économique*. Traduit par H.P. Bernard, Paris: Economica.

Ricardo, David (1817). *On the principles of political economy, and taxation*. London: John Murray, Albemarle-Street.

Robinson, Joan Violet (1942). *An essay on Marxian economics*. London: Macmillan and Co. Limited.

Robinson, Joan Violet (1966). *An essay on Marxian economics*. London and Basingstoke: The MacMillan Press Ltd, second edition.

Samuelson, Paul Anthony (1946). Lord Keynes and the general theory. *Econometrica, 14*(3), July, 187–200.

Say, Jean-Baptiste (1820). *Lettres à M. Malthus, sur differens sujets d'Economie politique, notamment sur les causes de la stagnation générale du commerce*, A Paris, Chez Bossange, Père et Fils, Libraires, rue de Tournon, n°6 bis. Paris: Bossange.

Schumpeter, Joseph Alois (1939). *Business cycles. A theoretical, historical, and statistical analysis of the capitalist process*. New York and London: MacGraw-Hill Book Company, Inc., 2 volumes.

Schumpeter, Joseph Alois (1966), *History of economic analysis (1954)*. New York: Oxford University Press, sixth edition.

Sen, Amartya (1986). Adam Smith's prudence. In Sanjaya Lall & Frances Stewart (Eds.), *Theory and reality in development. Essays in honour of Paul Streeten* (pp. 28–37). New York: Palgrave Macmillan, St Martin's Press, Inc.

Shackle, George Lennox Sharman (1967). *The years of hight theory. Invention & tradition in economic thought 1926–1939*. Cambridge (Ill.): Cambridge University Press.

Sismondi, Jean-Charles Léonard Simonde de (1827). *Nouveaux Principes d'Economie politique, ou De la Richesse dans ses rapports avec la Population* (1819). Paris: Delaunay Libraire, 2 Tomes, 2ème édition.

Smith, Adam (1761). *The theory of moral sentiments (1759)*. London: Printed for A. Millar, in the Strand; and A. Kincaid and J. Bell, in Edinburgh, second edition.

Smith, Adam (1913). *An inquiry into the nature and causes of the wealth of nations (1776)*. London and New York: George Routledge & Sons, Limited and E.P. Dutton and Co.

Smith, Adam (1795). *Essays on philosophical subjects*. London: Printed for T. Cadell Jun and W. Davies in the Strand; and W. Creech, Edinburg.

Smith, Adam (1987). The correspondence of Adam Smith. In E.C. Mossner & I.S. Ross (Eds.), *The Glasgow edition of the works of Adam Smith*. Indianapolis: Liberty Fund, Inc.

Smith, Henry (1937). Marx and trade cycle. *The Review of Economic Studies, 4*(3), June, 192–204, repris dans Wood John Cunningham (Ed.) (1988), chap. 35, 25–38, and "Marx and the Trade Cycle: A Reply", *Ibid.*, chap. 37, 47–48.

Sweezy, Paul Marlor (1952). *The theory of capitalist development. Principles of Marxian political economy (1942)*, with a Foreword by Maurice Dobb. London: Dennis Dobson Limited.

Vico, Johann Baptistae (1710). *De Antiquissima Italorum Sapienta ex Linguae Latinae Originibus eruenda*. Napoli: Ex Typographia Felicis Mosca.

Viner, Jacob (1927). Adam Smith and Laissez Faire. *Journal of Political Economy*, *35*(2), April, 198–232.

Wilson, John D (1938). A note on Marx and trade cycle. *The Review of Economic Studies*, *5*(2), February, 107–113, repris dans Wood John Cunningham (Ed.), (1988), chap. 36, 39–46.

Wood, John Cunningham (Ed.) (1988). *Karl Marx's economics. Critical assessments*, volume II. London and New York: Routledge.

Woolf, Virginia (1982). *The diary of Virginia Woolf*, volume 4 (1931–1935). Edited by Anne Olivier Bell and assisted by Andrew McNeillie. New York and London: Harcourt Brace Jovanovich, Publishers.

Index

Note: Page numbers followed by "n" refer to notes.

FSC
www.fsc.org
MIX
Papier | Fördert gute Waldnutzung
FSC® C083411

Kolibri 360 GmbH
Ferdinand-Jühlke-Straße 7
99095 Erfurt, Deutschland
produktsicherheit@kolibri360.de